ERASURISM

~~ERASURISM~~

LOUIS ARMAND

and

MICHEL DELVILLE

Bridwell Press

Southern Methodist University

Dallas, Texas

Bridwell Press is the professional publishing arm of Bridwell Library
(SMU Libraries and Perkins School of Theology).
Southern Methodist University

SMU Libraries SMU Perkins School of Theology

Series Editor: David Caplan

Design: Alicia Beebe

Cover art: Interior Ministry

Printed in the United States of America

ISBN: 978-1-957946-47-4 (hardcover)

ISBN: 978-1-957946-46-7 (paperback)

ISBN: 978-1-957946-48-1 (ebook)

SMU Project Poëtica

CONTENTS

ACKNOWLEDGMENTS

Earlier versions of some sections of this work appeared in *FPC – Formes Poétiques Contemporaines* 14 (2019); *Neo-Avant-Gardes: Post-War Literary Experiments Across Borders* (Bart Vervaeck, ed., Edinburgh: Edinburgh University Press, 2021); *Crossroads Poetics: Text, Image, Music, Film & Beyond* (Prague: Litteraria Pragensia, 2013); *Countertext* 6, no. 1 (2020); *Journal of Avant-Garde Studies* (2022), and *Philobiblon* XXX.1 (2025). They are reprinted here in an adapted and expanded form with kind permission from the editors and publishers.

CREDITS

Excerpts from Jochen Gerner's *TNT en amérique*, Martin Arnold's *Haunted House*, Bill Morrison's *Decasia*, and Christian Bök's *The Xenotext* reproduced by kind permission of the artists.

Excerpts from Tom Phillips's *A Humument* used by permission of SABAM, on behalf of the artist's estate.

Bob Cobbing's "Are your children safe in the sea" used by permission of the Bob Cobbing Estate.

INTRODUCTION

ERASURISM is omnipresent.

Traversing ideology, its gradients of power, apartheids, expropriations, suppressions, disappearances, displacements, ghostings, forced integrations, sterilization programs, genocides, redactions, revisions, subversions, plagiarisms. Erasurism is not an aesthetics but a complex of operations between inscription and erasure, in the ambivalence immanent to the exercise of control over meaning. To produce and abolish meaning. To represent and delete. To conjure and cause to vanish. To bring into being and consign to oblivion. Like all totalizing projects, the domination of language is constitutionally insufficient to its task. Despite every effort to constrain, discipline, or punish it, signification exceeds, deviates, will not conform. Despite every effort to expunge this unruliness, traces remain. Ideology is everywhere haunted by them. They multiply, not in ratio to the effort directed at their negation, but autonomously: they threaten to run amok, to invest the entire semantic field. The repudiated logos haunting ideology's dreams like a bad conscience. Innocuous, portentous, trivial, weird, parodic, solemn, infantile, concrete, monstrous, random, insurgent, unrequited, tender, vengeful, curious. An act of survival, a strategy, a making better use of, happenstance.

Erasure itself opens ideology to its other(s), like an exposed armature: negation-negated brings forth possibility.

Erasurism is the poetics of unwriting the impossible.

A road sign in Bucha with all the place names removed. The Old Jewish Cemetery in Prague, "preserved" by the Nazis as a monument to a vanished race. Stalin ordering Alexander Rodchenko to deface his own portraits of "renegade" Uzbek Communist Party members. A statue of James Cook covered in red paint.

Power always drags its trophies around with it, like Hector's corpse roped to Achilles's chariot: triumphalist kitsch. Erasurism is a corpse that gets up and sings: the kitsch of exquisite absurdities. For if, as Napoleon once said, power is never ridiculous in its own eyes, why grind lenses for it when broken glass would be more to the point?

The ongoing struggle against fascism, colonialism, corporate-statism, religious fundamentalism, globalization, pandemic, and genocide has profoundly inflected the meaning and scope of erasurism—enlarged from an obscure avant-garde vernacular to what may judiciously be called a universal paradigm: from the marginally literary to the broadly political; from *Kulturkritik* to culture war, on a spectrum with terms like extinction, cancelation, censorship, abolition, sanitation, yet posed in antagonism to them, as unclosed, generative, open-ended, ambiguous, indeterminate.

Today, the artifacts of a zero-sum ideological contest are everywhere visible, the ubiquitous signs of a confected "clash of civilizations" whose overtures to a philosophy of right haunt every claim and counterclaim to narratives of modernity and its myths of technosocial progress. The relentless industry in cultural pharmacology is like a general anesthetic administered to the mass mind, productive of historical dialectical amnesias. Language, formed of the ruins of such "utopias," builds vistas of cognitive dissonance into a music of the spheres: possible worlds not alien to this one but immanent to it.

It may be as simple as this: all writing—all *critical thought*—everything in fact that *cannot be ideologically predetermined*—begins in erasure and transfigures it into a poetics of being.

▪

This book investigates erasurism as the major critical praxis unifying the history of avant-garde, modernist, and postmodernist experimentation, and defines a radical poetics that extends beyond the confines of literature and the arts to cybernetics and the field of information broadly defined. Erasurism is implicit to inscription and in one way or another has accompanied the history of "writing" from its protohuman and paleolithic origins (Maltravieso, Lubang, Chauvet, Lascaux) to its intersection with modern computing (Turing's "halting machines") and quantum superpositionality (wave function collapse). While erasurism has been theorized in isolation, with regard to specific aesthetic developments from the nineteenth to twenty-first centuries, and to specific fields of study—including psychoanalysis (Freud's palimpsestic "Wunderblock"), the deconstruction of "grammatology" (Derrida), hypertext and hypermedia ("non-sequential writing": Ted Nelson), textual genetics (avant-texts), ecopoetics and indigenous erasure ("terra nullius"), gender abolition (Xenofeminism), and what might loosely be described as the "conservation of information" in the semiosphere ("erasures leave behind as much as they remove": Germán Sierra)—no unifying descriptive or theoretical approach to erasurism as a *general poetics* has yet been attempted.

For this reason, erasurism commands our attention.

The erasurist poetics of the late twentieth century and early twenty-first century by and large acknowledges a fundamental ambivalence underlying distinctions between concept and technique, rewriting and originality, self-reflection and aesthetic norms and values. Poised between effacement and defacement, concealment and revelation, erasure pursues a logic that considers the text as emergent and provisional: an inscribed teleology of future recyclings and re-inscriptions in lieu of a concluded status.

Recent and current developments in erasure art are closely associated with visual artists and writers appropriating existing texts with a view to discovering unforeseen semantic configurations, interfering in the transmissional logic of cultural artifacts, or new modes of legibility. As all "source texts" become the material for a permutational "open-source" remix culture, the apparent boundaries between any given cultural genome and its potential to be re-engineered come in turn to demarcate sites of generative "erasure." What once presented as fixed constraints between process and product, producer and consumer, thus comes into view as fluid recursive movements of feedback and obsolescence.

A contemporary poetics of erasure is rooted as much in a deconstruction of the history of writing as it is in the historical condition of discrete artifacts, from the found objects of Duchamp to the militant *détournements* of the Lettrist and Situationist Internationals to auto-encoded computer art and quantum poetry. As a constellation of a critical praxis—with antecedents in the work of Mallarmé and Sterne, the mass print media and the commodity critique of Marx—erasurism needs to be understood, however, as first and foremost a relation to history itself, in particular as a relation to a history of avant-gardism that coincides with the industrialization not only of modes of production and consumption, but of those operations of power expressed through mass surveillance, control, oppression, and disappearance. That is to say, by regimes of erasure. For it is here that the aesthetic, the ethical, and the *anesthetic* intersect with a dialectics of hard and soft power. If the course of the nineteenth and twentieth centuries was detourned, as Debord might say, by the "void" of modernity, that of the twenty-first may just as easily be said to be predetermined by modernity's supposed erasure—the condition of postmodernity, famously rendered by Jean-François Lyotard, in all its catastrophic ambivalence, as a perpetual "nascent state."

CHAPTER 1

Under Erasure: Black Holes, Holographs, and the Missing Letter

TRACING A NOMINAL GENEALOGY, from Robert Fludd's "Et sic in infinitum"to *The Life and Opinions of Tristram Shandy* to *Finnegans Wake* to Georges Perec's *La Disparition* and beyond, it is possible to speak of a "poetics" of constitutive erasure that comes to generalize itself, not as a literary device, but as a textual condition—whose theoretical elaboration is paradigmatic of the so-called poststructuralist turn: exemplified in the section of Jacques Derrida's *Of Grammatology* entitled "Writing Before the Letter" (1967) and the closely related essay "La différance" (1968). Like Malevich's *Black Square* (1915), Fludd's mimēsis of nothingness in *Utriusque Cosmi* (1617) and Laurence Sterne's "black page" (from one of the foundation texts of the modern novel; 1768–1769) pose questions about the representation of the negative and the limits of signification wherever writing *pushes into the domain of asemic interference*. In the case of Joyce's portmanteaux (emergent lexicality or lexical fusions: "word, letter, paperspace") and Perec's lipogrammes (systematic lexical omissions), this question of representation is literalized in the operations of inscription itself—as the complementary counterpart of that work of "erasure" seemingly depicted by "blacking-out."

Such complementarity (we might call it "ambivalence") is foregrounded in Derrida's appropriation from Heidegger's *Zur Seinsfrage* of a device for placing certain "inadequate yet necessary" terms—such as ~~Being~~—*sous rature*, or "under erasure," so that both the term and its erasure appear simultaneously. For Derrida, however, this is not a mere device to signal the "insufficiency" of privileged philosophical terms, but rather the sign of a general condition of writing/signification and the "total system"[1] of sense, since there is no *missing presence* of meaning before which language falters. Rather, there is what Derrida terms "trace," or again "différance": an "erasure" that is necessarily inscribed at the *origin of sense* in order that signification (writing) occurs *in the first place*. As such, *all writing is "under erasure."* Yet it is this conditionality of *sense* that is most often suppressed in the ideological claims placed upon its mimēsis (language as transparency). Within the discourse of the metaphysics of presence that Derrida's work critiques (from Plato's *Phaedrus* to Husserl's *Origin of Geometry* and beyond), writing is not simply "under erasure" but *erased* (at best a "secondary mimēsis")—such that Heidegger's literal crossing-out brings to mind a classic negation-of-negation ("it presents itself," as Derrida says, "in the dissimulation of itself"[2]). For Derrida, the ambivalence of the "signifier" (inscription, erasure, iteration) is radicalized as a lettristic, quasi-Joycean *ambiviolence*, indicative of what Derrida elsewhere terms "writing power"[3]—evoking the violence of a generative poiēsis capable of "soliciting" structure: simultaneously *perturbative* and, in a seemingly paradoxical movement, *constitutive* of a "system" of sense. Above all, this *ambiviolence* solicits a countervailing *systemic violence*: of reduction, interpretation, and of what (in an apparent absence of ideology) is called "readability." In this way, and despite their superficial differences, the texts of Sterne, Joyce, Perec, et al. interpolate a poetics of erasure as the very condition of writing *as such*—"origin of the experience of space and time," as Derrida says, "this writing of difference, this fabric of traces…"[4]

Derrida's conception of a generalized *writing* casts back, among others, to Mallarmé, whose work is the focus of an extended meditation in his 1972 volume *La Dissemination*, where Mallarmé's short text "Mimique" is read in juxtaposition to a fragment of Plato's *Philebus*, and from which Derrida constructs (in a single remarkable footnote) an intricate analysis of what he terms the "double inscription of mimēsis."[5] While himself constructing a series of diagrammatic or typographically "concrete" textual apparatuses (replete with deletions implied by blank space and discontinuous syntax), Derrida goes on to consider Mallarmé's *Un coup de dés jamais n'abolira le hasard*, evoking the idea of a "writing *en abyme*" or "writing in abyss" which cannot simply be reduced to a *phenomenon* by virtue of its becoming a black or white space ("the one and/or the other"):

EVEN WHEN TOSSED UNDER
ETERNAL CIRCUMSTANCES
FROM THE DEPTHS OF A SHIPWRECK
WHETHER
the Abyss
whitened
spreads out
furious

under an incline
hovers desperately
on the wing
its own
in

advance fallen in its pains to straighten its flight
and covering the upbursting swell
levelling off the surging leaps
very inwardly sums up
the shadow buried in the deeps by this alternative sail
to the point of adapting
to the span
its gaping depth as the hull
of a structure
listing to one or the other side...[6]

The radical ambivalence of Mallarmé's "spatialized" text (listing to one *or the other side*) calls back to the typographical logic that informed *Le Livre* (1842–1898), a project occupying the last three decades of the poet's life (commensurate in certain respects with Walter Benjamin's uncompleted *Passagenwerk*). In *Le Livre*, Mallarmé outlined a conception of the "ideal book" as a cosmic architectonics representing "all existing relationships between everything." It was to be a type of *Signatura Rerum*, an "open totality" which would depend for its *sense* not upon the revelation of a (divine) logos, but upon a signifying materiality—the "meaning of format"—a poetics of structure in which "artificial unity" would give way to "hesitation, disposition of parts, their alterations and relationships."[7] In this is represented the "true cult of the modern era."

Un coup de dés, completed just before Mallarmé's death and published in the journal *Cosmopolis* in 1897, can be regarded as a direct articulation of these ideas. Writing in the 1960s, Marshall McLuhan argued that the poem "illustrates…the exploitation of all things as gestures of the mind, magically adjusted to the secret powers of being. As a vacuum tube is used to shape and control vast reservoirs of electric power, the artist can manipulate the low current of casual words, rhythms, and resonances to evoke the primal harmonies of existence"—an effect mirrored in Mallarmé's *simultaneous vision of the page*.[8] *Un coup de dés* is thus less a "poem" in any conventional sense than a poiēsis—a cosmo-textuological spacetime machine. In the words of Cuban poet Octavio Armand:

> The poem seems to evoke the theology and science of distant centuries and to anticipate twentieth-century physics.…On the one hand it is impossible not to feel the ancient music of the spheres in the conjunction of musical score and star chart embodied in the poem. On the other hand, the idea of spacing reading so as to accelerate or diminish movement…links the notions of space and time so closely that it fuses them, creating a spacetime for poetry through the *simultaneous vision of the page*.…Finally, *Un coup de dés* places thought in an orbit very close to Heisenberg's principle of uncertainty. Thought fits, or rather falls, in the cage of chance; it is impossible to escape chance, despite a heroic effort to place a limit on infinity. The fundamental phrase, which is the title, "A throw of dice will never abolish

> chance," continues until the very last line, "All thought is a roll of dice."
>
> Typography underscores the idea that in essence we are reading a single, irrevocable, interminable, abysmal phrase. Scattered throughout the poem—on its only page—and mounted in the largest type used, the title is foregrounded continuously. The last verse, in the smallest type, occupies the background. This is doubly true in both instances: because of the order of reading and because of the spatial expansion or contraction implicit in working with different types. The throw of dice ends in another throw of dice that is the same one and the same as always. Dice, words, ideas, types run across the page until they are lost in the mind. Poem of blank spaces, music of silences. We see, read, hear the forms of absence. Verbal phrase and musical phrase tend towards extreme purity: they expand in silence and they express it… The idea empties in an abyss of infinite possibilities, as does the poem. Poem? Drawing? Score? The poem seems to embody the uncertainty of the throw of dice. It is a genre of genres. *Un coup de dés* that combines and generates genres.[9]

Thus the spatio-temporalizations of Mallarmé's text present themselves in a particularly "literalized" dimension, as an extruded palimpsest or *constellation* whose inscription in perspectival space erases itself under the sign of a temporal singularity. Flattened out, in other words, the twelve sheets of Mallarmé's poem become a single "black page," an abyss of illegibility, as in the Interior Ministry's *Un coup de désastre* (2018).

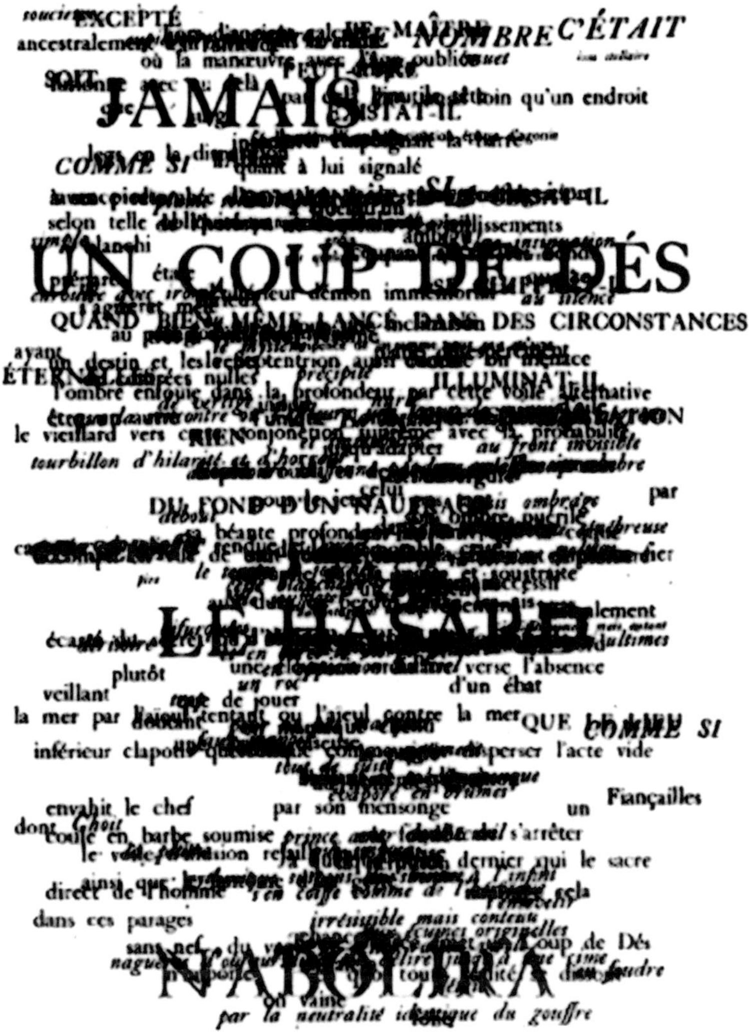

Interior Ministry, *Un coup de désastre* (2018)

It is this prospect that looms also in the background of Marcel Broodthaers's 1969 *Exposition littéraire autour de Mallarmé* (staged at the Wide White Space Gallery in Antwerp)—where, among a display of "industrial poems" on vacuum-formed plastic (like "oversized credit cards"), the artist first exhibited his erasure work *Un Coup de Dés Jamais N'Abolira Le Hasard*. Loosely referencing Robert Rauschenberg's 1953 *Erased de Kooning Drawing* and the rectified readymades of Marcel Duchamp, Broodthaers—in Johanna Drucker's account—"reduces *Un Coup de Dés* to its structure—or to put it another way he elevates the structure of the work to a concept worthy of study in its own right, thus acknowledging Mallarmé's own fetishistic attention to this aspect of his work."[10]

In Broodthaers's rendering, the twelve printed sheets of Mallarmé's poem are mapped onto a series of twelve anodized aluminum plates, engraved with rectangular black strips standing in for the "redacted" text. The result is a kind of "machine code," like a series of punch cards, or minimalist sculptural objects reminiscent of Donald Judd's anodized aluminum boxes (1968) and Elsworth Kelly's "Cité" studies ("Brushstrokes Cut into Twenty Squares and Arranged by Chance," 1951). Interestingly, Broodthaers's "text" also bears striking resemblance to another earlier work of not(at)ional erasure: Earle Brown's Cage-inspired piano piece *Four Systems* (1954) for David Tudor—in which the stave is transformed into a kind of distributed, vertical Malevich construction, where the "lines from left to right define the outer limits of the keyboard. The thickness may indicate dynamics or clusters." Almost inevitably *Un Coup de Dés* invites, as Jacques Rancière says, "a reflection on the relation between words and space"—or between what is called *writing* (including music) and what is called an *image*. "Yet this image," Rancière suggests, in consisting of "an erasure of the entire text and its replacement by black rectangles indicating its spatial distribution," renders Mallarmé's text only conventionally "illegible."[11]

For Rancière, Broodthaers's erasurism equates to a reduction of language to plasticity, a "spatializing mimēsis."[12] But at the same time, and precisely by virtue of this seeming reduction, its "plasticity" calls forth signification: it remains, first and foremost, an "act of erasure." Where Derrida's "sous rature" preserves the graphical ("readable") form of the text, here we're given its typographic distribution (erasure as diagram)—recalling Robert Smithson's "Map for Double Nonsite, California and Nevada" (1968) and Bern Porter's topographic erasure poems, or "map blank-outs," such as "The Inhabitant" (1945), produced while Porter was a physicist on the Manhattan Project and indelibly bound up with the work of compartmentalized state secrecy.[13] We can see Broodthaers's reversioning of Mallarmé in this way, too, not as simple "redactology," but as open encryption—a kind of significatory "hiding in plain sight."

Broodthaers's blacking-out of Mallarmé's *Un coup de dés* (itself an invocation of chance procedures against the "poetic" projection of originary meaning, originality, authorship, and authenticity) creates a field of open-substitution, of semantic dark-matter defined both by a stark materiality and radical ambivalence. The univocal command of meaning is placed, as it were, in suspense or "under erasure"—a stance (as Jerome Rothenberg says of the writings of Jackson Mac Low) "devoid of fanaticism" (it is discursively *blanked out*), yet whose concreteness is nevertheless "political"[14]—insofar as the *ambivalence* of this abyssal text suspends any hierarchy of reference.

Mallarmé's *lingua blanca*, as an exploration of typographics and syntactical recombination, likewise anticipates the atomization—or etymization—of language in Velimir Khlebnikov's *zaum* poetics and Joyce's *Wake*. The materiality of spacing and interval in *Un coup de dés* radicalizes the effect of writing as a form of field-phenomenon or constellation-effect: a simultaneous vision in which linear hierarchies of meaning devolve into a generalized transversality. As Mallarmé writes, "NOTHING WILL HAVE TAKEN PLACE BUT THE PLACE EXCEPT PERHAPS A CONSTELLATION."[15] This prototypical "field composition" is both relativistic (an interplay of inertial frames of reference) and complementary (a play of superposition and decoherence). In presenting itself to perception it simultaneously erases itself: from the particularization of "word, letter, paperspace" (in Joyce) to the semantic event-horizon of the "black page" (etc.).

Proceeding in this vein of reconstitutive erasurism, in 2017 Derek Beaulieu—following a project of decomposing Andy Warhol's *A* down to its punctuation (*à la* John Cage's *Empty Words*)—commenced a series of visual transcriptions of every page of *Finnegans Wake*, in the form of a blind contour drawing (graphite on paper) described as "records of readings" (in a comparable sense to the implied "readings" of Cage's 1976 *Writing for the Second Time through Finnegans Wake*—in which Joyce's text was "reproduced," in a manner of speaking, as a series of mesostics). Beaulieu's re-writing of *Finnegans Wake* situates itself in a constellationof relations to the fabric and contours of Joyce's text, and within a field of iteration in Western literature and art from Borges's conceptual rewriting of *Don Quixote* to the "appropriation art" of Sherrie Levine. Its status as *drawing* places it in a particular relation also to a certain *withdrawal*: as Derrida says, "a *re-drawing*, a *with-drawing*, or *retreat [re-trait]*, at once the interposition of a mirror, an impossible reappropriation or mourning, the intervention of a paradoxical Narcissus, sometimes lost *en abyme*…"[16]

This *erasure* in the act of repetition also implies a certain *blindness* (a blind contour) from which representation speaks (that which is given in place of that which withdraws, in the deferral of signification, etc.). In their most banal formulation, Beaulieu's "records of readings" are a kind of cenotaph, a memorial erected out of *a heap of language*—reminiscent of Smithson's 1966 work of that name and such visual-verbal "deformations" as Ulli Freer's "TORO" and Pierre Joris's "Five Translations from Arthur Rimbaud's *Une saison en Enfer.*" This "simultaneous vision of the page" lists to the side of *both* texture and textuality, in which (in a seemingly paradoxical movement) an act of semantic erasure or withdrawal stands at the center of its signifying possibility.

This paradox (or "paradox lust") is of course recognizable as one of the key tenets of Joyce's text itself—structured as it is around the allegory of ALP's "missing letter" (being the holograph of *Finnegans Wake* no less). This letter, having been lost under mysterious circumstances, is re-discovered (by a hen) in a garbage heap—a textual midden evoked in Robert Smithson's "A Heap of Language" (1966)—and subsequently subjected to a forensic process of exegetical defacement by a certain "grave Brofèsor" (*FW* 124.09). The "record of reading" ALP's letter thus produced resembles a textual fabric "pierced," or *parsed*, "by numerous stabs and foliated gashes made by a pronged instrument" (being the fork of "Brotfressor Prenderguest" [*FW* 124.15], with which he has eaten his breakfast):

> These paper wounds, four in type, were gradually and correctly understood to mean stop, please stop, do please stop, and O do please stop respectively. [*FW* 124.01-05]

At which point Joyce's text itself "breaks down" into a series of quasi-phonetic notations (on the edge of intelligibility), satirically analyzing the significance of the defaced letter's "punctuation":

> to=introdùce a notion of time [ùpon à plane (?) sù"fâç'e']
> by pùnct! ingh oles (sic) in iSpace?! [*FW* 124.12]

But this *defacement of reading* is already a general condition of the text: not, as in the allegory of ALP's letter, as something inflicted by interpretation, but as that which solicits and makes possible "interpretation" from the outset. The simultaneous *drawing* and *withdrawing* of the text—its "punctuation," so to speak—is everywhere evident in the *Wake*'s portmanteau, where terms like "riverrun" invite re-inscription as, for example, "river ran" in order to be conventionally "read"—in other words, to be *grammaticized*, *translated*, etc. Like Perec's lipogrammes, the *Wake* pre-programs and pre-cognizes, so to speak, the *deformations* of "reading" by encoding within itself the processes of its own inscription, deletion, reinscription, and computation. Such processes find an echo in Cage's recodings of the *Wake* and throughout the body of procedural/permutative poetics that eventually feeds into the OuLiPo, including the "concretion" of Ian Hamilton Finlay's serial lexical displacements—like "blackblock (Homage to Malevich)" (1970), whose method might well be described as "lack-and-lock":

lackblockblackb
lockblackblockb
lackblockblackb
lockblackblockb
lackblockblackb
lockblackblockb

—and such "erasure" poems as Jackson Mac Low's "7.1.11.1.11.9.3!11.6.7!4.,a biblical poem" (1955). The sequence "5 biblical poems" was the first occasion on which Mac Low employed chance operations, applied to found texts (Genesis, Numbers Judges, etc.)—though it wasn't published until 1968, in Bernadette Mayer and Vito Acconci's *0 to 9* magazine. The titles of the individual poems (e.g. "7.1.11.1.11.9.3!11.6.7!4.") referred to the poem's system of composition, described by Mac Low as follows: "each stanza has the same number of lines as the number of integers in the title, and each poem has as many stanzas as lines in each stanza. The integers show how many *events* (single words or silences) occur in each line of a stanza.... Silences are represented by boxes."[17]

bpNichol's *Translating Translating Apollinaire: a preliminary report from a book of research* (1979) extends Mac Low's chance and procedural operations of transmission, erasure, interference, etc., into a general poetics of *translation* ("memory translation," "sound translation," "acrostic translation," "re-arranging letters alphabetically," "musical translation," "homolinguistic translation," "stereo translation," "alchemical translation," "durability translation," and "typewriter translation") requiring a generalized logic of formal equivalence.[18] Calling to mind Duchamp's "Apolinère

Enameled" (1916)—in which the author of *Calligrammes* is not only "translated" into an advertisement for Sapolin Enamel paint, but depicted as a bed-frame drawn in a deliberately impossible perspective (an illusion produced by Duchamp's *erasure* of a piece of the frame)—Nichol's polyvalent "equivalence" systems hinge upon a simultaneous *ambi*-valence. As in Raymond Queneau's *Exercices de Style*, the "original" translation of Apollinaire to which the sequence "refers," is endlessly distributed between innumerable and increasingly bifurcating modes of *presentation* (like the *Wake*'s "genetic permutations" around the letters HCE and ALP, and Cage's mesostics on JAMES JOYCE), all the while constituting a "core" of *un*presentability—a "system" of recursive différance in which the so-called limits of intelligibility are placed under the constant strain of *translation*.

The genesis of Nichol's poem sequence began with an early translation-experiment entitled "Translating Apollinaire" (1963), which Nichol began reworking in 1975 by subjecting it to "as many translation/transformation processes as i and other people [including Dick Higgins, Steve McCaffery, Douglas Barbour] could think of": translation placed, so to speak, *en abyme*. Nichol conceived of the work as "openended" and "probably unpublishable," utilizing—among others—collaborative techniques like "alter-and-pass-on" and "alter-and-return" typical of the contemporary mailart networks (some sections of the *Report* were still circulating after Nichol's death in 1988, thereby evoking an ultimate gesture of *authorial erasure*).[19] Translating "translation" into a work of Derridian *dissemination*—across the (implied) entirety of the "verbi visi voco"[20] field of signifying possibility as a kind of cybernetic "communication system"—Nichol's project comes to describe something like a blueprint for a *potential writing*, an open-source poetic "operating system" in general development (see, for example, "TTA 30: poem as a machine for generating line drawings"). Yet *thereby* this blueprint, like the ambiguous "source" its translation system refers to, retains the status of an "originary"—which is to say *interminable*—erasure. It gives itself, as Derrida says, in the dissimulation of itself, as a translation-always-already.

Such generative erasure and reconfiguration of conventional exegetical frameworks (so to speak) evokes a quantum-like undecidability/irreducibility in delimiting a general field of signifying possibility. The record of such "reading"—as the inscription of a "disappearance"—*presents itself* in the form of a double erasure that, like ALP's missing letter, leaves traces (as the holograph *of its own disappearance*, the erasure of its erasure). The sign of "insufficiency" in this work of redaction is not a measure of the failure of "sense," but of a mimēsis of *an erasure at the origin*—"l'acte vide," as Mallarmé says—whose "singularity" is the mark of the unpresentable.

CHAPTER 2

Obliterations and Deviations: The Success Stories of Foundism and Erasurism

IF MARCEL DUCHAMP is universally credited as the inventor of found art, a fully fledged history of modern and contemporary "foundism" would reveal essential differences between the ready-made and the appropriationist strategies developed by artists in the second half of the twentieth century. Among those differences, the most notable are related to a tendency to write through, dis-figure, and refigure already existing works of art (as opposed to everyday objects or, say, samples of utilitarian prose) with a view to providing an alternative, often critical, reading of familiar texts which are often part of a literary or generic canon. As the examples below will show, what is at stake in appropriation in literature is less a gesture aimed at redefining the institutional parameters of what we call art than a revisitation—in the practical as well as in the hauntological sense made famous by Derrida's *Specters of Marx*—of the source text's original and/or accepted meanings. Such strategies can take the form of pastiche and parody, with various degrees of violence and intensity, or of more respectful intertextual homages and détournements.

A survey of found literature could possibly start with Tristan Tzara's famous randomist "How to Make a Dadaist Poem" (1920), which some champion as a precursor of the cut-up technique.[1] One could also begin with Kurt Schwitters's 1923 "P P P P P P P P P," which the author describes as a "pornographic poem" originating in an illustrated abecedarium for children[2]:

P P P P P P P P P
Pornographisches i - - Gedicht

Die Zie |
Diese Meck ist |
Lieb und friedlich |
Und sie wird sich |
Mit den Hörnern |

Der Strich zeigt, wo ich das harmlose Gedichtchen aus einem Kinderbilderbuch durchgeschnitten habe, der Länge nach. Aus der Ziege ist so die Zie geworden.

Und sie wird sich | nicht erboßen
Mit den Hörnern | Euch zu stoßen

The dotted lines indicate where Schwitters cut through the "harmless" poem, suggesting a rather different story replete with truncated innuendos which, as Craig Dworkin aptly puts it, remind us "that without censorship there is no pornography."[3] The meaning of Schwitters's saucy rewriting of the children's primer remains unclear insofar as the poet describes how the text came into being without accounting for its ultimate intention. Is it to undermine classical distinctions between high art and pornography? Is it an attempt to unveil the possibly repressed psychosexual content of the original nursery rhyme? And, if so, is the "pornographic" nature of the poem related to its overtly salacious content (as the abbreviated "go-at]" ["Zie-ge"] finds itself removed from its original, didactic context and evokes a world of satyrs, fauns, and other pansexual creatures)? Or does it refer to the fundamentally *ob-scene* act which consists in showing what happens behind the scenes of one of the best-selling avatars of bourgeois pedagogy? Irrespective of the interpretation, that one of the earliest examples of appropriationist poetry should come from the inventor of *merzbau* might suggest that literary foundism is a somewhat belated extension of the early twentieth-century visual collages of the Cubist or Dadaist variety.

The purpose of this chapter is not to study the collusion between collagist practices and found art; nor is it to suggest that a clean break exists between the historical and the post–World War II avant-gardes in terms of how writers have made use of appropriationist techniques developed by contemporary visual artists. Whether one looks for continuities or ruptures, the first significant post-Dada example of textual foundism occurs in the 1950s, at a time when Brion Gysin and William Burroughs started their experiments with cut-up and fold-in techniques. For Burroughs, the random juxtapositions generated by cut-ups, far from espousing the anti-art of the readymade or the shock tactics of conceptual, proto-uncreative art, are eminently mimetic in their attempts to capture the jolted cadences of contemporary urban life: "Cut-ups make explicit a process that goes on all the time. Every time we walk down the street or look out the window, our stream of consciousness is cut by random factors, random events, random people, random objects. In fact life is a cut-up."[4] For all its self-proclaimed novelty, the cut-up, which began with Gysin's experiments with sliced newspaper clippings, thus seems firmly rooted in Baudelaire's definition of the prose poem (which also grew out of the flâneur's experience of the dizzying rhythms of the "enormous cities" and was strongly linked, in its own way, with the rise of nineteenth-century newspaper culture), on the one hand, and in the uncompromising subjectivism of the modernist stream of consciousness, on the other. (It should come as no surprise that Burroughs acknowledged the influence of John Dos Passos's *USA Trilogy* [1930–1936], which constitutes an early, albeit late modernist, synthesis of the cut-up and the interior monologue.)

The second important category in postwar foundist literature is linked with the development of writing-through techniques, of which John Cage's and Jackson Mac Low's respective mesostic rewritings of Ezra Pound's *Cantos* constitute a foundational moment. The method used by both writers consists in producing a radical reduction of the source text (in Cage's case, the final version is only a few pages long) traversed and upheld by a central, capitalized word which can be read vertically. Cage's writing through of Joyce's *Finnegans Wake* emerges as another salient episode in the genealogy of the avant-garde's engagement with found texts. The "hidden" words can be likened to the poem's "spine" which has "JAMES" and "JOYCE" down the text's center. Cage describes his working method as follows:

> Taking the name of the author and/or the title of the book as their subject (the row), write a series of mesostics beginning on the first page and continuing to the last. Mesostics means a row down the middle. In this circumstance a

> mesostic is written by finding the first word in the book that contains the first letter of the row that is not followed in the same word by the second letter of the row. The second letter belongs on the second line and is to be found in the next word that contains it that is not followed in the same word by the third letter of the row. Etc. If a shorter rather than longer text is desired, keep an index of the syllables used to represent a given letter. Do not permit for a single appearance of a given letter the repetition of a particular syllable. Distinguish between subsequent appearances of the same letter. Other adjacent words from the original text (before and/or after the middle word, the word including a letter of the row) may be used according to taste, limited, say to forty-three characters to the left and forty-three to the right, providing the appearance of the letters, of the row occurs in the way described above.[5]

Cage explains the genesis of his work in terms that emphasize the need to break free from the "rigidity" of Joyce's grammar and approach the "floating" sparsity of classical Chinese and Japanese poetry:

> Reading *Finnegans Wake* I notice that though Joyce's subjects, verbs, and objects are unconventional, their relationships are the ordinary ones. With the exception of the Ten Thunderclaps and rumblings here and there, *Finnegans Wake* employs syntax. Syntax gives it a rigidity from which classical Chinese and Japanese were free. A poem by Basho, for instance, floats in space....Only the imagination of the reader limits the number of the poem's possible meanings.[6]

The reductionist impulse behind Cage's procedural aesthetics is thus geared towards the multiplication of the vectors of meaning generated by the poem, a method which is arguably more "writerly" in the Barthesian sense than its source text, that is, at least if we assume, like Cage, that the reader will fill in the gaps where the original text's syntactic telos was deleted. An "ideal" reader of Cage's mesostics would thus experience what Steve McCaffery describes as a kind of "return of the repressed," "induc[ing] uncanny configurations around themselves, precipitating extreme cognitive disruptions that decommission conventional methods of reading." "Although ordered and restrained by the axial structure," McCaffery adds, the mesostic "nevertheless resonates as a linear disequilibrium; there is a parsimonious quotient of meaning assembled, as if magnetically, around the theme name and beyond that disperses semantic degradations."[7]

McCaffery's analysis relates the sense of disorientation and defamiliarization encountered in Cage's mesostics to Léon Roudiez's Saussurean notion of "paragrammatics." For Roudiez, the paragram reading refers to any reading method or strategy which challenges the normative referential structure of a text from within by forming "networks of signification not accessible through conventional [i.e., linear] reading habits."[8] Praising the vertiginous "Saussurean sublime" afforded by paradigmatic composition, McCaffery describes "the percolation of words through the paragram" as a process which contaminates the notion of an ideal, unitary meaning and thereby counters the supposition that words can 'fix' or stabilize in closure,"[9] which seems an adequate description of the structural and reception patterns of Cage's mesostics.

Charles Bernstein cites Mac Low and Cage as influences behind his 1975 poem "Asylum," an early textual erasure which

I

wroth with twone nathandJoe
A
Malt
jhEm
Shen

pftJschute
sOlid man
that the humptYhillhead of humself
is at the knoCk out
in thE park

Jiccup
the fAther
Most
hEaven
Skysign

Judges
Or
deuteronomY
watsCh
futurE

uses Erving Goffman's 1961 *Asylums: Essays on the Social Situation of Mental Patients and Other Inmates* as its source text. Responding to Goffman's sociological critique of institutional life and the dehumanizing effects of mental institutions—where individuals are cut off from the wider society and subjected to strict regimes of control—the poem emerges as an interrogation of linguistic and social containment. Constructed entirely from the opening and closing fragments of sentences in Goffman's text, Bernstein's poem reconfigures the sociological prose of institutional life into a poetic matrix that reflects the ideological architecture of closed systems. In doing so, "Asylum" not only engages with the disciplinary logics of total institutions, but also stages its own formal analog to these structures through its fractured syntax and visually dispersed layout. The result is a linguistic bachelor machine, in Duchampian-Kafkaesque terms[10]: a closed-loop apparatus of textual production that replicates isolation even as it resists it.

By selecting fragments taken from the initial and terminal phrases of Goffman's sentences, Bernstein crafts a field of suspended transitions—each line a broken bridge between syllogistic coherence and semantic collapse. These fragments become simultaneously residual and anticipatory, ghosts of the discourse they once structured, the poem's syntax becoming the formal correlate of the asylum's own enclosures—words and phrases trapped mid-function, arrested before meaning can be fully enacted. Bernstein's method, while preceding by two years Ronald Johnson's foundational erasure *RADI OS*, discussed below, anticipates similar concerns: how to locate poetic space within the ideological detritus of preexisting texts, and how to make visible the violence of omission that sustains institutional power (or, in the case of Johnson, dominant reading strategies of canonical works). Ultimately, "Asylum" resists not only the institutions it draws from, but also the closure of interpretation itself. It is a poem that refuses to resolve, instead dwelling in the charged interstices of language and institution.[11]

The political and formal tensions activated by Bernstein's appropriation of Goffman find a broader theoretical framing in Craig Dworkin's *Reading the Illegible* (2003), which remains

-3-

culture" (to modify

of being "in" or "on the inside" does not exist apart

home world. Upon entrance

abesements, degradations,
humiliations and profenations

is mortified

of self. In civil life

taboo. Although

home. The role

such. It may not be

up, at a

cycle, the time

advancement, in

"civil death"

world. The process

well. We

life history, photographing, weighing, fingerprinting, assigning
numbers, searching, listing personel possessions for storage,
undressing, bathing, disinfecting, haircutting

nakedness. Leaving off

on, with

clothing, combs, towels, soap, shaving sets, bathing facilities

disfigurement, beatings,
shock therapy, surgery

dispossession

integrity. At admission

way. Given

movements, postures, and stances

demeaning. Any

regulation, commend or task

the most sustained investigation into the aesthetic and ideological strategies of literary foundism. Dworkin's study helps articulate the stakes of such appropriative practices, especially as they foreground the material and semantic fractures within inherited texts. As its title indicates, Dworkin's study is essentially about how we read "illegible" texts, texts that "appropriate and then physically manipulate a source text, employing erasures, overprintings, excisions, cancellations, rearrangements, *et caetera*, to render part of the source text literally unreadable."[12] Such formal and structural manipulations can be explored in the works of such diverse writers and artists as John Cage, Rosmarie Waldrop, and Susan Howe, works that encourage a "paragrammatic" reading, a reading that challenges normative grammar/syntax and forms "networks of signification not accessible through conventional reading habits."[13] In order to explore these issues, Dworkin proposes a method of analysis that seeks to unveil "the politics of the poem: what is signified by its form, enacted by its structures, implicit in the philosophy of language, how it positions its reader, and a range of questions relating to the poem as material object." Truly "radical formalism,"[14] Dworkin believes, is a practice which takes us beyond aesthetic considerations into the realm of politics. Ultimately, it urges us to (re-)consider poetry as a physical act and emphasizes how the range of a text's linguistic and political range depends to a large extent on the material conditions of reading/writing as well as on the mechanics of reproduction. In his chapters and sections devoted more specifically to erasure, Dworkin addresses, among other examples, the overprintings of Rosmarie Waldrop's *Camp Printings* (1970) and the procedural "writing-through" techniques of John Cage and Jackson Mac Low, with occasional forays into non-literary examples such as Asger Jorn's tactics of defacement or Robert Smithson's geolinguistic poetics. In doing so, he succeeds in demonstrating that these works, for all their apparent similarities, vary widely in methodology and theoretical position.

Dworkin's corpus remains centered on creative appropriations of already existing sources, beginning with the tactics of *détournement* deployed by the Situationist International, a movement which strove to develop a theory and praxis of micropolitical activity deriving some of its intensity from the "strategic misuse"[15] of source texts common to the works discussed throughout the book. Dworkin, however, remains critical of their enterprise and also addresses the contradictions that lie at the heart of Guy Debord's project to challenge the principle of passive reproduction and consumption that governs the "society of the spectacle." More specifically, Dworkin wisely acknowledges the danger of equating indeterminacy and "radical formalism"[16] with political radicalism as such—"even those works which encourage or require creative reader participation," he writes, "can operate in accord with hierarchies and manipulative control, and indeed that manipulation is frequently all the more insidious given its ulteriority." Such is the lesson to be drawn from the Situationists' recognition that, since acts of resistance are automatically incorporated as an integral part of modern capitalism, the only alternative left to the avant-garde is to "transform the geography in which one is (always) already trapped"[17] through a creative misuse of established norms and codes. Or, as Steve McCaffery puts it in terms more specifically related to the art of literary erasures and writings through, to seek an "incorporation of otherness in sameness," "a radical incorporation of alterity in which a work is defined in terms of another author."[18]

Dworkin's own selection of paragrammatic texts in *Reading the Illegible* comprises examples as various as Guy Debord and Asger Jorn's artist's book *Fin de Copenhague* (1957); Marcel Broodthaers's 1969 "edition" of Mallarmé's *Un coup de dés*, of which more will

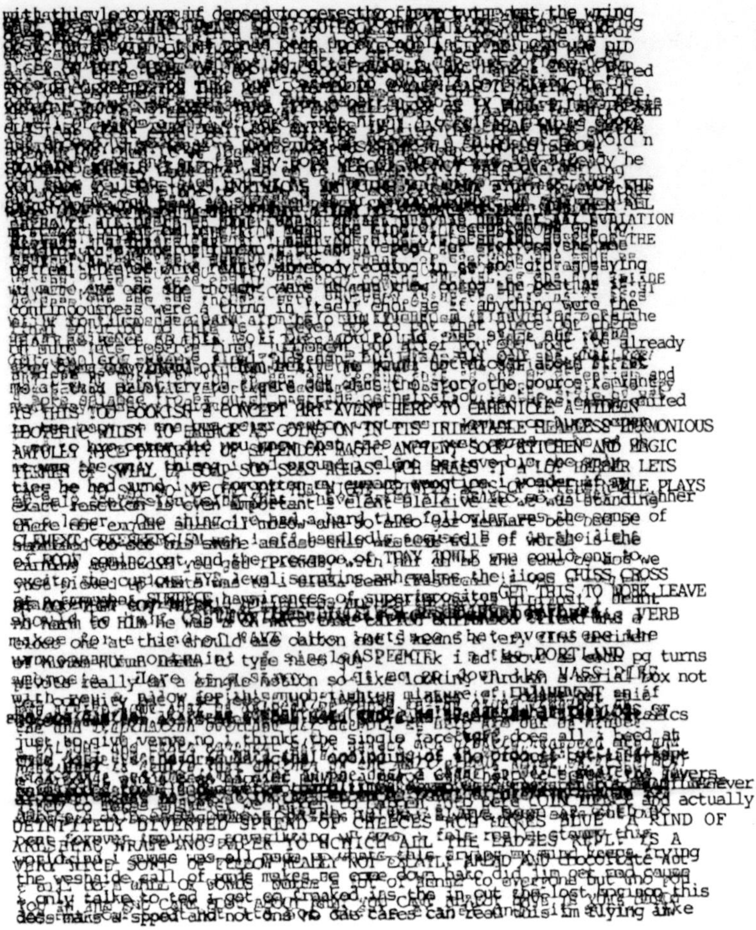

be said later; John Cage's *Writing through Finnegan's Wake* (1978), and Susan Howe's palimpsestic experiment, "Melville's Marginalia" (1993). At the center of both Dworkin's and McCaffery's work, the impact of Gertrude Stein's "composition as explanation"—in which discursive prose enacts its own critique insofar as interpretation is seen to emerge from the mechanics of writing itself—is far-reaching, as is that of Charles Bernstein's poem-essay "The

Artifice of Absorption," which advocates a poetics of opacity countering the ideals of transparency, sincerity, and directness of self-expression promoted by "official verse culture."[19] Bernstein's anti-absorptive mode reaches an intensified form in his own *Veil* (1976), a chapbook containing blocks of prose made of overtyped lines resulting in a typographical cover-up proclaiming its own self-effacing illegibility.

Bernstein's anti-absorptive model implicitly addresses the complexities of poetic foundism, which generally partakes of an aesthetics whose obliterative and deletionist tactics encourage heightened attention to the (opaque) materiality of the signifier. Such experiments are perhaps best understood in light of what Marjorie Perloff has described as the paradigmatic shift which takes us from modernist models of unmediated transparency to a postwar preoccupation with the fabricatedness of the aesthetic moment, one in which "natural" objects (whether they are concrete or affective) are always already filtered and processed by language and media.[20]

A similar emphasis on marked artifice, opacity, and (inter-) mediation offers foundist artists a crucial ground on which to experiment with something akin to Stein's "composition as explanation" method, revisiting found textual objects in a way which deconstructs their cultural authority while foregrounding their material and historical specificities. In Stein's own poetry, this process is driven by "a groping for using everything" (e.g., everyday objects, mundane kitchen talk alongside more elevated registers and concerns) and a desire to conflate temporality into a "continuous present," a fluid, relational reality enacting "an inevitable beginning of beginning again and again and again."[21] Stein's relational poetics; her obsession with repetition, difference, and variation; and her constructivist preference for non-hierarchical models of composition emerge as paramount moments for foundist poetics, an environment in which such strategies thrive on constant and continuous rewritings, de-writings, and disfigurations of already existing texts and artifacts.

Stein's "Composition as Explanation" begins with a recognition of the impact of World War I and a comparison between the art of warfare and the emergence of a new modernist sensibility in the arts. Marcel Duchamp's 1920 *Fresh Widow*—which, like Stein's essay, emerges as an odd fish in modernist waters and a precursor of postmodern and deconstructionist things to come—also addresses the aftermath of the war, albeit from a different perspective, that of the deaths of millions of soldiers and civilians alluded to in its tragi-comical erasurist transformation of "French window" into "fresh widow." Metonymically depicting a country of recent war widows locked up in their homes and mourning the loss of their husbands, the opacity of Duchamp's darkened openings suggests bereavement as much as it points to the illicit sex which may happen behind the secrecy of the black windows (another possibly saucy visual wordplay hinting at female spiders eating the male partners during sex). But Duchamp's pun- and innuendo-ridden object may also refer to the word "veuve" (the French word for "widow"), which famously designated the guillotine, or to the German word "frech," which further points at the sexual misconduct of the "cheeky" widows during or after wartime.

As for Duchamp's insistence that the black squares should be made of leather and be "shined every day like shoes,"[22] it smacks of foot fetichism and sadomasochism at the same time as it queers up the surviving wife's alleged confinement to domestic duties ("Fresh

Widow," incidentally, was the first work Duchamp signed under the pseudonym of Rrose Sélavy). Such historicizing of Duchamp's readymade reveals the differences between "Fresh Widow" and other apparently similar blackouts mentioned above, such as Robert Fludd's "Et sic in infinitum," Laurence Sterne's black page in *Tristram Shandy*, and Kasimir Malevich's "Black Square." It also serves to unveil the complexity and diversity of erasurist practices within the social, the aesthetic, and the political spheres, a subject to which we now turn.

Effacement, defacement

The examples examined so far attest to the ongoing influence of found material in postwar experimental poetics. The more specific—and more recent—success story of erasurist poetics also deserves our attention, if only because it has been ignored or relegated to the margins of literary and art history. There are two basic ways of practicing the art of erasure: the first consists in a partial or total crossing, blanking, or rubbing-out of the source text; the second involves covering up the text with extra textual or graphic material which can be credited with an added aesthetic value in and of itself, beyond its capacity to veil or conceal. Among recent literary examples, Crispin Glover's collagist *Rat Catching* (a humorous treatment of Henry C. Barkley's 1896 *Studies in the Art of Rat-Catching* characterized by the use of old prints and other found artwork) clearly falls into the second category, as do Will Ashford's *Recycled Words* (a rather undistinguished rehash of Tom Phillips's *A Humument*) and Matthea Harvey's *Of Lamb*, which was carved out of a biography of Charles Lamb, traversed by the nursery rhyme "Mary had a little lamb" and subsequently complemented with Amy Jean Porter's illustrations. The first, and significantly more represented, category comprises Stephen Ratcliffe's *[where late the sweet] BIRDS SANG* (another text cut out of Shakespeare's *Sonnets*), Mary Ruefle's correction fluid–covered *A Little White Shadow* (based on an anonymous nineteenth-century manual published "for the Benefit of a Summer Home for Working Girls"), Austin Kleon's self-explanatory *Newspaper Blackout*, Janet Holmes's further reduction of Emily Dickinson's already elliptical verse in *The ms of my kin*, Srikanth Reddy's *Voyager* (an erasure of Kurt Waldheim's memoirs), and Jonathan Safran Foer's artist's book *Tree of Codes*

(2010), which die-cuts holes in Bruno Schulz's *The Street of Crocodiles*, revealing "future" events and allowing the reader to read several pages at once in a way which is reminiscent of B. S. Johnson's 1964 *Albert Angelo*. (The lacunary structure of Foer's narrative tragically evokes Schulz's murder by the Gestapo and the loss of many of his unpublished works during World War II.)

As we have seen and will see, erasurism is rooted as much in contemporary philosophy's deconstructionist turn as in Duchampian found objects and Situationist *détournements*, of which most of the examples examined in this book constitute both an extension and a critique. Recent and current developments in foundist and erasurist art are closely associated with visual artists and writers (many of them poets) appropriating already existing texts with a view to modulating their meaningfulness and legibility. This says a lot about the relevance of found texts to late twentieth-century and early twenty-first century culture which, by and large, values concepts over technique, rewriting over originality, self-reflection over aesthetic norms and values. Poised between effacement and defacement, erasure pursues a logic which considers the artwork as an unfinished object that awaits future readings and negotiations to be provisionally refashioned, recycled, and reconsumed. As the source text becomes the model for the artists and the victim of their transgressions and violations, the boundaries between creator and creature, process and product, producer and consumer are dimmed in a haze of colliding gestures and interpretations. One example amongst many which appeared in the early 2000s, David Dodd Lee's *Sky Booths in the Breath Somewhere,: The ASHBERY ERASURE Poems* (2010), a collection of erasures of John Ashbery's poetry, follows a simple rule: the author reads through the source poem and selects words or parts of words ("as Ashbery ordered them (consecutively)" in a given collection) which he subsequently arranges into new lines, building upon the "incredible storehouse of language which is a John Ashbery poem" and "selecting language with an eye toward absurdity/humor" to create new patterns of suggestion and ambiguity.

Paul Ricoeur memorably identified Marx, Nietzsche, and Freud as the founding fathers of a "school of suspicion"[23] which steers readers, critics, and artists to read between the lines and deconstruct the strategies by which art can conceal its own constructedness and disguise its ideological complicity with dominant structures of power. Should erasure art practiced by Dodd Lee and countless recent foundist poets be considered as a casualty of the "terminal case of irony" in which the humanities find themselves at the present time, driven as they are by an "uncontrollable urge to put everything in scare quotes"?[24] Even though erasurism does not necessarily set out to destroy the art work per se, it is often prompted by a desire to revisit familiar, predominantly canonical genres and texts with a view to foregrounding and/or correcting their limitations and deficiencies.[25]

One of the most remarkable and in many ways unsurpassed examples of such a revisiting of dominant genres is Charles Coqueley de Chaussepierre's 1770 *Le roué vertueux*,[26] a work which contains four "chants" preceded by "arguments" sketching, in an elliptical manner, the premises of a convoluted plot "which puts before your eyes the reality of the most refined virtue, and the image of the most atrocious crimes."[27] The chants themselves, however, consist mainly of punctuation marks and a few words amounting to a catalogue of overblown, tearjerking clichés typical of what the author deplores, in his preface, as the fallacies and pitfalls of eighteenth-century melodrama. The emptiness of the pages, the author humorously argues, will protect him against criticism while encouraging the readers to fill in the blanks and "extend and embellish his ideas."[28] (The fact that de Chaussepierre was an official royal censor adds another twist to this unlikely tale of generic parody.) A literal precursor of Theodor Adorno's anthropomorphic praise of punctuation marks ("An exclamation point looks like an index finger raised in warning; a question mark looks like a flashing light or the blink of an eye"),[29] *Le roué vertueux* exposes the clichés of sentimentality and pathos used and abused by many of de Chaussepierre's contemporaries while foregrounding the expressive power of typographical signs.

An erasure of an imaginary performance, *Le roué vertueux* is a satire of the bombastic rhetoric and violent telos of sensationalized tragedy, which includes the need for unlikely situations and characters (such as the oxymoronic "virtuous scoundrel" mentioned in the title) whose purpose is to elicit increasingly intense and extreme emotions. If there was a successor to de Chaussepierre's erasurist hapax, it would probably resemble Kenneth Goldsmith's erasure of Stein's essay "On Punctuation," which only preserves the punctuation marks of the original text. By letting them spread themselves out freely on the physical space of the page, Goldsmith's "Gertrude Stein's Punctuation from Gertrude Stein on Punctuation" pays tribute to Stein's own claim that punctuation marks "have a life of their own," periods being particularly central to her poetics insofar as they do not "serve you in any servile way as commas and colons and semi-colons do." Goldsmith's reduction also stresses the crucial importance of visuality in reading Stein, an aspect of her writing which allies with Goldsmith's utopian vision of translinguistic appeal of concrete poetry.[30]

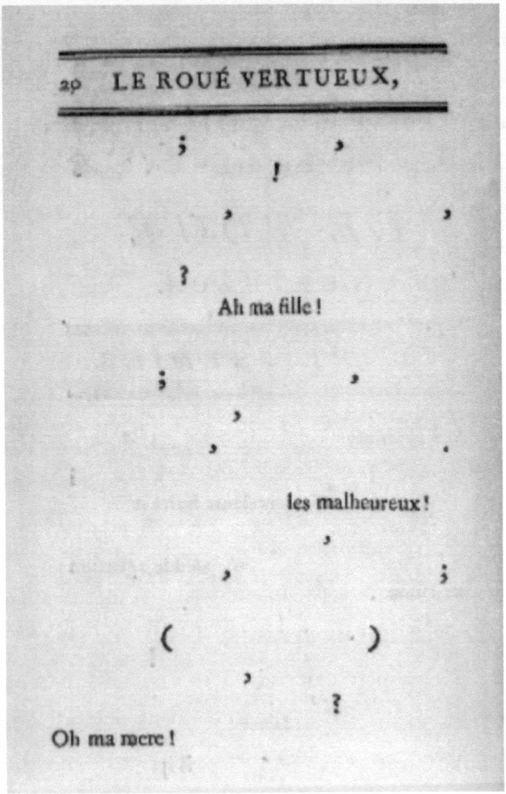

29 LE ROUÉ VERTUEUX,

; , ! , , ? Ah ma fille ! ; , , , . les malheureux ! , , ; ( ) , ? Oh ma mere !

More recently, Derek Beaulieu's *a, A Novel* (2017) is an equally "uncreative" rewriting of Andy Warhol's *a* (1968), a transcript of reel-to-reel tapes Warhol made of one his Factory collaborators (Ondine, aka the actor Robert Olivo) and produced by various typists in the mid-1960s. The text allegedly spans a period of twenty-four hours but consists of different recording sessions. Beaulieu scanned the 451 pages of Warhol's found text, digitalized it, and used Photoshop to manually erase all the spoken words, preserving only the interjections, onomatopoeia, descriptions of sounds and ambient noises, and other contextualizing indications inserted by the typists. The result is described by its publisher as a "visually powerful half score/half novel [that] highlights the musicality of non-narrative sounds embedded within conversation."[31] Beaulieu's work is a rather Steinian gesture conveying the "rhythm" of Ondine's personality as expressed by his compulsive talk and amphetamine-fueled ramblings.

Beaulieu has defined erasure as "a way of writing which mines existing texts; it is ultimately a readerly practice—the ultimate close reading."[32] This definition accounts for other reductionist works produced in the last few years. These include *Local Colour* (2011)—a visual translation of Paul Auster's novella *Ghosts* erasing all its words except those which designate colors and replacing them with swatches of the hues they designate—and *La disparition*, a similar chromatic reduction of Perec's novel applying the color spectrum of Rimbaud's "Sonnet des voyelles" to the vowels appearing in the first four pages of the source text.

As suggested above, the "ultimate close readings" that underlie erasure writing can be usefully related to the poetics of found art made famous by Duchamp's readymades. But where Duchamp elevated ordinary objects to the level of art by separating them from their context and use value, erasure artists have pursued rather different goals over the last fifty or so years as their main referent remains the original artwork itself, which is subjected to diverse forms of physical manipulations whose function and significance can only emerge from the tension between the found and the revised, the original and its "effaced" avatar.

What matters here is that even the most radical form of erasure is essentially a kind of rewriting. As with other more familiar forms of rewriting (Jean Rhys's *Wide Sargasso Sea* and countless other postmodern, perspectival neo-Victorian novels come to mind), the

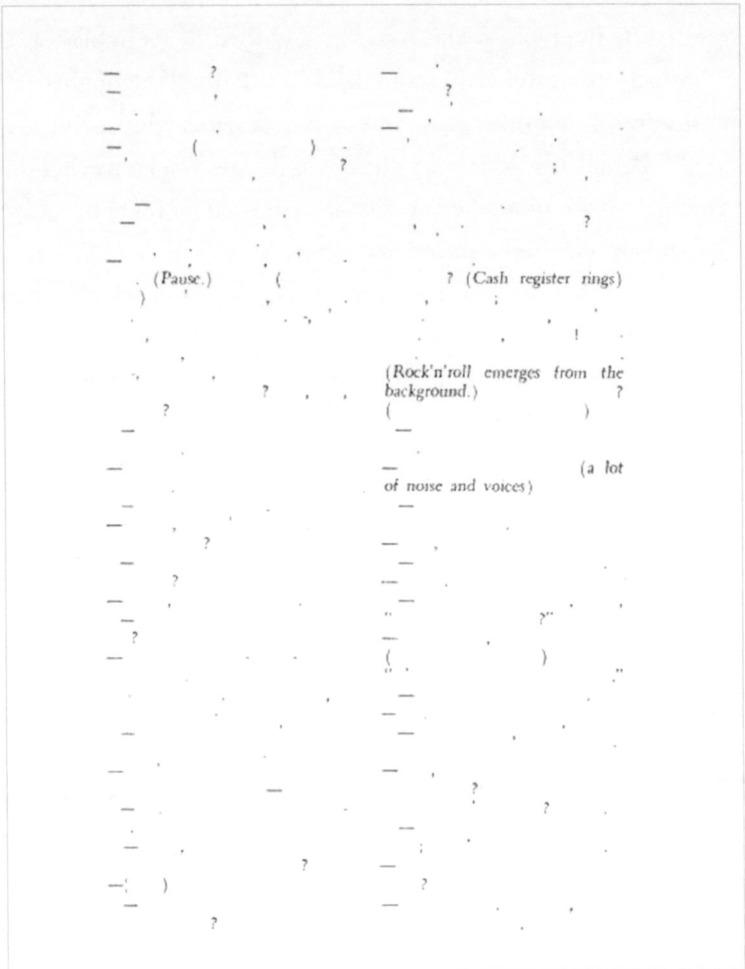

ghost of the source text is bound to continue to haunt its "treated" version. Its obliterated content is always likely to return with a vengeance as its previous vectors of meaning must leak through, in a more or less explicit and visible fashion, irrespective of whether readers or viewers are already familiar with the original text. That said, erasure poetics differs from postmodern rewritings insofar as

its act of undoing affects not only the content of the text but also (and primarily) textual matter as such. It is this concretist attention to the physical and material properties of language which unites all the diverse forms of deletion, obliteration, covering-up, canceling, scratching, rubbing out, blotting, etc., that are grouped here under the umbrella term "erasure." While much attention has so far been given to the practices of contemporary poets, examples abound in other, paraliterary genres such as graphic novels and comics. In the latter field, Jochen Gerner's oubapian blackout *TNT en Amérique* (2002) stands out. Gerner obliterates the pages of Hergé's 1932 *Tintin en Amérique* with black ink, substituting pictograms and isolated one-word balloons for the original panels. The selected details and micro-events of the plot and dialogue become the main focus of attention in the absence of a visible whole by which to contextualize them. Gerner's reduction of "TINTIN" to "TNT" evokes the exploded quality of the layout although the words preserved from Hergé's version are reinscribed in their original position on the original page. Gerner's reworking of the plot abstracts key moments and concepts mostly related to the themes of violence and corruption present in the original volume, published a year before Prohibition was repealed under Franklin Roosevelt. In doing so, it translates Hergé's popular story into an abstract, minimalist canvas, a semiotic reduction of the plot to its most basic "hardware" executed against a dark background, "black as a reference to censorship, nighttime, evil, the mystery of as yet unveiled things."[33]

The appeal of *TNT en Amérique* also lies in its intriguing and wittingly crafted "appendix," which converts Gerner's sixty-two pages into so many short poems, further reshuffling the book's narrative and ideological significance, as in the opening piece which remixes words selected from Hergé's bubbles into a delightful Cubist four-liner worthy of Pierre Reverdy or Max Jacob: "La production garde les volets fermés / Un adversaire reste à l'hôtel / La production reste à Chicago / L'hôtel garde l'oiseau."[34]

Whether in the form of Broodthaers's direct homage to *Un coup de dés* or in Gerner's Oubapian blackouts, Stéphane Mallarmé

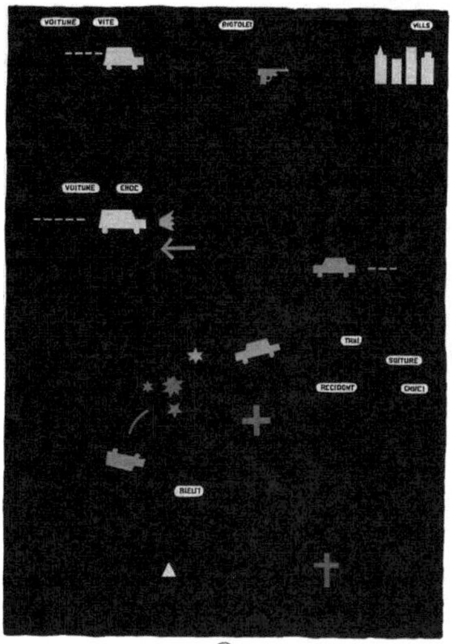

4

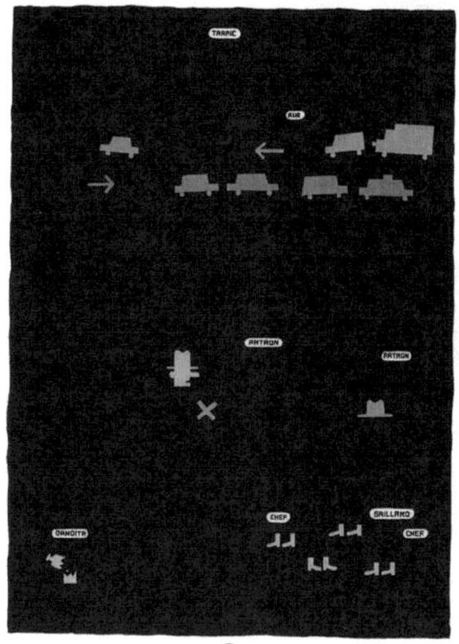

5

once again appears as the presiding consciousness of a constellation of poets who explore the relationship between absence and presence and for whom the spaces and silences between words matter at least as much as words themselves or the things they designate. Mallarmé's poetry is geared towards the creation of paradoxical objects which cancel themselves as soon as they are named (one is reminded of his "absent tomb," his "flights which have not fled," and the "abolished bauble of sonorous uselessness" of his aptly de-titled Sonnet allégorique de lui-même"[35]). Besides unsettling traditional notions of authorial control and controlled authorship in a space effecting the reciprocal annihilation of negativity and positivity ("confronting [the] existence [of chance], negation and affirmation fail,"[36] the poet writes in *Igitur*), the scattered spatial layout of Mallarmé's textual roll of the dice in his 1897 *Un coup de dés jamais n'abolira le hasard* would seem to afford endless readerly combinations and permutations multiplied by the "eternal circumstances of the dice throw" ("All Thought Emits a Throw of the Dice"[37]).

Marcel Broodthaers's 1969 version of *Un coup de dés* resubtitles the Gallimard edition of Mallarmé's poem into an "IMAGE," obliterating the entire text of Mallarmé's poem and replacing it with black typographical rectangles on the poem's double spreads. In doing so Broodthaers foregrounds the sheer spatial arrangement of the words in the book to the detriment of its referential potentialities.[38] "IMAGE" parenthesizes Mallarmé's prefacing claim that the page should be opened up as a canvas inviting a "simultaneous vision"[39] and upon which "the paper intervenes each time an image ceases or withdraws of its own accord."[40] It represents a literal extension of the poet's famous pronouncement that "verse should not consist of words but of intentions, and all words should efface themselves before sensation."[41]

Mallarmé's insistence on the (self-)effacement of words and the importance of "sensation" reflects his more general commitment to "paint[ing] not the thing itself, but the effect it produces" (Mallarmé 1959: 137). Born out of a conviction that artists can only work "by elimination…all acquired truth being born only from the loss of an impression (245)," Mallarmean poetics ultimately suggests that poets themselves are "merely empty forms of matter" in the face of "the Void which is the truth."[42] The first edition of Broodthaers's "IMAGE" further emphasizes this notion by printing the obliterated text on translucent paper conveying the depth as well as the two-dimensional plasticity of Mallarmé's verbo-visual experiments. The artistic and philosophical implications of this gesture are perhaps best summarized by Jacques Rancière when he writes that "IMAGE" "accomplishe[s] Mallarmé in his refutation," opposing several forms of artistic self-suppression resolved in an "indifferent spatiality" ruled by "the power of blankness."[43] In Broodthaers's "IMAGE," Mallarmé becomes both the victim and the perpetrator of a radical poetry of (self-)erasure.

The eraser as a concrete and aesthetic object reemerges in Jérémie Bennequin's ongoing *Ommage*, in which the French artist proceeds to rub out the pages of the Gallimard edition of Marcel Proust's *A la recherche du temps perdu*. The outcome of this process is a series of performances and photographs showing not only the blotted-out pages of the book but also the residue of the performance itself, with worn-out erasers and mounds of blue-gray eraser dust and crumbs being displayed as a miniature *arte povera* installation on the artist's desk. The title's pun on "gommage" ("gommer" = "to erase" in French) and "homage" is symptomatic of the ambivalent status of erasure as a poetic practice capitalizing upon the urge to undo and destroy while paying an ambivalent tribute to the object under attack.

Bennequin's erasurist obsession knows no bounds, and one suspects that he will never finish rubbing out Proust, even though he is rumored to work on a different page of the Gallimard printed text every day for about an hour. By forcing us to look at (rather than read) the fading words, *Ommage* foregrounds their physical vulnerability on the page. As for the creased and wrinkled pages themselves, they bear witness to the fact that any artwork carries the structural and material seeds of its own destruction. Perhaps more importantly, they also breathe a peculiar kind of nostalgia, albeit veiled with irony, which we associate with the dog-eared pages of well-loved books: only a worn-out book can become an object of affection, which is the measure of its fading physical integrity.

CHAPTER 3

■

Composing the Holes: Poetry sous rature

THE CANONICAL STATUS enjoyed by Mallarmé and Proust looms large in Broodthaers's and Bennequin's erasure experiments. Like Broodthaers's "IMAGE," Bennequin's *Ommage* suggests that such acts of undoing—whether affectionate, ironic, or both—often originate in an attempt to deal with the pressure of influence. In *The Anxiety of Influence*, Harold Bloom famously argued that poets since Milton have sought to escape from their predecessors' haunting importance. In view of the examples discussed so far the erasurist antidote to the danger of being derivative or of producing inferior work would seem to lie in deconstructive attempts to undo the past altogether through the disfiguration or correction of past works and/or the erasure of origin. In many of the works mentioned and analyzed in this book, the word "correction" carries an element of punishment as well as improvement and one is reminded here of Bloom's notion of the "clinamen,"[1] which designates a creative misreading which is likely to remedy the deficiencies and limitations of the source text.

Appropriately enough in the context of Bloom's model, one of the earliest examples of textual erasurism in contemporary poetry is Ronald Johnson's *RADI OS* (1977, reprinted in 2005),[2] which partially erases the first four books of John Milton's *Paradise Lost*, a volume at the heart of which lies another ur-story of erasure, that of the names of the fallen angels "blotted out and ras'd / by thir Rebellion, from the Books of Life" before they were worshipped by fallen men as pagan deities and given new names. Such theological considerations, however, seem absent from *RADI OS*, which seems less concerned by man's disobedience and its correlative moment, Satan's revolt against God, than with finding in Milton's poem what Guy Davenport aptly described as "those clusters of words which were originally a molecular intuition of the complex harmony of nature whereby eyesight loops back to its source in the sun, the earth, the tree, our cousin animals, the spiraling galaxies, and mysteriously to the inhuman black of empty space."[3] Johnson's excavation of Milton's poem carefully purges most of the religious references and debates that inform the source text, reducing Milton's Baroque epic to a succession of Mallarmean moments of ellipsis, wordless spaces, and visual silences. Deprived of its epic, moral, and biblical *ossature*, Johnson's excavation of *Paradise Lost* reads as an abstract choreography of elemental simplicity and monumental grandeur, a textual landscape in which Milton's vocabulary of myth, unfettered by the strictures of blank verse, emerges as a tribute to silence, the invisible, and the interstitial. Making meaning arise out of the spatial relationships between the words on the page and the vectors of meaning they "radiate" towards each other, *RADI OS* (excerpted below) abstracts Milton's use of natural imagery into what the author himself calls "a cosmology of the mind and a sort of Blakean exploration of the imagination."[4]

Who, from the terror of this

empyreal

Irreconcilable

of joy

answered

Too well I see

: for the mind

swallowed-up

entire

in the heart   to work in fire

words the Arch[5]

Even though Johnson can be placed in a line of other rewriters of Milton, ranging from William Blake to Charles Zukofsky, the main influence behind his reduction of *Paradise Lost* is a musical work: Lukas Foss's 1967 *Baroque Variations*. Foss's "perforated" rendition of Handel's Concerto Grosso, Op. 6, No. 12 features "groups of instruments play[ing] the Larghetto but keep[ing] submerged into inaudibility (rather than pausing)."[6] "The inaudible moments leave holes in Handel's music (I composed the holes)," Foss writes. One closer look at the sheet music reveals that the "holes" are indicated by two signs: *Nientes* meant to make the notes inaudible and smaller notes which, rather than indicating diminuendos fading into silence, require the string players to bow the notes without allowing the bow to touch the strings. Such moments in Foss's score (pictured here with *N* marking the inaudible notes) thus delineate a musical pantomime of sorts which does not separate the muted notes from the original context in which they appeared, nor does it convert them into silence ("no pauses"). Rather, the performers' half-executed gestures remind their audience of the original score, and one suspects that listeners familiar with Handel's opening Larghetto will mentally fill in the blanks upon hearing Foss's "perforated" version, in the same way as Milton scholars are likely to remember the source text from which Johnson's "Milton *imagiste*"[7] was excised.

The title of Johnson's collection also evokes medical radiographies: the caesura between RADI and OS in Johnson's title implicitly strips *Paradise Lost* to the bone. (Here, we could extend the discussion to contemporary music from Cage to wiping analog tapes to digital ProTooled remixes.) Wilhelm Conrad Röntgen's discovery of X-rays in 1895 affected the whole history of art, dividing contemporary painters into two categories according to their ways of representing the body, and the skull in particular: the "traditionals," such as Ensor and Cézanne, who continue to use the calvarium as a symbol of worldly vanities, and the "moderns," who are interested in exploring the inside mechanics of the body, unencumbered by metaphorical concerns, a option of which Meret Oppenheim's X-rayed skull wearing jewelry is a paramount example.[8]

Marjorie Perloff evokes radiography in her analysis of the uses of "arthrography" (an X-ray examination of the structure of a joint) in Johnson's later collection, *ARK*, arguing that Johnson's lettrist manipulation of textual material allows him to examine and diagnose "what lies beneath the surface" and the plural conditions in which meaning arises from the combination of neighboring words.[9] Johnson's X-rayed version subjects Milton's *Paradise Lost* to a similar treatment, revealing the lyrical backbone of the epic while isolating some of its vital semantic "organs," deriving its inspiration from the curvatures and asperities of their source text like "the painters of Lascaux found their horses in the rock... wherever there was a bulge in the cave wall that suggested equine solidity."[10]

Johnson originally blotted out Milton's words with a black pen, a method whose popularity with poetic erasurists has remained steady over the last thirty or forty years, as suggested by Travis Macdonald's *The O Mission Repo* (2008) and Austin Kleon's *Newspaper Blackout* (2010). While such works display the results of their deletions on their source texts, others, such as Janet Holmes's erasure of Dickinson, *The ms of m y kin* (2009), follow Johnson's example in cutting out words and leaving what is left of the text in its original place on the page. The poems erased by Holmes were all written during the first two years of the Civil War, a period during which Dickinson wrote nearly half of her works. Even though poems such as "It feels a shame to be Alive" and "They dropped like flakes" testify to her concern with the sacrifices and cruelties of the battlefields, Dickinson cannot be credited with having written explicitly about the Civil War, and her reclusiveness has done a lot to marginalize her contributions to war poetry per se. Holmes's collection sets out to combat Dickinson's public image by selecting words that underline the power of her war imagery at the same time as they invite a parallel with the convulsions of early twenty-first-century history. The following section, for example, is as much about Dickinson's own responses to the war as it is about our recent experience of world conflicts and crises. Holmes's intentions become even clearer when we learn that her erasure produces "occasional speakers" including George W. Bush, Donald Rumsfeld, Osama bin Laden, and journalist Daniel Pearl, as well as "soldiers, terrorists, occupiers, insurgents, and combatants on both sides of both the wars in Afghanistan and Iraq."[11] What emerges from Holmes's text is a tale of exile, brutality, and dispossession bringing to the fore the tragic reversals and repetitions of history. Holmes's reductionist approach to Dickinson's own radical minimalism produces a form of visual poetry in which the "lines" are held together by a structural and semantic glue which, while being already present in the source text, is further abstracted as it grows to represent presence within absence, the ghost of the source text haunting our present hurts, losses, and anxieties.

Now it may be argued that editing a nineteenth-century war poem into a poem about US foreign policy by singling out words such as "Shadows," "Death," "Camp," and "Desert" is no great accomplishment. (One is here reminded of Ron Silliman's recent rant against erasurism: "I'm not convinced that we need to have an 'erased' edition of every major work of the English language.... Do we really need *EAVES OF ASS* or *OWL* or any of the other 'edited' masterworks that must surely be in the offing? What is the value of a gesture when taken out of context?"[12]) And that works of canonical writers (including Shakespeare, Melville, and Dickinson herself) have been more profitably and challengingly revisited by the likes of Susan Howe, Jen Bervin, Stephen Ratcliffe, and Steve McCaffery. Among these revisions Shakespearean erasures stand out. And Vincent Broqua has emphasized how Stephen Ratcliffe's reworkings of the Bard's sonnets in *[where late the sweet] BIRDS SANG* are "inheritors of Mallarmé's poetics of the spatial page (via Marcel Broodthaers's already discussed erasure of *Un coup de dés jamais n'abolira le hasard*), as well as direct contemporaries of Larry Eigner's sculptural texts: by their rarefaction on the line, some of the words and syllables from Shakespeare's sonnets are left to their vibration, just as our memory sometimes retains a few words from a text and allows them to echo."[13] Rather than encouraging—or reflecting—some kind of speed reading of the source text, Ratcliffe's erasures "act as rhymes for the eye within the text and bring forward what might have otherwise been overlooked when reading Shakespeare's text as a whole."[14]

Jen Bervin's 2004 *Nets* undertakes something similar while granting the reader access to the original work which still appears in faded form. The poems in Johnson's *RADI OS* result from the complete deletion of the "unwanted" words, leaving no trace of the original text except for the layout of the page (the surviving words still appear where they belong in Milton's poem). Bervin belongs to a different category of erasure poets who have opted for a format which allows the reader total or partial access to the original work. In doing so, Bervin relegates Shakespeare's poems to a faded background text upon which the selected words appear in bold ink. Unlike Johnson's, Bervin's "reduction" does not stress the elemental and the natural but, rather, tends to strip the Bard's sonnets to abstract, self-reflexive musings bearing the mark of post-Language writing ("In singleness the parts / Strike / each in each / speechless song, being many, seeming one"[15]). Bervin's "reduction" strips Sonnet 8 down to a three-liner describing the polyphonic texture of the palimpsest through the coexistence and concomitance of its various enunciations: ("In singleness the parts / Strike / each in each / speechless song, being many, seeming one"). Sonnet 35 visually and verbally suggests (with the parentheses inevitably evoking the lettrism of E. E. Cummings) the "eclipse of meaning" resulting from an elusive poetic fort-da game, whereas Sonnet 63 paradoxically represents the disappearance of the speaker, diluted in black ink under the splitting effects of palimpsestic writing. As for Sonnet 64, it ventures into Bervin's personal experience of early twentieth-century American history ("I have seen / towers / down-razed / loss / loss" [16]), an aspect of her work which allies her with Holmes and, more intriguingly perhaps, with Tom Phillips's final version of page 4 of his "treated Victorian novel," *A Humument*, perhaps the arch-example of textual erasurism, of which more will be said later.

According to Bervin herself, her erasures are meant to "strip" the source text down "to the 'nets,'" with the aim of opening up the poetic space of the poem, revealing its porosity and multiplying its semantic vectors, opening the way to another place ("I stripped Shakespeare's sonnets bare to the 'nets' to make the space of the poems open, porous, possible—a divergent elsewhere"[17]).

"When we write poems," Bervin adds, "the history of poetry is with us, pre-inscribed in the white of the page; when we read or write poems, we do it with or against this palimpsest."[18] In other words, Bervin does not conceive of writing apart from rewriting, and Shakespeare, the source author of *Nets*, is the most salient example to date of the figure of the "rewriter," revising and adapting existing historical chronicles and plays to current tastes at a time when copyright did not exist and when notions of originality and novelty had not yet become touchstones of aesthetic value. In this sense, the examples of erasurism considered so far are perhaps best examined in light of Kenneth Goldsmith's "uncreative writing," which promotes the reappropriation, the re-visitation, the copy-paste, and the reiteration of found texts susceptible to be deconstructed, re-crossed ("written through"), and remixed in an age of digital dematerialization and globalization of contents. Such is perhaps one of the meanings of Bervin's "nets," which refer as much to the World Wide Web as to the webs of connections, interweavings, and correspondences outlining the "divergent elsewhere" to which her poetry aspires. This textile metaphor is presented in more a literal form in a more recent work, *The Desert* (2008), an artist's book in which the author embroiders a textilo-textual network through the work of art historian John Van Dyke's *The Desert: Further Studies in Natural Appearances* (1901), outlining a new aesthetic framework emerging from the text thus "crocheted".

Beyond Ratcliffe and Bervin, the Bard has continued to inspire erasurists and "writers-through." One thinks, in particular, of Jason DeBoer's 2016 *Annihilation Songs* (a volume of short stories written exclusively on the basis of the lexicon of *Hamlet*, *The Tempest*, and *The Two Gentlemen of Verona*) and Steve McCaffery's

2016 *Dark Ladies* (an Oulipian exercise in political and social criticism, summoning up the deleterious climate of the George W. Bush administration while incorporating the final rhymes of Shakespeare's 154 sonnets). Such experiments combine the joint strategies of rewriting and revisitation, in the aesthetic and spectral senses of "revisitation." They display a conflicted relationship with a canonical text whose intimidating presence evokes Tom Phillips's attempt to purge a Victorian novel from its conservative, misogynistic, and anti-Semitic biases.

In an article which appeared in *Jacket2* a year after Bervin's *The Net* came out, Travis Macdonald—himself a practicing erasurist—locates the emergence and proliferation of erasure poetics, especially in the United States, within a broader environment of moldering surfaces, corporate overlays, and palimpsestic residues:

> The poetry of erasure is taking place all around us. Underneath the pavement, behind newspaper headlines, on paste-layered billboards and graffiti-laden walls, our communal landscape is continuously peeling away and papering over itself. Its very surface is a living thing in flux between the dueling processes of decay and renewal, driven in the name of progress to adapt to the shifting contextual demands of culture or be replaced, removed, re-imagined. While this process can, at times, be artificially postponed, nothing escapes its effects forever. This world demands of its denizens a constant and vigilant revision of form.[19]

Central to this description is Macdonald's hypothesis that erasurism arises out of a need to acknowledge the syncopated rhythms of cultural and technological transformations as they affect our relationship with language itself. Language, Macdonald argues, "has been stretched, spread thin into a commercialized representation of itself" so that "as the means of communication quicken and advance the communal discourse, the demands of re-contextualization rise in direct relation."[20] By emphasizing the dialectical movement between decay and renewal which governs such a process, Macdonald points to the central paradox lying at the heart of erasurist poetics and politics, namely that "the poetry of erasure" is always already necessarily divided against itself, governed as it is by a principle of addition and subtraction, deletion and covering-ups, deconstructive and reconstructive strategies, however much this particular paradox is associated with the age of Global Information (the success story of artistic erasures begins largely in the 1960s with the foundational experiments of Tom Phillips and Emilio Isgrò and has grown exponentially ever since).

Travis Macdonald's own erasure, *The O Mission Repo* (an erasure of the *9/11 Commission Report* published in 2008), is another erasurist attempt to make sense of the contradictions of early twentieth-century American politics. Like Bervin, Macdonald allows the reader to return to the full textual source while simultaneously or alternately reading the new text that emerges from the partially obliterated words: the crossed-out parts of Macdonald's book can still be deciphered by readers interested in exploring the original document and/or in understanding the nature of the erasurist's adjustments and manipulations. In such works, the canceled words, instead of being deleted or rendered illegible by other means, are placed "under erasure" (*sous rature*) in a gesture reminiscent of Heidegger's and Derrida's typographical gestures signaling the presence of inadequate yet necessary words. In different but related ways, Heidegger's anti-metaphysical approach to language and Derrida's anti-logocentric *ratures* offer a useful model for an understanding of how erasure art "works," in theory as well as in practice. What is undone or "deconstructed" here is less the meaning of words—or, more generally, the relationship between signifier and signified—than the familiar deconstructive aporia that follows from the fact that the question of whether words can actually mean something can only be asked through language itself.

Macdonald's striking through of the *9/11 Commission Report* once again reveals the strong practical and conceptual connections between erasurism, censorship, and various forms of violence perpetrated against the source text which becomes the target of the rewriting. Certain pages of Macdonald's text can be read as a *mise en abyme* of the deconstructive and disfiguring strategies, the object of its "attack" being itself a response to the 9/11 trauma and an attempt to renegotiate the shifting parameters of counter-terrorism. The sentence (or poem) that appears between the redacted words of Macdonald's text ("All / aboard / the morning / that America's / 'Fasten Seatbelt' sign / turned / on"[21]) implicitly compares the United States with a drifting aircraft and conveys the urgency of action and panic which prompted the redaction of the final section of what was nominated for a National Book Award in nonfiction in 2004.

Conceptual artist Jenny Holzer's series of enlarged silkscreens entitled *Redaction Paintings*, which also proceeds to strike through and cover up declassified U.S. legal documents, evidences a similar impulse, one whose purpose is to give voice to the personal tragedies that were left out of the legal documents. The words emerging from Holzer's erasures refute the pretense to objectivity of the rhetoric of bureaucracy which characterizes "torture memos" at the same time as they attempt to give voice to those who experienced detainment, confinement, and torture.

One of the most discussed examples of archival erasurism is M. NourbeSe Philip's *Zong!*, an erasure of a late eighteenth-century Middle Passage legal report surrounding the drowning of some 150 African slaves, a massacre engineered by the captain of the slave ship *Zong* in order to collect insurance monies. Even though "Os," the first section of Philip's collection, comprises words exclusively taken from its source text and rearranged on the space of the page, the collection as a whole displays a wider range of deconstructive strategies culminating in increasingly disjoined and truncated word sequences. Such tactics, the author reflects, result in a new text which appears mutilated "as the fabric of African life and the lives of these men, women and children were mutilated."[22] Philip went on:

> I murder the text, literally cut it into pieces, castrating verbs, suffocating adjectives, murdering nouns, throwing articles, prepositions, conjunctions overboard, jettisoning adverbs: I separate subject from verb, verb from object—create semantic mayhem, until my hands bloodied, from so much killing and cutting, reach into the stinking, eviscerated innards, and like some seer, sangoma, or prophet who, having sacrificed an animal for signs and portents of a new life, or simply life, reads the untold story that tells itself by not telling.[23]

Here, the separation of subject from verb and verb from object is more than just a metaphor for the impersonal economic transactions which turn the slaves into mere properties of the colonizers. It also explains and justifies the nature of Philip's attacks against the syllogistic syntax of the legal text, whose disjointed residues confer to *Zong!* its commemorative and sacrificial value. What happened then on the global scale of colonialism and slavery is repeated at the level of the individual consciousness so that the reader skims the text for words and phrases "as one would cast one's eyes over the sea looking for bodies—so much flotsam and jetsam."[24]

Zong! straddles across erasurism per se and more complex and diverse writing-through techniques which are poised between textual deletion, selection, fragmentation, permutation, and redistribution. Philip's experimental archivism is likened to that of a censor working "like the law whose role is to proscribe and prescribe, deciding which aspects of the text will be removed and which remain."[25] In the recent development of poetic erasures, this process bears affinities with the archival method practiced by, say, Rosmarie Waldrop's writing through of Roger Williams in *A Key Into the Language of America* (1994), Susan Howe's *The Nonconformist's Memorial* (1993), or Tracy K. Smith's 2017 rewriting of Thomas Jefferson's Declaration of Independence into a document about the legacy of slavery, a reality carefully ignored in the source text.

Unlike most erasures published in the last quarter century, however, *Zong!* is as much driven by a deconstructive critique of normative linearity and cultural hegemony as by a desire to mend and amend the ways in which some essential parts of the history of the Middle Passage have been blotted out or relegated to the margins. Laurie Lambert captures the repairing nature of erasure in Philip's poem as follows: "These are poems of repair, meant to account for and counter the archival erasure of black life by creating textual and oral spaces in which structural erasures are acknowledged." Hence the author's decision to include the names of the slaves at the bottom of the pages of the volume's opening section, a reference to their relegation to the footnotes of history which points to their physical position in the ship hold ("the Africans on board the 'Zong' must be named. They will be ghostly footnotes floating below the text.... [The] idea at [the] heart of the footnotes in general is acknowledgement—someone else was here before—in *Zong!* footnote equals the footprint"[26]).

Zong! #6

question therefore

the age

eighteen weeks

and calm

but it is said . . .

– from the maps

and

contradicted

by the evidence . . .

question

therefore

the age

The spectral dimension of *Zong!* finds its ultimate expression in the last poems of the collection: in which patterns of overtyped, faded, washed-out words succeed each other in a jarring choreography of drowning typographies. It should, then, come as no surprise that Philip's collection opens with a quote from *Hamlet* and concludes with a reference to Derrida's *Specters of Marx*. Her acknowledgement of the hauntological dimension of erasure is explicitly addressed in the book's closing "Notanda":

> I come—albeit slowly—to the understanding that *Zong!* is hauntological; it is a work of haunting, a wake of sorts, where the spectres of the undead make themselves present. And only in not-telling can the story be told; only in the space where it is not told—literally in the margins of the text, a sort of negative space, a space not so much of non-meaning as anti-meaning.[27]

Philip's insistence on the spectrality of *Zong!* extends beyond the commonplace that phantoms of the past are bound to haunt the present. Her traumatology does not limit itself to unearthing the layerings of the tormented biopolitics of the slave trade. Rather, it seeks to capture and reactivate the paradoxical moment when the muted voices of the drowned resonate with the disjunct convulsions of modern and contemporary history. As we have seen and will continue to see, the entire history of erasurism, from its most trivial to its more crucial avatars, has been marked by such hauntological themes, from Tom Phillips's ectoplasmic revisitation of an obscure Victorian novel to Ronald Johnson's reduction of Milton's *Paradise Lost* and on to Jonathan Safran Foer's un-representations of the Holocaust in *Tree of Codes*,[28] Susan Howe's explorations of

Melville marginalia, Crispin Hellion Glover's Edward Gorey-ish, Tim Burton-ish spectral cover-ups of Henry C. Barkley's 1896 *Studies in the Art of Rat Catching*, and Marc Atkins's recent "Newspeak" series, which revisits Bede's eighth-century *Ecclesiastical History of the English People* while interrogating the broader themes of censorship and control.

The next chapter will continue to explore the nature of the hauntological in erasurist practices across other artistic disciplines, focusing on the Mallarmean interplay of concealing and revealing and its potential to unravel the complexities and complications of the vestigial, the ruinic, and the interstitial.

CHAPTER 4

On Detailism and Effacement

IN THE FIELD OF NARRATIVE PROSE, the detail is traditionally (albeit debatably[1]) associated with the accumulation of discrete and meticulously selected elements which confer to fiction an identifiable and "truthful" context by which to account for the characters' social, physical, and mental surroundings. This particular use of the detail as a documentary tool aimed at a global, panoramic description or suggestion of social and psychological conditions has been one of the mainstays of literary realism and has characterized many nineteenth-century novels setting out to produce the illusion of an unmediated representation of the outside world in a way that builds upon the dialectics of the general and the particular, as well as of the concrete and the experiential. In *The Rise of the Novel*, Ian Watt famously argued that the "exhaustive presentation"[2] that characterizes realist fiction "make[s] the words bring [the] object home to us in all its concrete particularity."[3] It is thus through the addition and accumulation of details that one paradoxically succeeds in capturing the objects and characters in their irreducible specificities: "through this generous heaping of particulars," Watt concludes, fiction produces the illusion that "the novel is a full and authentic report of human experience."[4] Such are the premises of "detailism," the dominant paradigm in studies of fictional realism from Lukacs's study of the "particular" to the Barthesian "effet de réel" and his later theory on the *punctum*. In the early decades of the twentieth century this mode of writing, in which the detail contributes to the "mimetic adequacy"[5] of the whole, was radically challenged by the more skeptical and disjunctive strategies of experimental modernism which sought to establish the notion that our perception of the world is fundamentally unstable and subjective and is therefore best described through fragmented utterances and multiple points of view.

Be that as it may, even the interior monologue, for all its attempts to convey the undifferentiated mental flow and sense perceptions of the characters "as they happen," continued to rely on a careful selection of discrete units (including memories, sense impressions, Proustian *madeleines*, etc.) which metonymically suggested a character's global personality and state of mind, no matter how discontinuous, dislocated, and disconcerting these narratives may appear at a first reading. Arguably, the final blow to the "detailist" paradigm outlined above was struck by the syndrome Robert Musil described in *The Man Without Qualities* as a mental condition which is marked by a process of "deterioration which transfers the will to live from the whole to the details,"[6] a condition not unlike that of the protagonist of Jorge Luis Borges's "Funes the Memorious," for whom the detail, far from eliciting a comfortable feeling of stability and verisimilitude, becomes a source of anxiety and alienation. Having mysteriously acquired a capacity for total recall following a horse fall which renders him blind, Ireneo Funes cannot help perceiving and remembering every detail of his real or imagined life ("A circumference on a blackboard, a rectangular triangle, a rhomb, are forms which we can fully intuit; the same held true with Ireneo for the tempestuous mane of a stallion, a herd of cattle in a pass, the ever-changing flame of the innumerable ash, the many faces of a dead man during the course of a protracted wake. He could perceive I do not know how many stars in the sky"[7]). For Funes, who soon becomes overwhelmed by what Baudelaire once called a "riot of details,"[8] the very notion of the detail becomes completely irrelevant and even incomprehensible precisely because he experiences his environment as a place where "there [are] nothing but details, almost contiguous details."[9] Funes, who lives in a world in which every single thing seems to exist on the same level of awareness, rejects any form of categorization, selection, and generalization, which leaves him intensely vulnerable and incapable of coping with the endless variety of the physical world as he becomes "almost incapable of general, platonic ideas,"[10] fails to "understand that the generic term dog embrace[s] so many unlike specimens of differing sizes and different forms," and is even "disturbed by the fact that a dog at three-fourteen (seen in profile) should have the same name as the dog at three-fifteen (seen from the front)."[11] In short, he succumbs to what Jean-Pierre Maurel has defined as the "Nausea syndrome" which has infected modern literature from Hugo von Hofmannsthal to Musil, Jean-Paul Sartre, Witold Gombrowicz, William Faulkner, Thomas Bernhard, and beyond: "Nausea is the loss of the unity of being and it is the fragmentation of reality into billions of little bits which no longer bear any relationship to each other and whose sensorial and perceptual sum can no longer give birth to a totality."[12]

In the field of poetry—a genre which requires the reader's attention to focus on the smallest compositional elements (the line, the word, and, in the case of certain forms of concrete poetry, the letter)—the detail is not an easy thing to locate or identify. An interpretive category potentially ingrained in each of the poem's basic units, it is both nowhere and everywhere. Because we have been taught that reading a poem amounts to paying equal attention to each of its individual parts, poetry does not regard the individual part as an element in a solid heap or aggregate of verisimilitude. On the contrary, contemporary poetry (at least in its most radical and innovative trends) has largely striven to hypostasize the "word as such" and consider it in its concrete materiality while multiplying its referential vectors. In such a context, the detail in poetry acquires the status of a linguistic fetish imbued with polysemic substance and mobility and which, representing itself first, increasingly draws attention to its own factitiousness, visuality, and artificiality.

The proximity of poetic practice to the production of concrete poets and visual artists facilitates an understanding of the detail in its relationship with a potentially totalized (or totalizing) whole, a preoccupation which is at the heart of all the erasurist experiments considered in this chapter. Before we start to look at the works themselves, it may be useful to distinguish the detail from other related categories such as the part (a strictly structural, ideologically neutral term which can be regarded as a hypothetical degree zero of the detail) or the fragment, whose contiguity to the detail has occupied the minds of art historians such as Georges Didi-Huberman and Daniel Arasse—suffice it to postulate, at this stage, that the detail, unlike the fragment, does not refer so much to the distinction between the part and the whole as to what separates what is seen from what is not seen by the reader or viewer.

Perhaps one of the most eloquent illustrations of this particular definition of the detail is acted out in Ernesto Sabato's short novel *The Tunnel*, in which the narrator, the artist and murderer Juan Pablo Castel, develops an obsession which begins when he sees a woman at an exhibition of his work focusing on one small detail of one painting of his "Maternidad," a detail which he himself considers the most important part of the work and which nobody besides him and the woman had so far paid attention to.[13] Since, to quote Master Sainclair in Gaston Leroux's mystery novel *The Perfume of the Lady in Black* (1908), the detail lies simultaneously in "what is hidden and what can be seen,"[14] or, even more paradoxically, in "all that can be seen and that is not seen" ("dans tout ce qui se voit et que l'on ne voit pas"[15]); the "oddness" of the detail, like that of Poe's "The Purloined Letter," indeed lies in its capacity to continually oscillate between concealment, disguise, and revelation.

Daniel Arasse has described the art historian as a "fireman of the detail": "A detail is shocking, it must be extinguished and explained so that everything becomes smooth again."[16] Such an approach urges us to resist the temptation to elucidate and *extinguish* the detail and focus instead on its irreducible and disturbing materiality while paying special attention to the oddities and "hidden narratives" that it may or may not conceal. In this, we will follow the examples of Georges Didi-Huberman and Daniel Arasse, who have both considered the detail's potential to "incarnate something"[17] as shown by the second anti-mimetic thread[18] of Johannes Vermeer's *Lace Maker*, an example used by both critics to emphasize the radical "living presences"[19] that emanate from the artist's paintings. "Doomed by the tyranny of matter," the stain-like thickness and "material opacity"[20] of Vermeer's lace thread creates an *effet de pan*[21] (the term "pan," which is derived from

Marcel Proust, could be translated as a "section" of a wall or a curtain) which designates "that part of the painting which ostensibly interrupts... like a crisis or a symptom, the continuity of the work's representative system."[22]

Reading A Humument

From E. E. Cummings's celebrated "leaf poem" to Eugen Gomringer's "wind" and beyond, the history of concrete poetry has been characterized by what Rosemarie Waldrop describes as a form of "reduction," a genre in which "both conventions and sentence are replaced by spatial arrangement."[23] Tom Phillips's *A Humument: A Treated Victorian Novel* (1966–2016)[24] stands out as one of the most accomplished, and also one of the most *literal*, examples of this spatialist turn, one which foregrounds the materiality of the word ("only the / word / pictures the / word"[25]) while problematizing and diversifying the function of the detail. The genesis of *A Humument* is best described by the author himself:

> Like most projects that end up lasting half a lifetime, this started out as idle play at the fringe of my work and preoccupations. I had read an interview with William Burroughs (Paris Review, 1965) and, as a result, had played with the "cut-up" technique, making my own variant (the columnedge poem) from current copies of the *New Statesman*. It seemed a good idea to push these devices into more ambitious services. I made a rule; that the first (coherent) book I could find for threepence (i.e., 1 1/4p) would serve.... [O]n a routine Saturday morning shopping expedition, I

> found, for exactly threepence, a copy of *A Human Document* by W. H. Mallock, published in 1892 as a popular reprint of a successful three-decker....I had never heard of W. H. Mallock....[H]e does not seem to be a very agreeable person: withdrawn and humourless (as photographs of him seem to confirm) he emerges from his works as a snob and a racist (there are some extremely distasteful anti-semitic passages in *A Human Document* itself)....However, for what were to become my purposes, his book is a feast. I have never come across its equal in later and more conscious searchings. Its vocabulary is rich and lush and its range of reference and allusion large. I have so far extracted from it over one thousand texts [out of the 367 pages the original comprises], and have yet to find a situation, statement or thought which its words cannot be adapted to cover.... When I started to work on the book in late 1966, I merely scored unwanted words with pen and ink. It was not long though before the possibility became apparent of making a better unity of word and image, intertwined as in a mediaeval miniature....Thus painting (in water-colour or gouache) became the basic technique, with some pages still executed in pen and ink only, some involving typing and some using collaged fragments from other parts of the book (since a rule had grown up that no extraneous material should be imported into the work). In some recent pages I have incorporated elements of their printed predecessors.[26]

The final version of Phillips's book was published in 2016, every single page of the first edition having been re-treated at least once, thus bringing the project to its full completion. It is unlikely to be superseded as an example of how erasure can be experienced simultaneously as negation of and as a prelude to the emergence of art. It is also a text which crafts a different, decentered kind of lyricism which surfaces from its saturated novelistic textual matrix ("Join / written / breath / to / written heart / to / the nerves / talking / in a / shirt / to / record / all physical maladies / and yet no / pains of the soul."[27]

A Humument differs from the radical post-representational thinking that informs, say, Johnson's *RADI OS*, as the "blanks" from which meaning can reemerge are filled with visual poems and poetic paintings which emerge as so many creative misreadings, extending rather than short-circuiting the process of interpretation. Phillips's cover-up "ex-humes" Mallock's novel, each page of the source text being partially painted and penciled over so as to foreground the remaining textual rivulets spoken by an impersonal "un-author" (as Phillips jokingly refers to himself). The sheer textural depth of *A Humument* is not evidently answerable to the shock tactics of any previous found art tradition either, even though his successors are many. In the recent history of the visual arts, another example of "overpainted books" is that of CoBrA member Pierre Alechinsky's aptly named "Dispaint, Describe" (1979), in which the artist's acrylic painting is framed by a series of smaller paintings executed on pages from old registers.[28]

According to Alechinsky himself, this method is dictated by the need to "draw over the italic scripts of a bygone age, as a way of escaping the blank page"[29]; like Phillips's work, it has also been likened to the art and style of comic strips. One essential difference between Alechinsky (who has extended his method to school work, stamped envelopes, and other found texts) and Phillips is that the former does not seek to manipulate or rewrite the text but, instead, often tends to use words primarily as an "expressive constraint": more often than not, the handwritten words and figures suggest forms and images that are implicitly present in the writing, as in the recent "Palimpsest, I-IX" series (2005) in which the overall form of the schoolbook divisions and multiplications inspire the painter to create diverse objects, animals, and characters, including, most prominently, his now world-famous snakes.[30]

Phillips's (de)compositional methods are significantly more eclectic. They range from chance procedures (including tossing coins or consulting the *I Ching*) to more controlled collages, writing-through methods, and various manipulations resulting in the creation of "textual characters" such as Bill Toge, whose last name derives from the words "together" or "altogether" ("the only words from which his name can be extracted"[31]). The sum of these techniques has been praised by Mary Ann Caws as originating in and prolonging "the most fertile veins of Surrealism, Concretism, Spatialism, Conceptualism, and the inexhaustible Symbolism."[32] Phillips's models and references are equally diversified—they comprise works as diverse as illuminated medieval manuscripts, Francesco Colonna's extravagantly arcane *Hypnerotomachia Poliphili* (the blueprint of Bill Toge's story, according to the author), and comic books.

A Humument generally posits and foregrounds the materiality of text prior to signification. But its concretist aspects should not obscure the fact that the poetic rivulets that traverse his treated pages are deeply rooted in a close reading of Mallock's novel and its underlying ideologies and representational strategies. The opening page of Phillips's book bears programmatic overtones (we are still referring to the 4th edition published by Thames and Hudson in 2005[33]). According the "bubbles"[34] of text that have been preserved ("The following / sing / I / a / book / a / book of / art / of / mind art / and / that / which / he / hid / reveal / I"[35]) the goal is to reveal by erasing. The pale yellow background which covers Mallock's text (*A Humument* is replete with painted interiors featuring walls, wallpapers, curtains, tapestries, and carpets) uncannily conjures the Proustian yellow wall section evoked by Didi-Huberman in the appendix to *Devant l'Image*. But it also reverses the logic of the *effet de pan*, since the yellow section is not the background of the "poem" (for want of a better word, I will refer to the textual "bubbles" as poems in the following pages) but, instead, the "plaster" that recovers it, as shown below.

Unlike Bergotte, the old writer of Proust's *The Captive*, who becomes overwhelmed and severely shocked by the "precious matter" of the yellow wall (which, incidentally, is actually not a wall but a section of a roof in the actual painting), the reader—busy as he is trying to decipher the textual elements on the page—does not succumb to the traumatic ecstasy of the *effet de pan* of Vermeer's "View of Delft" (Bergotte dies shortly after reeling from the shock of contemplation). Still, Bergotte seems to be anticipating some of the compositional strategies of Phillips's "treated novel" when he sadly recognizes that his "last books are too dry" and that he "ought to have gone over them with a few layers of colour, made [his]language precious, like this little patch of yellow wall."[36] One cannot help thinking that Bergotte is not using a metaphor here but reflecting upon the superiority of actual over linguistic "color" and deploring the literal "dryness" of (type)writing compared to the material freshness and organicity of the brush stroke.

In the opening page of *A Humument*, the big blue arrow directing the reader to the next page emerges as a rather humorous reference to Phillips's attempts to dismantle and reinvent the linearity

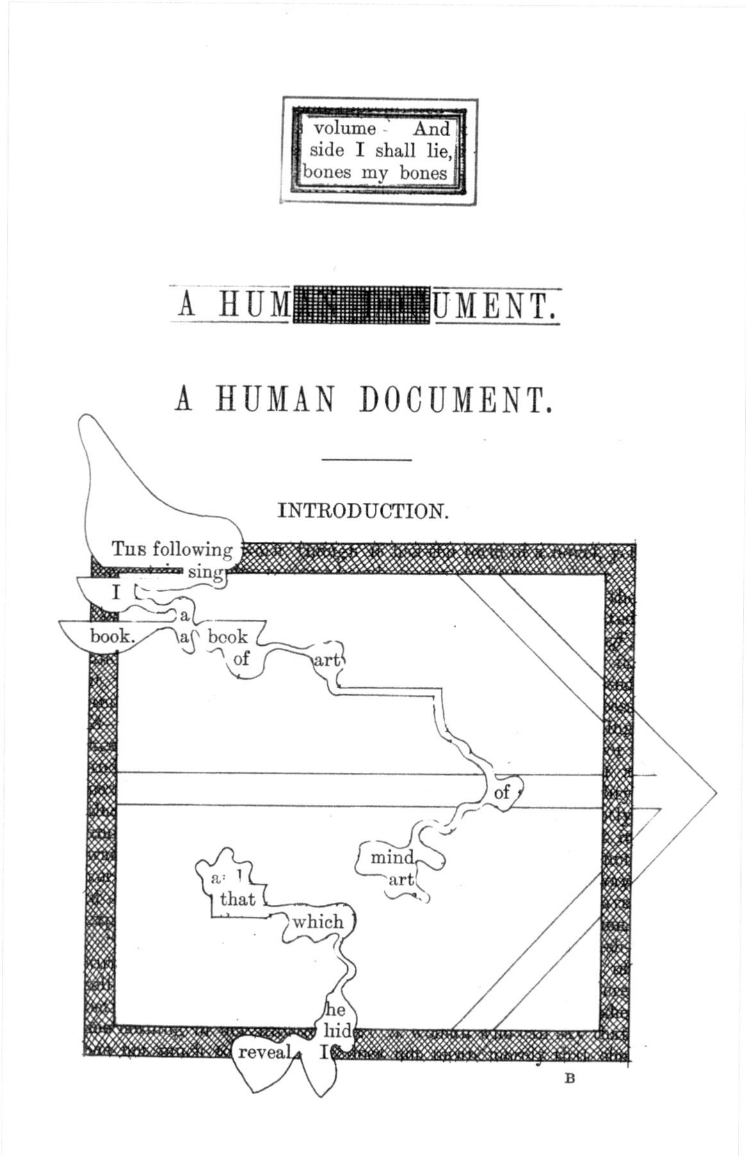
volume And
side I shall lie,
bones my bones
A HUM UMENT.
A HUMAN DOCUMENT.
INTRODUCTION.
The following
sing
I
a
book. a book
of art
of
mind
art
that
which
he
hid
reveal I
B

of the original text (although one cannot help reading the poetic bubbles themselves in a conventional, linear fashion).[37] Because they are "framed" by drawn bubbles and rivulets, the details in Phillips's book necessarily reintegrate the isolated words into the realm of the visible. Furthermore, the isolated words can hardly be described as "fragments" since they no longer refer to an implicit totality located within or outside the text—the original novel is no longer the main referent; it has been replaced by the new narrative created by the sequential arrangement of the comic-strip-like poetic "balloons" which come to the surface of the book's paint-covered pages. *A Humument* would thus seem to amount to a tribute to the non-descriptive materiality of a reversed *effet de pan* produced by the painted foreground of the page, a process through which colors gradually erase and substitute themselves to the text, thereby emphasizing its sheer materiality. In this respect, Phillips's book can also be seen to foreground the "tyranny of matter"[38] which Didi-Huberman can only see as the final aporia of the detail, at least in the context of his close analyses of pre-modern, figurative paintings. But in Phillips's clever and whimsical hands, this apparent aporia gives way to a singular dialectics of form and matter, meaning and suggestion, reading and seeing, which is at the core of the author's attempts to disfigure Mallock's novel.

A full-length reading of Phillips's book would have to stress its attempts to "doctor" Mallock's novel and purge it of its conservative, anti-Semitic, and misogynous tendencies (we / doctor / books / we / doctor / novels"[39]) while "unearthing" its repressed latent content. The abundance of sexual innuendoes in Phillips's "poems" and, more generally, the narrator's self-confessed purpose to reveal the hidden content of Mallock's novel ("that / which / he / hid / reveal / I") invite a short parallel with the Freudian take on the detail. To return to Didi-Huberman's analysis of the relationship between the visual and psychoanalysis (which sees the detail as a residual entity, the "rubbish of observation"[40]), it would not be far-fetched to argue that *A Humument* psychoanalyzes the original document, bringing out the symptoms[41] of the psycho-sexual frustration which lurks beneath the varnish of Victorian respectability of Mallock's fictional world and which the "realist" narrative tries to dissimulate. Phillips has claimed that his innuendo-ridden rewriting is meant to "tease the odd joke out of a novel which contains almost none."[42] Page 76 of the 4th edition shows a "shy" incarnation of Bill "Toge" trying to look up a lady's dress, a move to which the woman responds with a peculiar kind of "well-poised eagerness" (earlier in the book, a character, named Robert Grenville—who, contrary to "Toge," is present in Mallock's novel—is "scan[ning] the sofa, / to see / Miss Markham, / raising her / dress / half-parted"[43]). A confrontation with the source text produces its share of ironies and paradoxes, as the original page of Mallock's novel relates the "mirror story" of Phillips's text to that of the novel's protagonist, Grenville. On that same page in the original text, Grenville retires into his room to meditate on the traditional virtues of simplicity, modesty, and "shyness" which characterize Victorian representations of womanhood while examining "the photograph of a young girl, with a well-poised head, and eyes that looked with a sort of composed eagerness."[44]

■

As for the frame that hangs on the wall (unless it is a window giving onto the exterior of the room; one is reminded here of the mysterious, liminal quality of the detail which causes Bergotte to mistake a roof for a wall), it has been emptied of the "photograph" and thus creates another mise en abyme of the now familiar *effet de pan*, looking empty except for six small white bubbles that signify nothing but their own textless presence within the frame.

Phillips's half-confessed attempt to "cure" the original text of its stiff, humorless and racist dispositions through various forms of collage, displacement, falsification, overprinting/painting, and surinterpretation, point to a tactic which frees the detail from the constraints of Victorian "detailism" while providing a corrective to the master text's politics. It has to be noted, however, that, unlike other writing-through experiments (such as those of John Cage, Jackson Mac Low, or, more recently Ronald Johnson) Phillips's textual "rivers" do not give readers the illusion that they can enjoy the pleasures of a truly nonlinear and "uncertain" text, at least within each individual page-poem. The pleasure afforded by Phillips's text is of a different kind, one which mischievously destabilizes relationships between detail and totality, background and foreground, and which, in doing so, introduces an alternate kind of sinuous and labyrinthine linearity. Here, Didi-Huberman's distinction between the "visible" and the "visual" provides us with a useful starting point for a (re)definition of the function of the detail in Phillips's "treated novel" and, indeed, contemporary art in general. For Didi-Huberman, the detail is inextricably linked with the concept of singularity:

> … what can we know about the singular ? This question is central to the whole history of art which, from an epistemological point of view, is more akin to psychoanalysis, rather than to any kind of "psychology of art." This connection becomes crucial insofar as the destiny of the

> gaze is always connected with a form of memory which is all the more powerful *as it is not manifest.* The visible refers to what reveals itself. As for the visual, it tends to designate that irregular thread of symptom-events which, once they attain the visible, become so many traces or splinters…or clues…. Clues to what? To something—a piece of work, a memory in process—which was never completely written down, attested or archived, because its signifying "matter" originates in the image.[45]

Reflecting on the material "eventfulness"[46] and the work-in-progress quality of the visual, Didi-Huberman also insists on its non-manifest character, which is that of a kind of "trace, a "symptom event" or a "clue"[47] which allows the visual to reach and "mark" the visible and the manifest. The term "clue" is particularly relevant to Tom Phillips's *A Humument,* a work that seeks to "exhume" anxieties, frustrations, and aspirations that were implicitly expressed in the original novel. This aspect of *A Humument* underlines the darker dimensions of Phillips's rewriting of Mallock, which include the confusion of "art" and "he(art)," love and marriage, artifice and sentimentality ("does / modern marriage / require / the martyr's / art"[48]), and word and image ("only the / word / pictures the / word"[49]).

Here, as elsewhere, Phillips's *A Humument* reminds us that there are at least two basic categories of details: those which are supposed to be seen (these include various kinds of mannerisms as well as iconic or allegorical details, especially in pre-contemporary painting) and those which are not destined to be seen unless one actively engages in an operation of the gaze. For Daniel Arasse, the detail is "a small part of a figure, an object or a whole" which itself is "the result or the trace of the action of who 'makes the detail.'"[50] If one confronts Arasse's definition with the compositional strategies of *A Humument*, what follows is that Phillips's work clearly falls into the category defined by Arasse as a "detailling operation,"[51] an active process by which the (re)writer seeks to create a "reading event" which involves the reader's gaze in a paradoxical act of deciphering that is simultaneously analytical (the reader is looking for clues) and synthetic (the page is apprehended as a whole, unencumbered by conventional, linear reading methods, before he/she sets out to separate the part from the whole). In *A Humument*, this peculiar reading strategy is of course "orchestrated" (references to music abound in Phillips's poems) by the "windows" that immediately and inevitably attract the reader's attention to the poem that is born out of the fiction. Paradoxically, however, most readers will probably be tempted to "read back to" the erased parts of the original text in order to satisfy their curiosity and, in many cases, enjoy the ironical contrast between the apparent Victorian decorum and conventionality of *A Human Document* (although the latter is only relative, especially if one bears in mind that Mallock was well known at the time for his idiosyncratic views on religion, economics, and politics) and the whimsical and often sexually-charged overtones of Phillips's poetic "bubbles."

This reversal once again calls into question the issue of the return of the repressed or erased whole, which constantly urges us to examine the detail's relationship to an absent totality[52] which, in the case of *A Humument*, ironically refers to a Victorian novel whose effect on the reader was already far from being totalizing and unified. Indeed, Mallock's Introduction warns us that his novel—which originates in a "photographic scrapbook" found by the narrator, whose mission it is to "work up its contents into some presentable form, and publish"—does not really belong to a particular genre ("The following work, though it has the form of a novel, yet for certain singular reasons hardly deserves the name"[53]). This already points to the unusually self-reflexive and satirical nature of Mallock's fiction, an aspect of his work that undoubtedly augmented Phillips's attraction to the book as an infinitely deconstructable and subvertible piece of writing. More importantly, perhaps, Mallock points to the fragmented, disjunctive nature of his work when he remarks that "some single thread of narrative" needs to be unveiled by the narrator despite the truncated nature of the plot which is "broken by pages after pages of letters, by scraps of poetry, and various other documents"[54] as well as by "baffled and crippled sentences,"[55] "abrupt transitions,"[56] "odd lapses of grammar,"[57] and "mere nondescript fragments."[58] In light of these comments, it would be a mistake to consider *A Humument* solely as a satirical response to the late Victorian ideology that characterized its ur-text. The unusually heterogeneous, collage-like nature of Mallock's novel contains in nuce Phillips's treatment of the nineteenth-century text, which appears less as a subversive act than as a radical extension of the original work's unusual structure, a structure which already pointed to some of the main formal and/or thematic issues at stake in *A Humument*: the dialectics of revelation and concealment, the impossibility of a seamless narrative, the inherently unstable nature of the writing and the reading process, and the blurring of the boundaries between art and life (as testified to by Mallock's allusions to the inclusion of real documents, a "distancing" technique not unusual in the pre-contemporary novel but which acquires a special significance in the context of Phillips's contemporary revision of the text).

To conclude, Mallock's use of the word "fragment" returns us to the slippery question of whether Phillips's bubbles can acquire the status of details. They are not fragments in the traditional meaning(s) of the word, since they result from an active subtraction of linguistic units from the original text, thereby reversing the process that long characterized the accumulation of details in most pre-contemporary realist painting and fiction. They are not details in the more general "mimetic" sense either, since they do not refer to earlier visual models or partake in a particular form of representation that reflects a classical theory of mimesis. As we have just seen, Phillips's text can be seen as producing details that acquire the value of *clues* that obliquely reveal and exploit the subversive potential of the "master" text. This principle is the measure of Phillips's own capacity to disrupt the uniform intensity of prose in a movement which deliberately hesitates between poetic closure and (psycho)analytical disclosure.

CHAPTER 5

Hauntological Blurrings and Cancelations

MARK FISHER has explored the implications of haunting in a world governed by an overwhelming sense of melancholy and nostalgia in a late capitalist environment where the future is no longer seen as a space of possibility, but rather as a foreclosed horizon of repetitions and revisitations, whether on the political, the historical, or the aesthetic level. Writing of Afrofuturism and the legacy of slavery, he describes hauntology as "the proper temporal mode for a history made up of gaps, erased names and sudden abductions,"[1] a mode which evokes the already discussed memorial poetics of M. NourbeSe Philip's *Zong!* while being more broadly anchored in the realization that "while 20th-century experimental culture was seized by a recombinatorial delirium, which made it feel as if newness was infinitely available, the 21st century is oppressed by a crushing sense of finitude and exhaustion."[2] A general study of erasure in the arts needs to ponder this feeling of belatedness and the "slow cancellation of the future"[3] which ensues. It also calls for a discussion of how such a culture of retrospection and revisitation is liable to recover a sense of presence within that which has disappeared, that which is no longer, or that which has not yet happened. Lastly, building upon the Derridean opposition between hauntology and canonical understandings of ontology, it also has to address the question of whether there is a way of thinking of presence as other than self-presence, or the blank as other than the mark of absence, silence, or the void.

Derrida's hauntological model seems particularly relevant to an investigation of the palimpsestic dynamics of erasurism. Many, if not all, the works we have examined so far echo Derrida's deconstruction of the metaphysics of presence while bringing into play the question of how (partly) erased textual material can haunt us from beyond the grave or, in Tom Phillips's case, how a textual corpse can be exhumed from oblivion. While Phillips himself has admitted to practicing a form of hauntology ("I plundered, mined, and undermined [Mallock's] text to make it yield the ghosts of other possible stories, scenes, poems, erotic incidents, and surrealist catastrophes which seemed to lurk within its wall of words"), page 95 of *A Humument*, the most Derridean of Phillips's efforts, evokes the fall of the Communist bloc, with the headline "a spent Europe laden with serious history," itself haunted by the "laughing ghosts" of "the East" and "the serfs of the ruble." A full-length hauntological analysis of Phillips's work would reveal a veritable crisis of temporality akin to Simon Reynolds's notion of "dyschronia," a term coined to designate "the broken-time proper to hauntology, in which it is no longer possible to securely delimit the present from the past, in which the traces of lost futures unpredictably bubble up to unsettle the pastiche-time of postmodernity"[4]; similarly, the ghost of Mallock's novel is destined to haunt its "treated" version endlessly, whereas *A Humument* itself acts as another, retroactive specter crossing the themes of being and non-being, event and advent, illness and healing, possession and exorcism.

Perhaps more than any other field of study, popular music of the late twentieth and early twenty-first centuries has gained an unprecedented attention at this level, notably because the arts of cutting, scratching, remixing, and sampling problematize accepted notions of authenticity and authorship in an even more blatant way than literary and visual avatars of "uncreative" art. Discussing Little Axe's album *Stone Cold Ohio* (2006) Mark Fisher addresses the complicated and eerie relationship with the blues tradition and emphasizes band leader Skip McDonald's capacity to "mystify questions of authorship and attribution, origination and repetition":

> It is difficult to disentangle sampling from songwriting, impossible to draw firm lines between a cover version and an original song. Songs are texturally-dense palimpsests, accreted rather than authored. McDonald's own vocals, by turns doleful, quietly enraged and affirmatory, are often doubled as well as dubbed. They and the modern instrumentation repeatedly sink into grainy sepia and misty trails of reverb, falling into a dyschronic contemporaneity with the crackly samples.[5]

Fisher's general argument distinguishes the prioritization of presence and authenticity attached to classic avatars of live, "rockist" performance from the disembodied and deferred character of recorded music, and stresses the attention to sonic materiality and texture which characterizes other forms of popular music. Among these forms, dub stands out as a genre which does not conceal its own artificial re-cordedness and brings to the fore the disfiguring—and, in the best of cases, transfiguring—effects of recording technology. Fisher's choice of dub as the quintessential music of Derridean hauntology is hardly surprising given the genre's heavy use of reverb, delay, echo, and tempo-altering effects achieving a spectral deferral of their source performance and original material, not to mention dub artists' predilection for remixed revisitations of familiar or less familiar songs. Fisher's penchants for artists attempting to recover the "repressed" physicality of popular music is clearly in line with an already well-established tradition of contemporary materialist poetics which finds its literary correlative in Marjorie Perloff's critique of the unmediated, transparent lyric (*Radical Artifice*, 1991) and Charles Bernstein's non-absorptive poetics (*A Poetics*, 1992), to name but two prominent theoretical models challenging accepted notions of the immediacy of self-expression and focusing on the signifying hardware of art production rather than (merely) its signified purposes.

Central to Fisher's anti-expressivist poetics (sound should be explored and enjoyed "as a medium in itself rather than as a carrier for Meaning"[6]) is the dyschronic element in dub that forces and reveals its capacity to convey the alien, uncanny, and untimely powers of recording technology.[7] This process allies hauntology with Derrida's critique of the privileging of "the essential and immediate proximity"[8] of voice to consciousness. It also echoes his deconstruction of the logocentric dismissal of writing as "mediation of mediation and as a fall into the exteriority of meaning."[9] Like writing, recording technology can be understood as a form of mediation which challenges any theoretical and ideological model predicating the creation and consumption of meaning on an identifiable, if not transcendental, origin. Such assumptions are of course cardinal to musical performance per se, a field of expression which traditionally relies on models of vocal and instrumental vicinity, synchronicity, and authenticity. By foregrounding the process of mediation instead of concealing its own methods of production and dissemination, hauntological music counters logocentric assumptions of (self-)presence insofar as the latter can only be reconstructed belatedly, in a *nachträglich* gesture of provisional definition which happens against a background of myriad formal, thematic, and material interconnections. "Since there is no point of pure origin," Fisher argues, "only the time of the 'always-already', then haunting is the state proper to being as such."[10] Hauntology thus refers to songs which are "texturally dense palimpsests, accreted rather than authored," "doubled as well as dubbed," songs that amount to "sonic phantoms detached from live bodies, [transforming] the voice of the living into the 'ghosts of ghosts of effects'"[11] through extended trails of delay; deep, body-numbing sub-bass, and other, even more specifically hauntological devices such as the use of crackle, of which more will be said later.

Fisher's untimely death in January 2017 put an end to his critical documentation of pop culture's hauntological tropes. One suspects that a sequel to *Ghosts of My Life* would have included a close reading of Kanye West's "Ghost Town" (2018),[12] an exemplary case study in "depression, hauntology and lost futures," to cite the subtitle of Fisher's volume. The song begins with a sample of Shirley Ann Lee's unfinished gospel hymn "Someday" (1968) only to unleash another extended sample, Chicano soul group the Royal Jesters' version of "Take Me for a Little While," a song originally written by Trade Martin in the 1960s and since then covered by artists as diverse as Evie Sands, Vanilla Fudge, and

Dusty Springfield. The track preserves a substantial amount of the lyrics of the original songs intertwined with West's own ruminations about fame and depression. The sheer number of "songwriters" credited in the album's liner notes (no less than sixteen including the authors of the two main songs sampled by West and his co-producers) conveys the radical reshuffling of notions of authorship performed by a song whose inception can only be reconstructed retroactively, its origins being lost in a multilayered whirlwind of revisitations and retrospective reconfigurations. Far from merely eliciting nostalgia for its samples' worn-out charm and vintage appeal, "Ghost Town" strikes a disarming balance between an overwhelming sense of claustrophobic sadness and the promise of a mysterious state of sublime quietude and suspension unimpeded by delusions and "half-truths" ("just naked minds / caught between space and time"). The song's Wordsworthian moment of childhood nostalgia ("Oh, once again I am a child / I let it all go (go), of everything that I know, yeah… And nothing hurts anymore"), however, is undermined by the suggestion that the narrator's Fentanyl-induced relief gives way to a state of tedium and numbness ("I put my hand on the stove, to see if I still bleed"). As the song unfolds, "Ghost Town" continues to convey the trauma of being imprisoned in locked grooves and memories. The track's fatigued sense of foreboding increases as its harmonies, rhythms, and lyrics begin to feel fraught and wrong and create uncanny frictions between the sampled music and the vocal additions of West and his guest singers. While this anomalous impression is painfully perceptible in the rather ungainly live rendition of the song delivered on a 2018 episode of *Saturday Night Live*, it is also perceptible in the studio version's far from seamless mix, in which West's voice sounds detached from the musical background, as if he was performing a karaoke version of his own composition.

A song about schizophrenia and depression, "Ghost Town" is a sonic collage of dysphoric fragments interrogating the speaker's relationship to his past selves while failing to gesture towards a consoling present. The track's dyschronic complexities evoke one of hauntological music's foundational moments, the ballroom music of the Gold Room in the Overlook Hotel of Stanley Kubrick's *The Shining* (1980), a music subsequently warped, spliced, and remashed in another influential hauntological work, the Caretaker's 1999 album *Selected Memories from the Haunted Ballroom*. The affinities between *The Shining*'s appropriation of Al Bowlly's foxtrot and West's recycling of Shirley Ann Lee's gospel song are perhaps best understood in the context of Fisher's distinction between hauntology and postmodernism: "sonic hauntology similarly 'blurs contemporaneity' with elements from the past, but, whereas [Jamesonian] postmodernism glosses over the temporal disjunctures, the hauntological artists foreground them." In other words, whereas postmodernism's weakening of historicity produces a culture of seamless stylistic heterogeneity placed under the banner of nostalgia and pastiche ("a formal attachment to the techniques and formulas of the past, a consequence of a retreat from the modernist challenge of innovating cultural forms adequate to contemporary experience"[13]), hauntology draws attention to the temporal displacements, deferrals, and distortions which allow listeners to "hear that time is out of joint. The joins are audible in the crackles, the hiss."[14] Fisher's Hamletian hauntological pantheon (which he shares with other foundational hauntologists such as Simon Reynolds, Joseph Stannard, and Ian Penman) include artistic endeavors as diverse as the Caretaker, Tricky, Philip Jeck, Burial, the Ghost

Box label, and William Basinski, most of whom emerged in the late 1990s and early 2000s and share a preoccupation with "the way in which technology materialized memory—hence a fascination with television, vinyl records, audiotape, and with the sounds of these technologies breaking down." Musing about the dialectics of digital and analogue recording and playback systems, Fisher remarks that "so many hauntological tracks have been about revisiting the physicality of analogue media in the ear of digital ether."[15] Nowhere is this more apparent than in Basinski's *The Disintegration Loops* (2002), where the joint strategies of disfiguration of hauntology and erasure culminate in a serendipitous experiment in self-defacement and material decay. The story is well known to ambient and electronic music lovers. Since the 1980s, Basinski had been collecting audio tape loops containing various samples ranging from fragments of radio programs to shortwave white noise. In 2001 these short snippets of music and sound which had been stored away for years were digitized for preservation. Basinski realized that the magnetic tapes were deteriorating during the process and began repeating the experiment, recording the samples further as the tapes were slowly disintegrating. The result is a four-volume release of elegiac meditation on the poetic nemesis of recorded archives, capturing the passage of time while literally recording the different stages of decomposition of its source material. Basinski describes the genesis of his project as follows:

> I came across these big cases back in the storage room—The Land That Time Forgot, we used to call it—and I found all my old tape loops. By then I had a CD burner, and knowing what happens to old tapes, I started to archive the loops to digital. In the summer of 2001, in late July or

> August, I pulled this one loop out that I didn't remember at all, and put it on the machine…and I turned on the recorder and started recording. After about 15 minutes, I realized something was changing—and I looked, and I could see dust in the tape path on the ReVox that was playing the tape loop. I sat there watching the recorder, monitoring it as this thing over the length of a CD-R completely disintegrated in the most profoundly beautiful way. The sustains sort of fell away, and yet somehow the core of it stayed—the attack and the basic rhythm of the melody—hanging on desperately until the very end.[16]

As Basinski's erasures gradually fade out into crackle and noise, the pieces explore the beauty of decline and the aesthetic transformation of sonic degradation into a landscape of crepuscular sonic mist and crumbling harmonies. The loops are rendered even more uncanny by the gradual blurring out of the sustains and the attacks, which makes it increasingly difficult to recognize the source samples, the movements of the repetitions (each piece is composed of one single short sonic snippet looped hundreds of times) happening in a Steinian "continuous present," a timeless narrative which has neither beginning nor end, haunted by the ghosts of its previous and future dis-incarnations. This peculiar form of sublime aesthetics evokes the ambivalent mixture of boredom and shock, dysphoria and euphoria, tedium and terror Sianne Ngai has termed "stuplimity," a condition which seems fit to describe works which exceed the capacity of the human mind to distinguish the parts from the whole, the causes from their effects, the sources from their variations. Among Ngai's principal literary models, the examples of Gertrude Stein's *The Making of Americans* and Samuel Beckett's later prose, stand out as texts where "narration is repeatedly forced to 'begin again'" and where—in Beckett's case—"the theme of survival and endurance in the wake of a traumatic loss is conveyed...through a drastic slowdown of language, a rhetorical enactment of its fatigue."[17]

The slowdown of narrative movement (Basinski uses mostly scraps of slowed-down Muzak, as do, by the way, the Caretaker's spectralized disfigurations of Kubrick's ballroom music) and the themes of trauma and resilience are also inextricably linked with the production, the dissemination, and the reception of *The Disintegration Loops* as they were used by Basinski to negotiate the convulsions of time and history. In an ironic reversal of the Derridean concept of hauntology—which posits that we are haunted by events which did not actually happen and paradoxically make us feel nostalgic for futures which will never materialize—Basinski claims to have completed his project on the morning of September 11, 2001, and later released his finished work to mark the specific historical moment of the 9/11 attacks, which he witnessed and filmed from the rooftop of the Brooklyn building he occupied at the time before synching the images to his music. Responding to the overwhelming sense of numbness and exhaustion which followed the attacks, Basinski retrospectively conferred to his loops an elegiac power which has since then become a landmark of American memorial art (Basinski's loops are now part of the permanent collection of the 9/11 Memorial & Museum in New York City). According to Stein herself it is the sheer length of her prose which conveys meaning and affect ("sentences are not emotional but paragraphs are"), a theory which finds its musical near-equivalent in Basinski's looped samples, whose critical success story can be accounted for, at least in part, by their insistent, "stupefying" capacity to interrogate the signifying logic of musical composition while exploring the emotional, cultural, and political resonance of the mechanical degradation of sound and meaning (however problematic the latter term may be in the context of instrumental music) against a background of rubble and mass destruction.

The loop is in itself a paradigmatic structuring device of hauntology, one which, unlike mere repetition, "returns upon itself" and thereby resists linear categories of narrative progression and closure. As a result of this process, the elements revisited within the loop lose their status as the primary source. Instead, they can only be seen as duplicates or revenants of their initial appearance in the artwork, as they undergo further repetitions, alterations, and shifts in later sections of the piece. Loops, whether of the musical or the literary variety, thus serve to organize, complicate, and transform what is already present in the concepts of repetition and recurrence. Much like Stein's repetition-with-variation technique, Basinski's work, by relentlessly revisiting its own previous compositional segments, embodies such a striving towards a mode of representation where the artist's approach to knowledge and memory can develop through an investigation of musical or literary language itself.

More ruinist cracklology and visual turntablism

Reflecting on the significance of glitches and crackle, the "principal signature" of sonic hauntology, as an alternative to unmediated notions of aesthetic experience, Owen Hatherley writes of the paradox encountered in listening to blues musician Robert Johnson's recorded work: "you have, rather than the expected in yr [*sic*] face earthiness and presence, layers upon layers of fizz, crackle, hiss, white noise, as if its [*sic*] been remixed by [German techno-dub duet] Basic Channel rather than recorded in a room in some mythologised deep south."[18] Likewise, the surface noise foregrounded by Tricky's retro-Afrofuturist trip-hop and countless other hauntological musicians from the 1990s and 2000s unsettles the distinction between presence and absence while investigating the interplay of past and present temporalities persisting within a dislocated narrative made of eerie glitches, jagged gaps, and raging echoes.

Basinski's loops encapsulate such a condition, but decayism and cracklology go rampant in other spheres than musical production. At least part of their appeal and popularity lies in their capacity to address our culture's sense of belatedness, its declinist melancholy, and its fascination with the spectral and the dilapidated, a condition which returns us to the papyrus scrolls of Sappho, Aeschylus, and others, whose remnants exhibit blank spaces which invite contemplation and extrapolation. In recent literary history, Armand Schwerner's *The Tablets* (1999) seeks to reproduce this very process of material degradation, incorporating process into procedure ("the right words wait in the stone / they'll discover themselves as you chip away, / work faster, don't think as long as you want" [Tablet VIII]) while furthering the interstitial dynamics of the readerly text with accompanying "translator's notes" speculating about the missing passages.

Besides being an important precursor of recent developments in erasure poetry, Schwerner's "translations" of fictive Sumerian clay tablets also suggest that the growing popularity of erasurism—whether in the form of eroded poetry, crackled music or, say, spectral photography—may have something to do with our post-Romantic taste for the fragmentary, the unfinished, and the ephemeral.[19] (Do we enjoy Schwerner's *Tablets* over more finished forms of poetry in the same way as some preliminary sketches by Renaissance masters are just as appealing to us, if not more, than the actual paintings?)

To this date, the most famous literary example of hauntological erasurism is undoubtedly Tom Phillips's earlier-discussed *A Humument*. To better understand the complex relationships between Mallock's novel and the "unauthor" of *A Human Document*, a return to the introduction of the source text is essential. We learn there that the genesis of the text, which, according to the narrator himself, "barely deserves the name of a novel," is linked to a chance encounter with a mysterious Countess Z_____, who entrusts him with a collection of texts and fragments related to her private life and hopes that he can transform them into a work of fiction. What we know about the "scrap-book," which constitutes the raw material for this story, amounts to a proleptic mise en abyme of Phillips's rewriting, which also produces a narrative made of letters, pieces of plot, poetic fragments, and "disconcerting and unfinished sentences."[20] Mallock specifies that the fragments of the manuscript pasted on the pages of the Countess's notebook are "of various sizes and appearances" and include various found documents whose collage-like qualities prefigure, in their own way, Phillips's appropriationist aesthetic. As for the "narrative thread" sketched by a feminine hand running through the volume, it is reminiscent of the "rivulets" that, tirelessly coursing through Mallock's text, sketch out a similarly singular plot, one that drifts in a perpetual state of the unexpected, marked by abrupt shifts and broken syntax. In light of this reading, it would not be an exaggeration to claim that Mallock's source text haunts Phillips's work as much as it is haunted by it, and that any attentive reading of *A Humument* is marked by this double spectrality. Gill Partington indirectly addresses this question in an interview with Phillips, saying to him, "People now will read Mallock after reading *A Humument*, and so they're reading Mallock as a secondary text. You've become the original."[21] Phillips also calls upon the lexicon of spectrality to characterize the eruption of his "rivers" within a doubled textual universe that, paradoxically, grants them the status of images: "Once more I emphasize the fact that I regard texts as images in their own right: treated as they are here with words *ghosted* behind words to form a (literal) subtext they are all the more image for being doubly text."[22] Such a method—traversed as it is by poetic digressions and paranoid-associational leaps—might evoke Henry James's "figure in the carpet," a visual trope which has become a symbol for obsessional critical strategies seeking to unveil the definite meaning of a literary work. Phillips explains:

> The joy of learning is to find that one is not alone. I remember reading when I was about fifteen (and already condemned or committed to the artistic life) in the notebooks of Leonardo da Vinci his instruction to young painters to stare at stains on the wall and to find in them figures and fantastic landscapes. One thing a London house in wartime did not lack (for decoration was considered, if not merely wasteful, a challenge to fate) was blotchy wallpaper and plaster with spreading islands of damp. I unwittingly obeyed Leonardo by spending hour upon infant hour summoning up angels and demons amid tortuous clouds or craggy terrain, thinking somehow I was the only

> person peculiar enough to invent such worlds. Wonderful then to discover that this commonplace of fantasy was in fact an early professional engagement.[23]

Phillips's pareidoliac poetics relentlessly explores the resources of the materiality of the text in order to extract what can be represented and re-figured through his verbi-voco-visual explorations. Positioned at the intersection of the hybridization of artistic imagery and textual experimentation, Phillips's "treated novel" seeks to bring forth from Mallock's novel objects and characters suggested by the typographical roughness and angularities of that novel. This process recalls Paleolithic cave paintings (a model foregrounded earlier in connection with Ronald Johnson's *RADI OS*), whose shapes were partly dictated by the reliefs of the walls and the roughness of the concretions. It also brings to mind the hypothesis of a "torn anthropomorphism"[24] that, according to Georges Bataille, would relate the self and the world within a dialectic governed by the desire for incompletion elicited by an artwork placed under the sign of revision, reworking, reappropriation, and revisitation, as evidenced by the successive versions of *A Humument*. From a hauntological perspective, the eruption of ectoplasmic characters, whose outlines follow the curves, angles, and breaks of the prose in *A Human Document*, is further testimony to this.

If we are looking for artworks which foreground the potential for self-effacement of the moving image, we might begin with Stan Brakhage's experimental short film *Mothlight* (1963), which bridges the conceptual gap between erasure techniques and (self-)destruction per se. *Mothlight* differs from Brakhage's trademark hand-painted films in that it incorporates insect wings, petals, leaves,

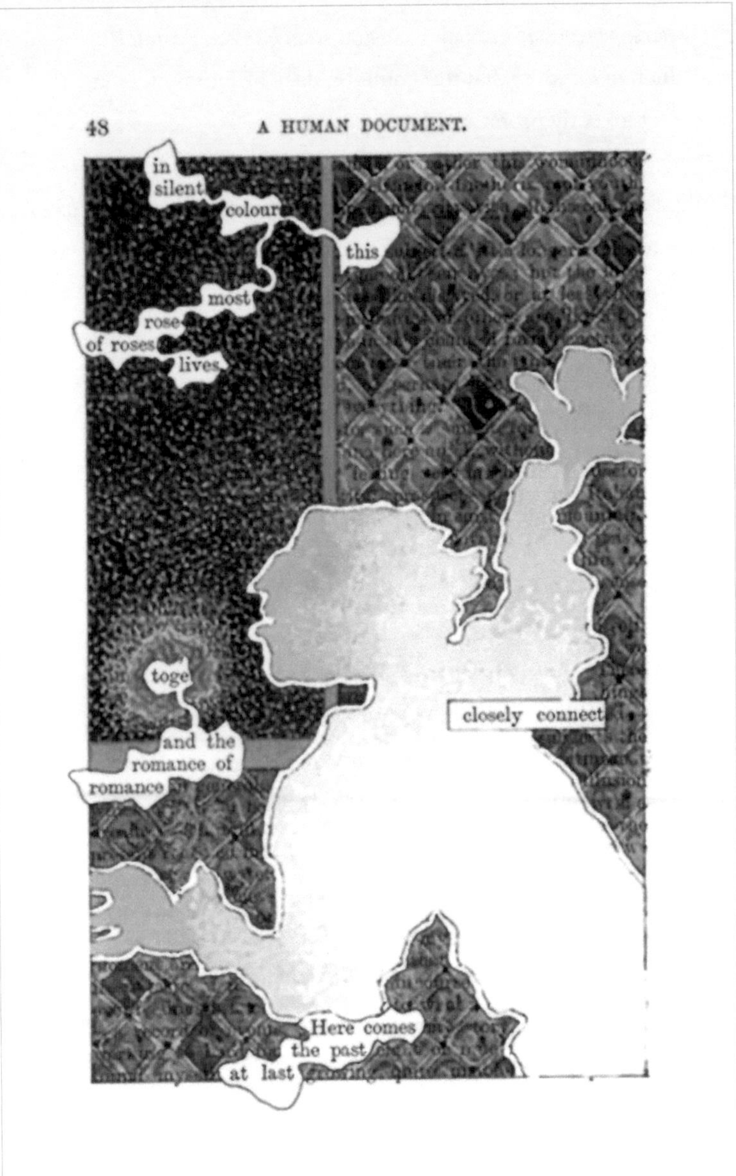
48
A HUMAN DOCUMENT.
in
silent
colour
this
most
rose
of roses
lives
toge
and the
romance of
romance
closely connect
Here comes
the past
at last

and blades of grass pasted upon the strips of celluloid. Brakhage has made the connection between the film's form and its content clear. His account of how his film originates in personal suffering deserves to be quoted in full:

> Here is a film that I made out of a deep grief. The grief is my business in a way, but the grief was helpful in squeezing the little film out of me, that I said "these crazy moths are flying into the candlelight, and burning themselves to death, and that's what's happening to me. I don't have enough money to make these films, and…I'm not feeding my children properly, because of these damn films, you know. And I'm burning up here… What can I do?" I'm feeling the full horror of some kind of immolation, in a way.[25]

The moth's suicidal flight towards light thus represents the agony of the starving artist whose personal life is sacrificed on the altar of his creation. As for the dead moths' wings stuck on Brakhage's filmstrip, they are paradoxically "reanimated" after being fed into the projector. Whereas the murmur of the silent film can be likened to that of the fluttering of wings or the sound of the wind blowing through leaves, Brakhage's close inspection of the veined textures of the flickering fragments of nature which appear on the screen progressively coheres into a single organic environment of shrouded, unreadable shapes.

In Paul Sharits's *Bad Burns* (1982), a very short film recycling some of the artist's own outtakes, burning is not so much a cathartic or sacrificial ritual as a meditation on how the film medium itself confronts its inevitable decay, making the physical corruption of celluloid its main subject matter. In order to document the different steps of their degradation, Sharits proceeds to re-film strips of film until some of them become corroded and dissolve into abstract shapes, unidentifiable forms blurred into formlessness. Sharits's *Bad Burns* documents cinematic death itself at the same time as it depicts the death of the subject captured by film (a human face seems to emerge from the decomposing celluloid at one point before disappearing into a haze). The flicker effects created by the vertical strips traversing the screen convey the acceleration of the film's erosion, whereas the rare frozen images capture the most "tragic" moments occurring when the stillness of celluloid exposes it further to the forces of acidic degradation.

Twenty years later Bill Morrison's haunting sixty-seven-minute *Decasia* (2002) took its viewers on a different but related kind of decaying found footage roller coaster ride, jigging to the ragged and fractured cadences of Michael Gordon's soundtrack. One brief but memorable scene shows a dancing couple who seem to be struggling with their fading environment while keeping smiles on their faces as they try to brush away the blots and blemishes which threaten to liquefy them. The film uncorks strange hysterical outbreaks as the tragic, materiological slapstick plays out in a riotous celebration of distorted and dissolving forms.

Eric Rondepierre's recent appropriations of film images have done a lot to redefine the practical and aesthetic modalities of erasurism beyond now familiar strategies of obliteration, disfiguration, and (auto-)destruction. His early 1990s series *Excédents* (French for "surplus" or "extra" as in "extra luggage") consists of frames taken from black-and-white films with French subtitles. The stills are photographed on a TV screen and captured on a VHS video player by using the pause button. The subtitles are the only thing visible on an entirely black, interstitial background which is

impossible to perceive while watching a movie in normal circumstances since they only last for a fraction of a second: *Excédents* thus predicates the persistence of meaning upon the disappearance of the image blurring the line which separates the seen and the unseen (or the subliminal), the significant from the insignificant.

Rondepierre's later series comprise photographs of frames selected from various cinematic archives. His "Précis de décomposition" (1993–1995) departs from his monochromatic obsessions and concentrates on silent film stills eroded by time and the circumstances of their storage conditions. It also prefigures the equally arresting and convulsive beauty of his "Moires" (1998) series, based on carefully selected images from colorized films. The resulting images are always moving and often tragic, the actors' faces and bodies morphing into monstrous, ghostly shapes not unlike Francis Bacon's deformed portraits. Rondepierre's more recent "DSL" (2010–2013) project does not explore the perishability of celluloid but the pixelized textures of digital film. "DSL" (an initialism for Digital Subscriber Line) is composed of unretouched screenshots of classic movies by the likes of Ophüls, Hitchcock, Truffaut, Godard, and Lynch broadcast on the television screen by means of a computer connection. "This passage by the web," Rondepierre explains, "can provoke dysfunctions in the relation between the flow of lines and the decoding."[26] The scattered and dislocated pixelizations of "DSL" yield startling results. As Rondepierre further explains, "'DSL' is a work anchored in contemporary technology, and at the same time it sends back to more older practices as painting, the art of stained glass or mosaic."[27] This aspect of his work is apparent in the retrospective illusion which at a distance makes us mistake the blurred, divisionist textures of a still of Tippi Hedren in Hitchcock's *Marnie* for an impressionistic portrait à la Manet ("No 4, 2011").

Rondepierre's work sits between cracklologist found film and hauntological photography. In the latter field, the equally ominous erasurist art of Francesca Woodman displays a different kind of ruinist approach applied to the art of self-portraiture. Her "House" and "Space2" series, created during her time in Providence while she was studying at the Rhode Island School of Design between 1975 and 1978, displays her in various states of undress obscured by movement and long exposures, investigating the interplay between her body and her environment, which mainly consists of the decaying interiors of dilapidated buildings. Woodman's photographs explore themes of decay, abandonment, and the passage of time in ways that address hauntology's deconstruction of ontological models prioritizing being and meaning as presence, the photographs staging themselves as captured moments of failed self-definition turning the violence of material decay against itself.

As the ruined house becomes the site of a self-engineered blurring and cropping of the self, Woodman implicitly references Gilman's *The Yellow Wallpaper* and Kafka's *The Metamorphosis* while building on the work of earlier explorers of photographic spectrality (from Victorian times[28] to Duane Michals's 1973 *The Bogeyman*).

Martin Arnold's experimental short *Shadow Cuts* (2010) undertakes a similar erasure experiment through the medium of cartoon, taking found film to a paranoiac-critical level. Besides their use of different media, one of the main differences between Arnold and Rondepierre lies in the former's radical treatment of psychosexual "buried" narratives. *Shadow Cuts* stretches and scratches (in the musical, deejaying sense) the happy ending scene of a Disney short to an intense narrative performed on a black background over several minutes, which constantly threatens to fade it out of existence. The scene, which features Mickey and Pluto laughing out loud in a friendly embrace, becomes destabilized through multiple repetitions and rewindings affecting both sound and image. Arnold's ruthlessly analytical eye erases parts of the characters' bodies, forcing us to contemplate isolated body parts, gestures, looks, and facial expressions severed from their original context (this technique is also deployed in Arnold's equally perturbing Disney-based *Haunted House* and *Soft Palate*).

Psychoanalyzing Disney in a gesture reminiscent of Phillips's unveiling of the latent meanings of Mallock's Victorian prose, Arnold produces a schizophrenic narrative, a stammering remix of a familiar domestic scene which does not capitalize on paratactic shifts, as a less subtle collagist Disney deconstruction could have led to, but in an affectless commentary on the medium's own obsession with sheer physicality and its obsession with the infinite plasticity of cartoon characters. Arnold's *effets de pan*[29] force us to see details as the symptoms less of a visual crisis than a crisis of faciality (the reference here is Deleuze and Guattari's concept of "visagéité"), a de-facing and dismantling of "what gives the signifier substance: it is what fuels interpretation, and it is what changes, changes traits, when interpretation reimparts signifier to its substance."[30] Seeing this operation at work in the anti-absorptive blurs of Vladimir Židlický's photographs, Craig Dworkin writes of the necessity to deconstruct the face as "the system by which sheer materials are legible as media"[31] and allow Deleuze and Guattari's critique of interiority to deploy itself through the production of heads without faces. Likewise, Arnold's blanked out visages and silhouettes evoke the mechanics of the body-without-organs, a condition characterized by the "pure intensity" of "poles, zones, thresholds, and gradients" and "traversed by a powerful, non-organic vitality" manifested in the enucleated stares of the blanked out Disney figures. The pure, Anti-Oedipal energy of Arnold's grotesque turntablism disconnects the body from its cozy social and cultural environment as it manifests itself in the original plot of the cartoon. Arnold's convulsive choreographies envision a state where the body exists outside any determinate condition, ready for any potential action or transformation, a hysterical spectacle of stuttering shapes, gestures, and configurations which, as Grafton Tanner has remarked of another work by Arnold, *Passage à l'acte* (a mashup of the family breakfast scene from *To Kill a Mockingbird*), anticipates recent satirical subgenres of vaporwave as well as the fashion for absurdist low-tech remixes known as YTP (YouTube Poop) which, like Arnold's films, draw the viewer's attention to "the darker, peripheral moments of transition that go unnoticed by the casual viewer."[32]

Like the earlier discussed subtitles in Rondepierre's "Excédents," such a slow reading of familiar movies forces us to focus on the interstitial rather than the detail, on the glitchy, Duchampian infrathin moment that makes the imperceptible perceptible, suspended between presence and absence, rather than on plot progression. Arnold's obsessional mise-en-scène of the interstitial within the interstitial has become a trademark of his own idiosyncratic brand of repetition-with-variation technique which spotlights micro-events and (albeit debatable) visual lapses which remain unnoticed in the original version and generate a feeling of unease and discomfort as to what the rewriting actually "means." The hysterical jerks and panting cadences generated by Arnold's grimacing turntablism balance Disney's sentimental narrative of friendship against the neurotic, possibly erotically charged content of an endlessly rehearsed (and reversed) flickering counter-narrative which also amounts to a mise en abyme of our incapacity to watch a film without interrupting the performance by blinking our eyes.

Arnold's quirky turntablism provides an appropriate point on which to conclude this chapter. The haunted Disney shorts return us with a vengeance to the ex-humed linguistic and characterological ghosts haunting Phillips's *A Humument* and, more generally, to the aesthetics of the spectrality which has characterized the recent history of poetic foundism and erasurism. In a digital age where language has arguably become "a provisional space, temporary and debased, mere material to be shoveled, reshaped, hoarded and molded into whatever form is convenient, only to be discarded just as quickly,"[33] foundist art can be seen as an alternative to what Fisher diagnosed as the "pious cult of indeterminacy" and

the "pathology of skepticism"[34] which characterizes some deconstructionist and post-deconstructionist paradigms. In the works of Basinski, Arnold, and others, foundist erasurism thus conceived of as a hauntological trope and method addresses the psychoanalytical trauma which echoes Hal Foster's Freudian sense of the neo-avant-garde as a *nachträglich* reprocessing of earlier shocks revisited and reinterpreted through anticipation and reconstruction, much like trauma that only becomes meaningful after the fact.[35] With varying degrees of hauntological intensity, foundist erasurism has also given several generations of artists a way to deal with the despondent feeling of emptiness that seizes artists for whom "stylistic innovation is no longer possible, [where] all that is left is to imitate dead styles, to speak through the masks and with the voices of the styles in the imaginary museum."[36] In this sense, also, contemporary erasurists seem increasingly interested in finding ways of transforming paralyzing misology (in the Paulhanesque sense) into more productive revisitations of past texts, not in the spirit of a post-Fordist, Jamesonian culture of constant pastiche and retrospection, but in a critical investigation of an artistic practice that capitalizes on the uncanny reciprocity of relationships between the past and the present, the canonical and the new, the living and the dead.

CHAPTER 6

No Thoughts but in "Things"

Charles Olson's manifesto of spatial poetics, "Projective Verse," was addressed as much to the still-prevalent anachronisms and parochialisms of the contemporary American poetry scene as it was to its historical antecedence in the materiality, technicity, and futurity of Pound, Mallarmé (and Marinetti), proclaiming itself as:

(projectile (percussive (prospective.

The manifesto famously quotes Robert Creeley: "FORM IS NEVER MORE THAN AN EXTENSION OF CONTENT," implying likewise its inverse in a McLuhanesque equivocation of medium and message, also to be understood as *process* or *kinetics*—an interrelation of what Olson calls OBJECTS in a FIELD—whose *medium* is therefore *composition*.[1] Composition or "recognition"—the terms, for Olson, become synonymous, and we can understand why, since this mode of *composition by field* is also a mode of thinking. While Olson's starting point is the potential of "breathing," of a certain breath-formed rhythm (articulated via the keyboard as technopoetic prosthesis), versus the sort of dogmatic metrics Pound railed against, the major argument in the manifesto rests (pace McLuhan) upon a *typographic consciousness*—specifically, the impact of the typewriter upon a general poetics.

If Stéphane Mallarmé's *Un coup de dés* (1897) signaled the first major acknowledgement in poetry of the potential represented by the printing press and the mass-circulation newspaper (poetry's belated recognition of what McLuhan termed, in honor of Gutenberg, "typographic man," the modern *human condition*), the poem itself was nevertheless composed in manuscript—painstakingly, with directions inserted for the printer, to indicate spacing, font size, italics, etc. Likewise Marinetti's *Parole in Libertà*, Khlebnikov's *Zaum* poems, and (when they weren't composed of newspaper cut-ups) Hugo Ball's *Lautgedichte*. The novelty for Olson is the direct role of the typewriter in composition, in part accomplished by the post-war mass product of cheap portable typewriters which, by removing the intermediate role of the professional typist, transformed the writer's relationship to the published artifact, producing in turn a notional equivalence between compositing and composition, printing and typing. "The machine," Olson writes,

> leads directly…towards projective verse and its consequences. It is the advantage of the typewriter that, due to its rigidity and its space precisions, it can, for a poet, indicate exactly the breath, the pauses, the suspensions even of syllables, the juxtapositions even of phrases…[2]

Here, in a certain sense, is the emergence of what amounts to a "new media poetics" *avant la lettre*—erasing the binary of form vs. content—whose "consequences" encompass not merely the formal *technics* of composition and the potentialities embodied in a given hardware (here represented by the typewriter), but the *poetics* of that technicity itself. Such a poetics is evinced already in the time-and-motion studies of Frank and Lillian Gilbreth, and in the "photodynamism" of Anton Bragaglia (e.g., "Typewriter" [1911]). It is perhaps more than coincidental that Olson's "Projective Verse" was written during the historical moment which saw the emergence of modern computing and cybernetics, marked as it is by an attempt to reconcile, in a sense, the futurism of Pound with the condition of what Olson himself termed "postmodern man," centered upon the integration of body and machine (breath and writing). At stake here is in fact a belated confrontation of language with *industrialization*, understood as a process of abstraction and standardization of interchangeable elements—a process inaugurated with the advent of writing (for Ong, it begins with alpha-numerics; for Pound, following the lead of Fenollosa, it begins with the ideogram; for McLuhan, with the invention of moveable type and the Gutenberg printing press—the first mechanized production line[3]).

Olson's immediate point of reference for the typewriter's regularized *spatial notation* is the arrangement of notes on the musical stave—such that the relative distribution of type *signifies* in addition to the conventional semantics, echoing Mallarmé's *meaning of format* and Joyce's "word, letter, paperspace"—suggestive thereby of a general semiotic *system*, one directly contingent upon the typewriter's "space precisions." The musical comparison also implies a certain "instrumentality," which is not that of a utilitarian regard for language, but of a *prosthesis of consciousness*. Or, we might say, *prosthetic* consciousness. For the typewriter doesn't merely avail the poet of a set of practical controls over the visual appearance of words on the page; it is, quite literally, a *writing machine* whose operations, like those of a musical instrument, define an entire *logic* of composition. Of composition *as such*. We move from the machine as an instrument for notating breath (or *rhythmos*[4]) to a breathing *by way of the machine*. This "language technology" is, therefore, both a *condition* and the *articulation* of a poetics.

Collocations

Early in what has come to be known as *The Blue Book* (1933–1934), Ludwig Wittgenstein poses a series of dilemmas regarding language and technicity, in the form of questions about the *locality of thinking*. These dilemmas, focused as they are upon problems of *situating* discourse, provide the foundations for an inquiry into the particular material and signifying conditions that are taken to define consciousness. "It is misleading," Wittgenstein says,

> to talk of thinking as of a "mental" activity. We may say that thinking is essentially the activity of operating with signs. This activity is performed by the hand, when we think by writing; by the mouth and larynx, when we think by speaking; and if we think by imagining signs or pictures, I can give you no agent that thinks. If then you say that in such cases the mind thinks, I would only draw your attention to the fact that you are using a metaphor, that here the mind is an agent in a different sense from that in which the hand can be said to be an agent in writing.[5]

The equivalence between "thinking" and "operating with signs" is made more explicit by Wittgenstein in his subsequent demystification of "mind" metaphysics—in which "thought" might be located outside or beyond the materiality of its own operations, like the Cartesian homunculus. "If again we talk about the locality where thinking takes place," Wittgenstein suggests, "we have a right to say that this locality is the piece of paper on which we write or the mouth which speaks. And if we talk of the head or the brain as the locality of thought, this is using the expression 'locality of thought' in a different sense."[6]

But between these senses of agency and locality, how do we say that the page or mouth differ from the brain? For it is not simply that Wittgenstein is arguing against the Cartesian idea of a ghost in the machine, as it were, operating the gears and levers of "mental" activity, just as the little voice in the head is supposed, by way of intention or command, to direct the hand that holds the pen that writes on the page (or connects to the typewriter). Rather, it is primarily a matter of how a certain reasoning has obscured the relationship between *thinking* and *operating with signs*. To operate with signs, Wittgenstein tells us, has nothing to do with subordinating (or even equating) the material conditions of writing and what "takes place inside the brain," since thought itself is *contingent* upon precisely such material conditions and is in fact *articulated by them*.[7] To paraphrase William Carlos Williams: *no thought but in "things."*

The implications of this line of argument for Olson's "Projective Verse" are clear enough: the typewriter doesn't simply *represent* the movement of thinking/breathing, but is itself the *locus* of that movement, which is to say the locus of a signifying operation *and its negation* (consider, in extremis, Conroy Maddox's *Onanistic Typewriter* [1940]—a masochistic fetish machine whose keys have nails stuck to them, threatening to pierce or mutilate the typist's fingers). This in turn gives rise to a number of important questions. One such can be found in the third part of Foucault's *The Archaeology of Knowledge*, entitled "The Statement and the Archive," posed in the following terms:

> Can the letters of the alphabet written by me haphazardly onto a sheet of paper, as an example of what is not a statement, can the lead characters used for printing books—and one cannot deny their materiality, which has space and volume—can these signs, spread out, visible, manipulable, be reasonably regarded as statements?[8]

By "statement" Foucault means a "function of existence that properly belongs to signs," which is "neither entirely linguistic, nor exclusively material," but represents a *potential* for *making sense.* "The statement exists…neither in the same way as language… nor in the same way as objects presented to perception…"[9] It is on the basis of this appeal to an idea of something which, by its non-objectivity, may be said to coincide with what Wittgenstein terms a "sign operation" that Foucault then seeks to effect a key distinction. "When looked at more closely," Foucault says, "these two examples [the haphazardly written letters and the pieces of movable type] are seen to be not quite superposable":

> This pile of printer's characters, which I can hold in my hand, or the letters marked on the keyboard of a typewriter are not statement: *at most they are tools* with which one can

> write statements. On the other hand, what are the letters that I write down *haphazardly* onto a sheet of paper, just as they *come to mind*, and to show that they cannot, in their disordered state, constitute a statement? What figure do they form? Are they not *a table of letters* chosen in a *contingent* way, *the statement of an alphabetical series* governed by other laws than those of chance? [Emphasis added.]

A little further along he refigures the problem in relation of the letters printed on the keyboard of a typewriter and the letters A, Z, E, R, T "listed in a typewriting manual," being "the statement of the alphabetical order adopted by French typewriters." The latter is considered a statement, while the former isn't. We may recognize two forms of the problem: in the first, we have an apparently haphazard writing versus a generalized potential *for writing*; in the second, we have the synecdoche of a typographical organization (the string A, Z, E, R, T—whose Anglophone equivalent is QWERTY) and that organization itself (the letters distributed across the entire keyboard).

Foucault's error is to ignore that the keyboard itself is in fact the statement of an organizational complex, with an evolutionary history, in which the distribution of lettered keys is coded to the statistical frequency of individual letters and combinations of letters within a given language, as well as to the physiology of typing. That is to say, the keyboard itself and the operations implied by it are a statement of an entire semiotics—or, we might say, *techno-poetics*. In the first example, a "pile of printer's characters" are distinguished from letters "written down haphazardly" on the false assumption the former are *at most* tools "with which one can write statements." If Foucault's "haphazard" writing constitutes a "table of letters *chosen* in a contingent way," how is it the case that the "alphabetical series" to which they belong is not also *contingently chosen* and itself *a table*, so to speak—or rather a matrix—of *possible significations* to which it also belongs and whose *operations* thereby describe a *poetics*? I am speaking of the fact that both movable type and the alphabet as such are metonyms of a series of "social texts" that are technologically, historically, *ideologically* situated. To the extent that *every writing* represents its own potentiality *as writing*, every "statement" is also an "*en*statement."

Foucault's "pile of printer's characters," like Olson's typewriter, is a language machine *because it is also a matrix*, just as every one of Foucault's "statements" is also a prosthesis of language *as such*. One writes "by hand," just as one writes "with" a typewriter, or "with" an entire cultural system. Moreover, this matrix is somewhat reminiscent of Schrödinger's box: to "choose in a contingent way," as Foucault says, simply means *opening the box* in order to observe the given state of what it contains, which is thus its *statement*—a statement which is not an "example" of anything but its own hypothesis, produced by the very *act of observation*. For if writing, in its broadest array (which is to say, *language*), constitutes the *possibility of a statement*, the statement itself is nothing but the *enstatement* of this possibility. "Language," Foucault says, "exists only as a *system for constructing* possible statements"[10] and yet this inversion of terms, of "possibility" and "system," belies the ultimately instrumentalist rationale behind Foucault's thinking: a rationale which is itself internally incoherent by virtue of its unacknowledged appeal to an agency (that which chooses, which writes, which adopts conventions) located in some other dimension outside language.

Wormholes through the Gutenberg galaxy

There's an anecdote related by Jonathan Swift in the Academy of Lagado section of *Gulliver's Travels* (published in 1726) which provides an interesting counterpoint to Foucault's argument, since though its avowed intent is satirical it nevertheless exposes a key aspect of the relationship between language-as-technology and the assumptions of Reason. The anecdote is worth citing at length:

> The first Professor I saw was in a very large Room, with forty Pupils about him. After Salutation, observing me to look earnestly upon a Frame, which took up the greatest part of both the Length and Breadth of the Room, he said perhaps I might wonder to see him employed in a Project for improving speculative Knowledge by practical and mechanical Operations....He then led me to the Frame, about the Sides whereof all his Pupils stood in Ranks. It was twenty Foot Square, placed in the middle of the Room. The Superficies was composed of several bits of Wood, about the bigness of a Dye, but some larger than others. They were all linked together by slender Wires. These bits of Wood were covered on every Square with Paper pasted on them, and on these Papers were written all the Words of their Language, in their several Moods, Tenses, and Declensions, but without any Order. The Professor then desired me to observe, for he was going to set his Engine at Work. The Pupils at his Command took each of them hold of an Iron Handle, whereof there were forty fixed round

> the Edges of the Frame, and giving them a sudden turn, the whole Disposition of the Words was entirely changed. He then commanded six and thirty of the Lads to read the several Lines softly as they appeared upon the Frame; and where they found three or four Words together that might make part of a Sentence, they dictated to the four remaining Boys who were Scribes. This Work was repeated three or four Times, and at every turn the Engine was so contrived that the Words shifted into new Places, as the Square bits of Wood moved upside down.[11]

As with Foucault's "haphazard" writing, Swift's random-text generator is in no way *random*: the constraints of an entire cultural system are at play, from the logic of its construction as a "word machine," to the delegation of Reason to it. But what first appears as a satire about technological *irrationalism* transpires as a critique of Rationalism as such, and a reversal of the instrumental view of technology *as prosthesis of thought* in order to expose the *programmatic* character of Reason itself (by virtue, we might say, of the possibility of satire itself). In short, Swift's anecdote presents a scenario in which the operations of this "writing machine" determine the "forms of thought," just as the operations of philosophical discourse determine, so to speak, its object. This machine, of course, is a metaphor for the contingent structure of language *per se*, which *by virtue of its probabilistic and permutational nature* assumes, at the "level" of discourse, the appearance of a *system*, while at the "level" of the statement, retains the character of being ambivalent or "haphazard"—like Foucault's A, Z, E, R, T.

In the 1950s, while Olson was advancing the theory and praxis of "Projective Verse" in Gloucester, Massachusetts, the Lettrists in Paris were exploring a technique of writing which, somewhat under the influence of Joyce, pursued the atomization of "words into letters" which in turn could be substituted *haphazardly* by signs and symbols (in fact any kind of graphic mark at all), resulting in what they referred to as hypergraphy—a restatement, loosely speaking, of Gödel's theorem in semiotic terms. In his introduction to *Rules of Hypergraphy* (2014), Paul Gangloff compares the practice to a type of urban runic graffiti:

> Imagine we are in a train. The carriage is full of people all talking in a foreign language. Although the sounds of words are very clear, we do not understand their meaning. As the train pulls into Rotterdam Central Station, the group of people leave the train. In a metro, this time in Seoul, a man observes his neighbour covering a page with symbols, in compact rows, with astonishing speed, calmly and with precision from top to bottom, leaving no white spaces in between.…Again, in another train, through the window, two people spot signs on panels used to regulate the trains' circulation.…And at some point, in some train, a conductor comes along, and with the laser beam of some black device scans the printed Quick-Recognition code of the tickets. Above the frantic mosaic of the QR code is written: "quxf bgfk fngo qmf."…On the concrete walls along the tracks it reads: FGR SERAZ FGR FGR RE!…As the train approaches Brussels, the graffiti covers the walls in a more and more dense succession of letters. At walking distance from Brussels South Station, one can read: "DU JA MA IS VU" on the blue wall of a building that houses the Ligue Braille…[12]

These cryptic, virological texts advance the idea of a "foreign element" at work in the assimilation of "sign operations" into Foucauldian "statements" wherein writing retains something of the quality of a mirroring agency (in Foucault, the "statement" is always exemplified by a discrete *choice*, the non-statement by having been *programmed in advance*, which is to say, *systematized*). What hypergraphy demonstrates, as with Swift's textual machine, is that every statement is *always already* translatable into a non-statement: just as every sign harbors within it an *asemic* existence, and vice versa. We find this in the ideograms, hieroglyphs, and gestural calligraphy of Henri Michaux just as we find it in the mesostics and I-Ching "cut-ups" of John Cage (between overly determined and random distributions of type across the page: letters, punctuation marks), such as in the five *Writings through Finnegans Wake* (1978–1980) and *Empty Words* (1974). We find it in the kinetic text/pattern dissolves of Duchamp's *Anemic Cinema* (1926) and *Rotoreliefs* (1935), in Brion Gysin and Ian Sommerville's eidetic-stroboscopic *Dreamachine* (1959), and in the cinematographisms of Stan Brakhage and Jean-Luc Godard. We find it in the "noise" of Bob Cobbing's typestracts—in (and between) the "ear"/"eye" permutations of, for example, *Are your children safe in the sea* (1966).

Ear version:

Are your children safe in the sea?
Are your children safely in the sea?
Are your children safe? In the sea
Are your children. Safe in the sea
Are your children. Safe? In the sea?

Eye version:

Verbi-visi-voco "hesitancies" of this kind also characterize the palimpsestic type-dissolves of Steve McCaffery's *Ur Carnival* scroll (1966) and *Carnival* (1967–1970); the calligrammic arrangements of Bill Griffiths's *Fragments of A History of the Solar System* (1978); the earlier typewriter poems of Diter Rot, Emmett Williams, Dom Sylvester Houédard, Ulli Freer, Lawrence Upton, and Susan Howe; John Furnival's "Babel" overlaps of the early 1960s; the spatial "deletions" of Man Ray's "Lautgedicht" (1924) and Marcel Broodthaers's redacted *Un Coup de Dés Jamais N'aAbolira Le Hasard* (1969); the corroded typographics of Reinhard Döhl and Heinz Gappmayr's black squares; and the techno-hieroglyphic "noise" of Nam June Paik's *Dream TV* (1973).

The question that recurs here—and which ultimately defines the very idea of a "spatial poetics"—has to do with an implied "location" of contingency. What presents itself in Olson as a typographic (encoding of) subjectivity—*rhythmos*—becomes for Cobbing an operative technicity; what for Foucault is "caught up in a logical, grammatical, locutory nexus" becomes for the Lettrists a prototype literate technology. Such "contingencies" evoke an open-ended system of substitutability which assumes the status of *writing* precisely because of the possibility of its *not being able to be read*—since it is precisely the phenomenon of *illegibility*, of an experience of the *asemic*, which guarantees, as it were, the possibility of "making sense"—just as "operating with signs" implies its contrary. In Dom Sylvester Houédard's "Chronology" for the 1965 exhibition at the Institute of Contemporary Arts *Between Poetry and Painting* (the first exhibition of concrete poetics in the UK), it is suggested that only on a basis of material contingencies can language escape reduction to a metaphysics—or the interjection of "mind" into the signifying equation—while at the same time inscribing authorship as a *techno-poetic* locus that is always already "under erasure." Which is to say, a *locus of ambivalence* between that which writes and that which is written.

Nothing is what it seems?

In 1962 Christian Dotremont began designing what he termed "logogrammes" or "word drawings"—visual poems intended to restore a "tactile" dimension of poetry "in order to replace it amongst the objects of reality."[13] As with the Lettrists—Isidore Isou, Maurice Lemaître, and Gil Wolman—Dotremont sought erasure of the "representational paradigm" of so-called phonetic writing.[14] The logogrammes were developed in collaboration with Asger Jorn, Pierre Alechinsky, Karel Appel, and Corneille—particularly Alechinsky's lithographies from 1960 and the "peintures-mots" and "dessins-mots" that Dotremont produced with Asger Jorn and published under the title *La Chevelure des choses* (1961). While the logogrammes appeared to follow on chronologically from the Lettrist hypergaphics of the 1950s, they are more generally a continuation of a tendency towards "asemic" practices by the CoBrA group (Copenhagen, Brussels, Amsterdam), founded in 1948, of which Dotremont's collaborators had been members until 1951, when several became peripherally or directly involved with Lettrism and, later, the Lettrist International.[15] CoBrA was initially referred to as Revolutionary Surrealism, and the principal writers and artists associated with it were Dotremont, Jorn, Alechinsky, and Serge Vandercam, having in common a profound interest in gesture and the physical act of writing. Derived from the combinatorial and heterogeneous logic of Surrealist objects and Dada cut-ups, glossolalia, and collage, words were not treated as an accompaniment to images and vice versa, but fused in the "physical substance" of the work.

These shared "asemic" tendencies developed in a number of directions during the postwar period, casting back to Mallarmé's

Un coup de dés and Apollinaire's *Calligrammes* (1918)—particularly by the "Noigandres" group in Brazil (Augosto and Haroldo de Campos, Décio Pignatari, et al.) and Grupo Neoconcreto (Lygia Clark, Hélio Oiticica, Franz Weissmann, et al.) in the 1950s—and, in the more "expressionist" vein, to Henri Michaux's *Narration* (1927). In contrast to the Surrealists, Michaux regarded "automatic writing" *as such* to be an impossibility—and, in the bastardized form employed by Breton, insufficient to the task of translating the unconscious. To this end, Michaux pursued a more *calligraphic* (versus what Pound called *ideogrammatic*) method, a kind of "pure writing" that seems to anticipate the work of the "Abstract Expressionists" Mark Toby and Jackson Pollock, and the "graffito" paintings of Cy Twombly. But if the Lettrists and CoBrA find any sort of analogue in a contemporaneous art scene in the U.S., it would arguably need to include the exemplary "action" painter, Willem de Kooning's seemingly transitional canvases of the late 1940s, such as *Orestes* (1947) and *ZOT* (1949)—loosely textual works of excavation, erasure, and overwriting that anticipate the poetico-painterly collaborations of Kenneth Koch and Larry Rivers (e.g., *New York, New York* [1950–1960]) and of Grace Hartigan and Frank O'Hara (*Oranges* [1952]), with their forecast of Jean-Michel Basquiat's "graffiti" paintings of the early 1980s. But a more radical incorporation of the ideas of Michaux and "Revolutionary Surrealism" can be found in the calligraphy of Brion Gysin's *Saharan Notebook* series (1952–1958) and his cut-up, tape-splice, and permutational experiments in collaboration with William Burroughs and Antony Balch.

As a critical term, "asemic writing" was first defined by two visual poets, Tim Gaze and Jim Leftwich, in 1997. Prior to this, "asemic" had appeared (in French as well as in translation) in

Jacques Derrida's *Dissemination* (1972) and Roland Barthes's *The Rustle of Language* (1984). Barthes applied the term to a "word" produced by a typographical mistake, for example "offiver" instead of "officer."[16] Barthes had previously employed the term "contra-écriture," in the context of a discussion of Cy Twombly, to refer to typos and misspellings that produce generative lapses in lexicality.[17] The result was considered a "pure signifier" that, free of any preordained signification, is released into "efflorescence."[18] This efflorescence has a technopoetic dimension. As Francesco Aprile and Cristiano Caggiula write:

> It is possible to analyse the evolution of asemantic writings, by deepening some sociological concepts brought forward by the Canadian sociologist M. McLuhan, who theorized the advent of a post-literary society. He claimed in fact that the continuous evolution of technology would have changed man himself, who would have evolved in "media literate," "multimedia literate," "visually literate," "trans literate." As a matter of fact, the mere alphabetisation would have given space to a universal immediate communication founded on the culture of images and sounds. A sort of return to a tribal society, that would have enhanced the culture of image over the verbal one. With the development of technologies, we experience the passage from a written culture to a verbal one, which is at the same time visual and digital, hence much more dynamic. The founders of the first historical avant-gardes had already introduced in their productions violations of the text, a tendency which will also characterise the future avant-gardes.[19]

A conspicuous outlier in the genealogy of technopoetics is Alan Turing's 1936 article "On computable numbers, with an application to the Entscheidungsproblem," in which he famously proposed the idea of an automatic textual machine—subsequently known as a Turing machine—able to serve as a mathematical model for a simple abstract computer. Turing described his machine as, in effect, an automaton capable of reading, writing, and erasing symbols on an infinitely long tickertape. This tape was divided into squares and each square contained a symbol. Turing's automatic machine could only read one symbol at a time, using a set of rules to determine its next action, based on its current state and the symbol it was reading. It would then perform one of three actions: erase the symbol and write another symbol and move on; move on without modifying the symbol; or come to a halt. The halting state represented an element of undecidability, indeterminacy, or ambivalence.[20]

As a universal cybernetic apparatus capable, in principle, of articulating any computational state, Turing's machine broke with the standard "positivistic" view of infallible logic and—as the later "Turing Test" was to further explore—devolved upon a certain ambiguity that might even be described as self-satire. The Turing machine wasn't bound by the notion of "productive" outcomes—the hallmark of utilitarianism and functionalism: the algorithmic or feedback systems determining each of its discrete states weren't reduceable to a simple binary of "positive" or "negative." Whether the machine continued indefinitely, halted indefinitely, or completed a calculation, its teleology was, as it were, accomplished (*all* feedback was ostensibly "positive," even if it caused the machine to apparently "break down"). Like Duchamp and

Picabia's Dada contraptions, the Turing machine operated on the verge of the "irrational"—recalling Lacan's assertion that the word "irrational" is only meaningful in the way it is applied in the expression "irrational number."

In Seminar XIV, Lacan gives the example of the *unwritability* of the golden number ϕ—(1 + Square root of√5)/2—which is both real and irrational and for which there is no object or signifier that can supply the remainder and thus resolve the infinite series into a whole. In this respect, Turing's writing apparatus can be regarded as a type of "desiring machine," and from this seemingly fortuitous encounter a whole spectrum of poetics can be seen to emerge, from Nanni Balestrini's *Tape Mark 1* and Gustav Metzger's Auto-Destructive Art (ADA) manifesto (both 1961)[21] to Ilse and Pierre Garnier's *Poèmes Mécaniques* and Bruce Lacey's poetic robot *R.O.S.A. B.O.S.O.M* (Radio Operated Simulated Actress—Battery Or Standby Operated Mains—constructed for the International Poetry Incarnation at Albert Hall) (both 1965) to Jiří Valoch's computer poems (1968) and Douglas Davis's *World's First Collaborative Sentence* (1994–). In *Tape Mark 1* (a computer-generated "poem" consisting of a mixture of randomness and simple deterministic rules to shuffle sentence fragments from *Hiroshima Diary* by Michihiko Hachiya, *The Mystery of the Elevator* by Paul Goldwin, and *Tao Te Ching* by Lao Tse) and *Tristano* (1966; a "novel" in 109,027,350,432,000 permutations), Balestrini attempts to erase the singularity of the original/text by situating the "work" itself in its recombinability. Like Beckett's late "cybernetic" theatre pieces (*Quad* and *What Where*, but also *Krapp's Last Tape*), a general grammatological schema emerges from the insistent materiality of the text in its physical operations.

Unfolding extra dimensions

The advent of hypertext opened the path of a corresponding "digital poetics," which on the one hand recycled ideas of materiality vs. dematerialization from 1960s conceptualism and computer art (see, for example, the ICA's 1965 *Cybernetic Serendipity* exhibition) and on the other hand produced artifacts like Francesca da Rimini's *Doll Yoko* (1998) and VNS Matrix's *Cyberfeminist Manifesto* (1991)—a polemic against Big Daddy Mainframe and for "gender abolitionism"—whose critique of phallogocentrism went some way towards the evolution (and subsequently recuperation) of codework, net.art, and glitch poetics (just as the internet itself, as a liberatory space for radical poetics, was recuperated into the commercial sphere at the end of the 1990s).

In his introduction to the October 2001 "Codework" issue of *American Book Review* (22.6), Alan Sondheim coined the term codework to designate the writing practice of a genre of "computer poetry" by a number of writers emerging from the "electronic writing" scene of the previous decade. These included da Rimini (aka Doll Yoko and GashGirl), Mez (Mary-Anne Breeze aka net. wurker), jodi, Talan Memmott, Ted Warnell, Brian Lennon, Kenji Siratori, Netochka Nezvanova, lo_y, and John Cayley. Codework served to designate a type of writing in which the terminological and formal aspects of computer programming would assume an aesthetic or ornamental function which at the same time would be productive of aesthetic and semantic disturbance within the "field" of signification: tree-structures, Booleanisms, Unix shell commands, html, ascii, bracketing, and directory slashings, etc. Mez in *Datableed* (2001):

> 2 uze computer kode kon.[e]vent.ionz spliced with irc
> emoticons and
> ab[scess]breviations....
> 2 spout punctu[rez]ationz reappropri.[s]ated in2 sentence
> schematics....
> 2 illustrate the x.pansion of software potentialities of co:d]
> [iscours][e
> in an environment x.clusively reliant on it.[22]

For Sondheim, codework designated a type of writing which de-semanticizes while at the same time exposing the material armature of the semantic "program." It works, according to Sondheim, by "using the syntactic interplay of surface language, with reference to computer language and engagement" and "works in which the submerged code has modified the surface language—with the possible representation of the code as well."[23] This in many respects resembles the material considerations of contemporary textual genetics with its formal analysis of "avant-texts." The program, as what comes in advance of writing, denotes that which, consequently, withdraws from writing, just as the avant-text denotes that which withdraws from the text at the same time as "haunting" it in the form of a genetic trace, a signature code, a specter. Kenji Siratori writes:

> In my writing the language cell is able to be distorted by the infinite hyperlink of the synapse—"a new language" is the conceptual pain—all the data act as the hardweb character as if I dissect subjective writing, I'm striking the nude brain to a screen.[24]

In the material environment of digital poetics, this entails not just "theoretical" notions of dematerialization, but the vulnerability of "electronic writing" to constitutive forms of erasure, such as datableed, link-rot, and script redundancy—being, as Mez writes, "alt[.ctrl.delete]etered" (the Web is nothing if not full of holes or "Puzzle Pieces of a Datableede Jigsaw"[25]).

In a later article entitled "Codeworld"[26] (2006), Sondheim discusses "codework, code writing" in terms of "the alterity of a substrate which supports, generates and behaves as a catalyst in relation to its production." This reconnects with the legacy of Turing via the route of cryptographic automation during the Second World War, in the form of the Colossus (a brute-force permutational text machine designed to break the German "Enigma" code), and the function of randomness as both a technique and an artifact of encipherment. Such artifacts—like the data traces that haunt modern computing—could not simply be regarded as residual echoes within the machine, but required accounting for as characteristics of transmission itself, thus assuming a veritable "semantic" function. From its advent, codework has thus been concerned not with "codes" per se, but with the spectrality of code and the haunting of the "pro-gramme," just as the work of Cage (situated at the intersection of Dada and cybernetics) was concerned with chance operations, redundancy, and noise.

No longer the site of metaphysical detours into a mimetic elsewhere, these works erase the denotative subjection of the signifier to the rule of the signified, as Derrida says. And while this has at times been treated as a "phenomenon," such as the conveniently outposted body of writing called Concrete Poetry, it is by no means isolated—to the contrary, what we see is a general condition (the sublimated Kantian *technē*) that has made itself visible *in the present[ation] of the work itself* (to speak in Kantese). From Mallarmé's throw of dice to Olson's projective verse, from Pound's erasure of metronomic division in the "line" to the divisionism of Cagean mesostics, from Cendrars's trans-Siberian prose to Kerouac's continuous typewriter scroll, from Khlebnikov's molecularized *zaum* to Joyce's wakean *poeta—and beyond.* A genealogy of erasure unfolds like curled-up extra-dimensions, not to instate a new teleological poetics—one "more authentic" than the rest—but as the articulation of a *field of possibility* itself hitherto erased under the critical mass of mimeticism.

CHAPTER 7

Radio Pictures, Blank Transmissions

Concretion from within creates the specific place,
Taught, radiant, articulate, but strange to language,
The absolute strains to become aware.
Eye, standing at extreme perimeter listens,
Becomes the medium of the heard;
Touch makes it move: returned to motion,
Light, stopping from its latent anonymity,
Explodes in sound.

BOB COBBING, May 1978

Avant-gardism can be summarized as a critique of social and cultural power. What this often amounts to in practice is a critique of the abstract and concrete relations between medium and genre—not genre understood in the limited sense of aesthetic categories, but as categorical thought in its broadest ramification—beginning with questions like "what is art?" and extending by way of questions like "what is meaning?" to the possibility of questioning as such.[1] Contrary to the dogmatic "modernism" of Clement Greenberg—which insisted upon an abstract (almost eugenic) purity of form over medium—the tendency of avant-gardism has been towards the synergetic and transmedial, and to a critical self-consciousness that even in its more rigidly constructivist turns disputes categorical thought. It is for this reason that "genre" is primarily evoked for polemical purposes: for example, Rauschenberg's telegram "This is a Portrait of Iris Clert if I Say So" (1961). And at a certain point also, for all its resistances, avant-gardism tends to the acknowledgement that in the final instance all "medium" is commodity—perhaps nowhere more flagrantly demonstrated than in Yves Klein's "The Specialisation of Sensibility in the Raw Material State into Stabilised Pictorial Sensibility, The Void" (1958; exhibited incidentally at the Iris Clert gallery in Paris), which took the form of an empty room; the following year Klein began selling a series of "Zones of Immaterial Sensibility" (i.e., empty space) for 20g of gold each, half of which was then tossed into the Seine. One of the buyers wrote of the transaction ceremony that "no other experience in art equal[led] the depth of feeling it evoked," and that there was a "shock of self-recognition and an explosion of awareness of time and space."[2]

While exploration of synesthesia and a skepticism towards genre characterize the so-called historical avant-garde from its origin, the categorical distinction of a *neo*-avant-garde (itself not immune to this skepticism) makes appeal to a particular critical self-reflexivity in which the question of art *work* (medium, form, practice, etc.) is subsumed in a broad-reaching "conceptualism." The line of argument from Marcel Duchamp to John Cage, Yves

Klein, Robert Rauchenberg, Nam June Paik, and Joseph Kosuth not only posits the internal contradictions of such formulations as "avant-garde art," "avant-garde literature," "avant-garde cinema," "avant-garde theatre," and "avant-garde radio"—thus exposing them as categorical artifacts *a priori*—but puts these contradictions to work in the construction of a "neo-avant-gardism" in which the status of any given medium is attributable to an arbitrary taxonomy of forms, including (but not limited to) broadcast metadata, written sets of instructions, technical schemas, definitions, photographs, collages, sign language, braille, and spectroscopy—and all of these simultaneously.

The problem, for example, of avant-garde (or so-called neo-avant-garde) "cinema," "ciné-roman," "ciné-poetry," "*Schauspiel*," "*Hörspiel*," and "radio play" is therefore not one of periodizing and cataloguing works produced *for* or even *with* cinematic or radiographic apparatuses—composed within formal constraints that correspond (however experimentally) to such genres or even genre-hybrids, and whose aesthetic in some way reclaims or continues "avant-garde tendencies," whatever these may be—but one of a necessary reconfiguration of the question of genre itself (and consequently of hybridity), of medium, and of the institutionalization of the "avant-garde" as a mode of production of artworks (no matter how "subversive"). Such a reconfiguration must go beyond a mere attempt at synthesis—as, for example, such seemingly paradoxical "centaurs" as *ciné-radio*—to an examination of propositions in the form of a cinema-without-images, silent radio, and so on.

These imperatives have not prevented historians of the avant-garde—perhaps beguiled by a proliferation of antithetical "art movements"—from attempting to supplant a limited categorical view with a more pluralistic one, on the false assumption that this in any way problematizes the insistence upon art *form*. Without any apparent irony, arguments are made for a broader representation, despite the history of avant-gardism itself disclosing a critique, precisely, of mimeticism. It is as if all that had been in question was the inadequacy of existing categories either to realize or account for a plenitude of media, or of the discipline of art history to adequately document their genealogy. Perversely, such a line of reasoning extends to the idea that art itself is the cause of this inadequacy. As Douglas Khan and Gregory Whitehead lament in their preface to *Wireless Imagination: Sound, Radio and the Avant-Garde* (2010):

> the deafening silence of sound-in-thought is mirrored by the absence of anything remotely resembling a coherent tradition of audio art. Instead, we are left with an odd assortment of isolated moments and cultural marginalia: the fantastic acoustic scenarios projected through the texts of Raymond Roussel; the impossible aural objectives of Marcel Duchamp; Dziga Vertov's proposal for a phonographic "Laboratory of Hearing"; the zaum language and Radio Sorcery pronounced and promoted Velimir Khlebnikov; the brazenly iconoclastic castaways of F.T. Marinetti's and Pino Masnata's *La Radia*; the antimusics of the Surrealists; the noise bands of Russolo, Foregger, and Cage; the contorted radio talk show delivered by Antonin Artaud; the labyrinthine inner journeys invoked by German Hörspiel; the razor contamination and cut-up ventriloquism of Gysin and Burroughs.[3]

The idea that "the avant-garde" embodied a coherent tradition had been famously advanced by Greenberg's principal rival, Harold Rosenberg, in a book ornamented with a cover by Willem de Kooning, called *The Tradition of the New* (1959). Rosenberg conceived this anti-tradition around the paradigm of radical discontinuity as *action*, in contrast to Greenberg's vulgar Hegelianism in which art progressed by continuous historical-materialist refinements towards an apotheosis in pure abstraction. Rosenberg's *discontinuity principle* implied—as McLuhan was soon to point out—that all innovation is therefore *contiguous* across a generalized field of *possibility*, and that this field is traversed by what we call *media*. Such an idea (less *opposed to* than *radicalizing* Greenberg's "resistance of medium") is articulated precisely by way of a discontinuity that is not necessarily historical (and by way of a counter-appeal to the "kitsch" of mass media culture) that broadly corresponds to what is sometimes called the neo-avant-garde (retrospectively characterized by Rosalind Krauss *à la* Lyotard—under the influence of Conceptualism and its "new media" avatars of *disembodiment* and *dematerialization* from Bruce Nauman to Christian Marclay—as a "post-medium condition" [2012]).[4]

With the nineteenth-century advent of novel technological "prostheses of experience," like photography, sound recording, and film, and new experiential environments like radio, cinema, and television—as well as the quotidian sign-space of commercial advertising and mass print media—contiguity itself increasingly became the preoccupation of an art that, before being "avant-garde," was already, in a certain sense, *neo*-avant-garde. From the chronophotographs of Eadweard Muybridge and Étienne-Jules Marey to Nam June Paik's "Experimental TV" in the 1960s, an intuitive vanguardism with regard to form was accompanied by counter-intuitive (ab)uses of medium and the concomitant resistance to a subordinate illustrative function (even of "art movement"): simplistically, it marked "the transition from staging traditional forms of performance within emergent media, towards the creative use of *new media* on their own terms."[5] While the question of technology was conventionally viewed within a rationalist-utilitarian framework, a more radical, "poetic" (critico-satirical or even "cybernetic") understanding of the emergent "new media" began to develop symbiotically within the "historical avant-garde"[6] and converged, via Cubism, Futurism, and Constructivism, upon the "irrationalism" of Dadaist anti-art and its descent, by way of Surrealism, Lettrism, and Situationism, to "telematics" and "computer art" in the 1960s.

Autodestructive media

Largely overlooked in this genealogy of (neo-)avant-garde experimentation within the institutional framework of broadcast radio and the so-called "radio play" is the emergence in 1951 of the Jarryesque proto-/neo-Dadaism of Spike Milligan, Peter Sellers, and Harry Secombe (in collaboration with the BBC's Radiophonic Workshop). Often misconstrued as popular "light entertainment" (as was Dada itself on occasion), *The Goon Show* had its origins in the wartime subversive humor of Milligan and evolved its name from "the Goons" in E. C. Segar's 1933 Popeye cartoon storyline "Plunder Island" (the show was originally billed as the needlessly prophylactic *Crazy People* because of objections at the BBC). Milligan had adopted the term "Goons" as a denotator of jingoistic military stupidity (indeed, of the stupidity of authoritarianism generally). In his World War II memoir *Adolf Hitler: My Part in His Downfall*, Milligan recounts an episode involving a group of like-minded barracks subversives called the Clubbers:

> The way the Clubbers were assembled was by a trumpet call based on the Fanfare from the *Boys from Syracuse* film. Immediately the gang would do "Hollywood Rhubarbs," rush forth, grab their clubs, run into the woods hitting trees and shouting "Death to the Goons."[7]

The Goons' evolution from homefront anti-militarist "humorists" to a crypto avant-garde has echoes of Dada's founding political aesthetics during the previous war, represented in the personages of Hugo Ball, Emmy Hennings, Tristan Tzara, and Sophie Taeuber-Arp, among others, with its roots in cabaret and street spectacle. In *Spike Milligan's Accordion*, Rick Cousins emphasizes the similarly radical experimental character of *The Goon Show* as belying *its* status as merely an extension of variety theatre for radio, or as a simple parody (replete with irrealist plot and narrative devices, sound effects, relentless puns and verbal gags, musical interludes, and so on) of a mainstream radio play *genre* that had frequently served as propaganda during the war and afterwards was pressed into service for national reconstruction. Cousins likens Milligan's "desire to force a change" in the medium of radio—and in a society eager for escape from food-stamp austerity—to what Lyotard and others later theorize under the rubric of postmodernism: "a 'search for new presentations' in ways which consistently 'denied itself the solace of good forms.'"[8]

At times evocative of Jarry's *Ubu Roi* and James Joyce's *Finnegans Wake*, *The Goon Show*—which nevertheless sustained a hugely popular run on the BBC over a nine-year period—served as a catalyst (though one often uncredited in the discourse of "serious" cultural history) for an emerging London underground scene—contemporaneous with the Lettrist International, Nouveaux Réalistes, Viennese Actionists, Fluxus, the PANic movement, the Provos, and others elsewhere. This loosely configured and largely unacknowledged neo-avant-garde would have included, in addition to Milligan and company, figures like vaudevillian Bruce Lacey, sound poet Bob Cobbing, "autodestructive" artist Gustav Metzger, and acolytes of Bryon Gysin and William Burroughs's tape-splices, fold-ins, and cut-ups (such as COUM Transmissions), as well as nonpareil cultural subversives and wreckers of western civilization like Screaming Lord Such and the Who's Pete Townshend.[9] Jeff Nuttall's *Bomb Culture* attributes this collective effect around *The Goon Show*'s to its origins "in the absurd compulsory National Service in an era dominated by the H-bomb," serving as "the most important bridge" linking "hitherto alien traditions" within an emergent pop culture. It was able to do this not merely by force of aesthetic argument, but due to the seemingly anomalous fact of its extremely widespread influence (over two million listeners already during its initial incarnation as *Crazy People*).[10] As Nuttall recounts, "*The Goon Show* catchphrases and *The Goon Show* caricature voices spread into everybody's conversation and provided us all with schizoid subterfuges, vocal disguises." He also states, "*The Goon Show* was protest. *The Goon Show* was surrealist and therefore art, and *The Goon Show* was every National Serviceman's defence mechanism, was therefore pop."[11]

This hybrid sub-culture, fused by the sensibility of the Goons, found further analogue in the show's transformation of "medium," in no small part through Milligan's sound-effect logics, realized by the technicians of the BBC's Radiophonic Workshop—whose innovations were subsequently integrated (recuperated) into the soundscape of more conventional radio dramas. Cousins attributes a spatiotemporality to the overall structure of Milligan's work that is "fluid and indeterminate: boundaries between different times and different spaces dissolve, allowing mutually inconsistent chronologies and scales of size and distance to coexist."[12]

This assault upon a mimetic paradigm that assigns, in radio, a function analogous to the predominant *visuality* of the spacetime constellation across theatre, cinema, and TV recalls Joyce's polysemic "soundsense" experiments in *Finnegans Wake*: "What can't be coded can be decorded if an ear aye sieze what no eye ere grieved for. Now, the doctrine obtains, we have occasioning cause causing effects and affects occasionally recausing altereffects."[13] Through its minimal resemblance to, and evocation of, variety theatre, the Goon "show" inflected the idea of the radio "play" with a substantially non-verbal synesthetics of the medium's dimension of *unpresentability*. It is in this respect that Milligan, Sellers, and Secombe most anticipate Lyotard's thinking of a nascent postmodernism. And just as Joyce, who serves as something of a paradigm case for Lyotard, "allows the unpresentable to become perceptible in his writing itself, in the signifier"—thereby putting "the whole range of available narrative and even stylistic operations…into play without concern for the unity of the whole"[14]—so too the entire technical apparatus of *The Goon Show* was pitched towards a type of critical transmediality: not as a *transcendence* of medium, but as a *subversion* of its generic logic, wherein this subversion itself becomes its own mode of production.[15]

In his 1970 study *Expanded Cinema*, Gene Youngblood would go on to identify such a synesthetic logic as the defining trait of a general cybernetics of sense, evolving from the advent of the earliest techno-mechanical systems of producing and recording the spectrum of what Joyce called "verbivocovisual presentment."[16] By 1970, the radical possibilities traceable through the neo-avant-gardism of Milligan and others had achieved their most striking formulation in what Nam June Paik called "Experimental Television" (1963). "Television," Youngblood quotes video artist Les Levine as saying, "is the most obvious realization of software in the general environment. It shows the human race itself as a working model of itself. It renders the social and psychological condition of the environment visible to the environment."[17] And if this is so, it is because synesthesia (as the feedback of contiguous modes of experience into a "unified *Gestalt*"), rather than *mimēsis*, is the mode of its "realization." The medium being, if not "the message" (per McLuhan), an *articulation of signifying possibility*. One of the notable explorations of these synesthetic "tele-" effects was initially envisaged as a spatially composed synthesis of textual montage and sound-work—this time quite explicitly mediated by Joycean polysemy—eventually entitled *Roaratorio: An Irish Circus on Finnegans Wake*, by polymath composer John Cage. Paik's "Experimental Television" was, in fact, an explicit synthesis of, and homage to, both Cage and McLuhan.

Playing by ear, an eye-mime

Cage's *Roaratorio*, originally conceived as a radio drama, was commissioned in 1979 for Westdeutscher Rudfunk (WDR-Köln) by Klaus Schöning, who had already in 1968 commissioned George Perec's Hörspiel *Die Maschine*. *Roaratorio* was produced at the Institut de Recherche et Coordination Acoustique/Musique (IRCAM) in Paris, which also produced algorithmic works by Pierre Boulez as well as the "computer music design" of Alexis Baskind. The title of Cage's "radio play" derives from a passage in *Finnegans Wake*—"this longawaited Messiagh of roaratorios."[18]—as do the content and key aspects of the composition's formal method. The groundwork for the *Roaratorio* began when Cage was invited to provide musical accompaniment to another project based on Joyce's text, which he had begun in 1976 as a contribution to an issue of *TriQuarterly*, entitled "7 out of 23," and which later evolved into the book *Writing for the Second Time through Finnegans Wake* (and thence into a third, a fourth, and a fifth—the last of which, produced in 1980, is entitled *Muoyce*, a portmanteau of "music" and "Joyce"—*Muoyce II*, produced in 1992, is subtitled *Writing through Ulysses*).

In 1979 the forty-one-page text of *Writing for the Second Time through Finnegans Wake* became the "score" for *Roaratorio*, which was composed as a sixty-minute soundscape, directed by references to place names in Joyce's text. As Cage recalled: "places mentioned in the *Wake* are identified in Louis Mink's book *A Finnegans Wake Gazetteer*....And so a sound coming from Nagasaki, or from Canberra in Australia, or from a town in Ireland or a street in Dublin—could be identified by page and line and then put into this hour, where it belonged in relation to the page and line of *Finnegans Wake*."[19] Cage and his assistants then went to many of those places and recorded the sounds they found there, and obtained a number of other recordings by contacting radio stations around the world. Cage then made a recording of himself reading various passages from the *Wake*. A third set of tapes was made of Irish music. Finally, a sound collage from all of these source tapes was produced, divided into four parts with each part representing a book of the *Wake*. The sixty-four tracks of Cage's *Roaratorio* produced a "reading" of *Finnegans Wake* of comparable complexity to the *Wake* itself and evocative of the "complex branching and interconnected chains of causation" explored in cybernetics.[20]

For *Roaratorio*, Cage turned to a combination of mechanical means to select and combine elements of Joyce's text, initially subjecting the *Wake* to a series of chance operations determined by a computer program called *Mesolist* (based on the *I Ching*), which ultimately produced "a 41-page mesostic text, using the string JAMES JOYCE."[21] In Cage's lexicon, a mesostic is a type of hermetic, "found" acrostic poem, which emerges in the form of textual fragments constellated around the capitalized proper name of the author (or any other arbitrarily determined string or set of terms). Cage describes his methodology for "writing through" Joyce's text as follows:

> I would look for a word with a J in it that didn't have an A because the A belongs on the second line for JAMES. And then a word with A that didn't have an M, and an M that didn't have an E, and an E that didn't have an S and in this way I made a path through the entire book...[22]

Cage uncovered 862 instances in which Joyce had "signed" his text in this manner, collecting them in a single volume under the title *Writing through Finnegans Wake*—later subjected to additional constraints and eventually published under the title *Writing for the Second Time through Finnegans Wake.* The idea of mesostics is interesting for a consideration of synesthesia for many reasons, not least because it mimics—in the intersection of the aleatory and the over-determined—those structural schemata of Joyce's own "hypertext," while at the same time critiquing the mystical idea of revelation through divine *logos* or authorial signature effect. Comparable procedures are at work in *Roaratorio*:

Jiccup
the f**A**ther
Most
h**E**aven
Skysign

Judges
Or
deuteronom**Y**
wats**C**h
futur**E**[23]

Cage's "Irish circus on *Finnegans Wake*" pursued a diametrical trajectory to Perec's *Die Maschine*, which has been described by Ulrich Schönherr as "one of the most radical attempts to construct a literary text that is in close affinity to musical techniques."[24] Based on Goethe's "Wanders Nachtlied II"—and, like *Roaratorio*, recorded at IRCAM—*Die Maschine* was staged as a "computational simulation" that "replaces the alphabetic code" of Goethe's text with an algorithmic one, dramatizing (so to speak) the "historical transition from symbolic through analogue to digital media." In consequence, Schönherr argues, Perec's Oulipian procedures "succeed in producing a polyphonic acoustic artwork that transcends the intermedial boundaries between the two distinct semiotic systems of music and language"[25]—just as *Roaratorio*'s "chance" combinatorial procedures do.

Indeed, *Roaratorio*'s structure harks back to an earlier sound-piece produced by Cage in collaboration with Marcel Duchamp and sound engineer Lowell Cross at the Ryerson Institute, Toronto, in 1968, entitled *Reunion*. This performance consisted of Cage and Duchamp (in his last public performance) playing chess on a chessboard fitted with sixty-four photoresistors and nine contact microphones.[26] In addition, Gordon Mumma, David Tudor, and David Behrman[27] operated an array of sound-generating systems by way of accompanying "electronic music." Visual monitoring of sound events passing through the chessboard was produced by having the resistors and microphones feed into several modified black-and-white and color TV sets. The resulting oscilloscopic effects served as visual analogues to Cage and Duchamp's otherwise "minimalist" soundscape, in which the algorithmically patterned arrangement of the chess game's "score" was interpolated and counterpointed by frequent approximations of silence, which—in an echo of Cage's best-known piece, *4'33"* (1952)—remained the focus of a certain visual spectacle: a non-verbal TV that wasn't "silent film" but instead a kind of notional, even notational, synesthetic *radio-graphy*.

Notably, *Reunion* was the opening event of the Toronto "Sightsoundsystems" Festival, organized by composer Udo Kasemets. But while this original performance of *Reunion* was recorded and videotaped for CBS/Columbia, the video's whereabouts is unknown while the audio was only partially released on vinyl as a twelve-minute flexi-disc LP, *John Cage and Marcel Duchamp*, in 1970. However, in 1982 Cage did produce—again at the invitation of Schöning—a radio play for WDR entitled *James Joyce, Marcel Duchamp, Erik Satie: An Alphabet* (a collage of fifteen mesostic "dialogues"), raising the question of what synthesis of ideas might otherwise have resulted had *Reunion* been designed "for radio," and how such an element of intentionality might even be considered operative outside the technological situation of the "performance" itself. In other words, it raises the question—in which a distinction must be made from mere avowal of a *being-for* radio: thus "conceived" but nevertheless able to do without, or be detached from, "its medium" (as if this were possible: a pure concept able to "assume form" at will: pure *mimēsis* in other words)—of the possibility of *transmitting* what Cobbing called a "concretion from within." A question of the immanence, here, of a certain radio-graphy in its very structure, in its eventness (and in no respect a *vehicle*). To *détourne* an expression of Debord: "Radio without radio, if necessary."

Reunion's deployment of the chessboard as site, occasion, instrument, and composition logic had a particularly arcane quality—a mannerist austerity, even, pedantically at odds with the burden of spectacle placed upon it by the theatrical setting. In his 1978 opus magnum, *La Vie mode d'emploi*, Perec utilized a similarly ironic reliance upon the apparently anti-dramatic trope (or rather, tropic mechanism) of a modified chessboard to generate, precisely, a narratological system of "spectacular production" (Debord) inseparable from its schematics. Perec's schematics bear uncanny resemblance to those of Lowell Cross's design for the electronic chessboard: a constraint-based cybernetic mechanism, in effect, for producing a radiographic environment. In both works, the generative logic—like that of *The Goon Show*—was not mimetic, but situational, procedural, and synesthetic.

As a "system" of generative operations, the chessboard's gamespace and state-based temporality also served to foreground the relationship between the transversality of the work's "textual" array (and its probabilistic arrangement), amounting to a deconstruction of the idea of such categorical distinctions as *artwork*, *performance*, *novel*, and *radio play*, within a general field of *textuality*. On the one hand tending to an abstract minimum (Cage's "empty words," Klein's "void") and on the other to a maximalist polysemic "broadcast" (*Finnegans Wake*, *The Goon Show*, *La Vie mode d'emploi*), the neo-avant-gardism of this gesture is vested precisely in those counter-indications of the term *play* that escape presentation within any generic system which—among other things—denotates radio as a form of prosthetic speech-technology: the electronic logos. Incisive in this respect is Derrida's critique of mimeticism in *Of Grammatology* (1967) and *Writing and Difference* (1967: in particular the essay "Structure, Sign and Play in the Discourse of the Human Sciences"), in which "speech" itself is reconceived as a form of *inscription* under the influence of a disseminative, polysemic/synesthetic play of difference and repetition. Derrida's deconstruction of "play" touches directly upon the *radical* character of the categorical unmooring that takes place with regard to the conjunction of the terms "radio" and "play" in the work of Perec, Cage, and Milligan, and their production of what Derrida calls "genetic indetermination"[28]: "a field of infinite substitutions"[29] in which a *signifying possibility* takes the place of the generically *presentable*.

This short-circuiting of the mimetic paradigm is at the core of the neo-avant-garde project, yet it is arguably in the domain of "expanded cinema" that it achieves its most emphatic articulation in a culture so utterly immured in the image. From the anti-retinalism of Duchamp's *Anemic Cinema* (1926) to Paik's "Experimental Television," a critical impulse within the avant-garde itself pursued a yet more radical repurposing of the dominant technological media of sense-transmission. Developing earlier approaches to radio as a "site of broadcast performance" into a general synesthetics of "indeterminate electronic sound [and image],"[30] there emerged a reconception of the verbo-visual dichotomy as *cinemato/graphy* in a broadly semiotic continuum (or "broadcast"). By the time of *Roaratorio*'s production, this generalized field of synesthesia had been mapped by Youngblood not simply as a terrain of trans-medial and trans-generic hybrids, but as in fact an art of the unpresentable. While so-called new media tended towards a fully-immersive Virtual Reality, mimetic technologies in general remained haunted by what *does not* transmit—between sound/image, speech/writing, and in the work of erasure, silence, blankness, and noise—all of which have nevertheless acquired the status of aesthetic information.

Information is radiation

One particular outgrowth of this examination of transmissibility was the "flicker film," a structuralist reduction of Duchamp's anti-retinal anemia to the stroboscopic interplay of alternating black and white or monochrome frames—exemplified by Tony Conrad's thirty-minute-duration 1966 film, *The Flicker*, consisting of only five separate frames: a warning notice, two title cards, and a black frame and a white frame (which alternate in forty-seven arrangements repeated ten times). A custom-built synthesizer soundtrack, pitched at 20Hz, using heavy reverb and tape-delay, accompanied the film. *The Flicker* calls attention to the optics of moving-image technology—and what it is that in fact constitutes a "cinematic" image—while at the same time constructing a (nominally) visual, "synesthetic" environment for the transmission of sound and vice versa. Analogous effects could be produced by slowing or accelerating conventional film reels below or above the sixteen-to-twenty-four-frame per second threshold that defined the silent or talking "moving image": beyond this threshold of optical illusionism, structural (machinic) effects take over, tending—via the stroboscopic, in one direction, and the static, in the other—to a general "radiographic" effect of the projection apparatus itself. These thresholds become indistinguishable: the acceleration of optical flicker into sonic Morse code ultimately produces (at its extremity) a sense of stasis accompanied by an effect of pure sound or noise (a semiotic "event-horizon").

Debord's *Hurlements en faveur de Sade* (1952)—a proto-flicker film heavily indebted to Gil Wolman's *L'Anticoncept* of the previous year (made notorious by a screening at London's ICA)—along with *Société du spectacle* (1972), recodes this effect within an explicit aesthetico-ideological critique. It is composed mostly of still images overlaid by an almost monotone reading of sections of Debord's text of the same name; the former composed of alternating white and black screens, ending in twenty-four minutes of silence (wherein it is announced that "there's no more cinema, cinema's dead"): a blank cinema broadcasting—like the cryptic radio signals emanating from Hades in Cocteau's *Orphée*—from beyond the grave. "The only interesting undertaking," Debord was subsequently to write, "is the liberation of everyday life, not only within a historical perspective, but for us and right away. This entails the withering away of alienated forms of communication. The cinema, too, has to be destroyed."[31]

This announcement of cinema's death—repeating the gesture of Duchamp in a signification that this death is an interminable one that indeed bears repetition—in turn poses the question of what *cinema amounts to*, through a deconstruction of those generic boundaries that were meant to separate it from radio, photography, and text. "There's no more cinema," Debord says—which could equally be understood as, *there's nothing more to cinema: this is all there is.* (A stance later appropriated by Jean-Luc Godard in his 1967 film *Week-End*, which ends with the words FIN DE CINÉMA in "International Klein Blue" blazoned on the screen.) Like Magritte's 1929 painting "The Treachery of the Image" *(Ceci n'est pas une pipe)*, *Hurlements* questions the status of the cinematic image itself—and, by direct implication, its *radiographic* analogue—beyond any *mimēsis*: *c'est tout*, that's all it is. To which, in a seminar three years later, Lacan gives the impression of responding with the observation that,

> When we say, then, *that's it*, we imply that that's all it is, or that that's not what it is, namely, the appearance that we stopped at. But this proves to us that everything that has subsequently emerged, the *that's all it is* as well as the *that's not what it is*, was already implied in the *that's it* at the beginning.[32]

By an interesting coincidence, shortly before Wolman and Debord's experiments in anti-cinema, Yves Klein had begun producing a series of monochrome blue "paintings"—contemporaneous with the composition of a sound-piece, *Symphonie Monotone-Silence, 1947–1948* (comprising two halves: a single continuous sound and an equivalent time of silence)—intended to express, as Klein in a gesture of proto-conceptualist neo-dadaism insisted, "what I wished my life to be." The symphony was of forty minutes duration and "consisted of one unique continuous 'sound,' drawn out, and deprived of its beginning and of its end, creating a feeling of vertigo and of aspiration outside of time":

> Thus, even in its presence, this symphony does not exist. It exists outside of the phenomenology of time because it is neither born nor will it die. However, in the world of our possibilities of conscious perception, it is silence—audible presence.[33]

This first half of the symphony was intended to prepare the listener "to transform the experience of silence," in the second, "into fullness":

> Silence… This is really my symphony and not the sounds during its performance. This silence is so marvellous because it grants happenstance and even sometimes the possibility of true happiness, if only for a moment, for a moment whose duration is immeasurable.[34]

As with Cage's *4'33"* before it, the *Symphonie*'s play between monotone and silence echoes the play in the *Monochromes* between entropy (or equilibrium) and non-image: a "diptych," as Klein said, that is "the exact transposition of the articulation between the visible and the invisible."

In the early 1970s, these ideas became the basis of Derek Jarman's attempt at an investigation of the monochrome which, while nominally "cinematic," pursued a radically *radiographic* agenda. Initially inspired by the tonal quality of both the *Symphonie* and IKB (International Klein Blue),[35] Jarman's "blue film for Yves Klein"

(1973),[36] conceived under the working title *Bliss*, materialized some twenty years later as the director's final work, *Blue* (1993). In his notes, Jarman described the monochrome as "an alchemy, effective liberation from personality. *It articulates silence*. It is a fragment of an immense work without limit. The blue of the landscape of liberty."[37] Jarman's approach was to be by turns metaphysically abstract and—after he was diagnosed with AIDS in 1986—insistently materialist, initially envisaging the work (in the spirit of Warhol) as a single long-take of a Klein painting, "no image, simply a field of blue," intended to evoke, as Jarman's biographer puts it, "an elegiac journey towards immateriality," "the admirable austerity of the void."[38] Ultimately it was to pose the problem of "the impossibility of visualising an unseen virus" even while its visible effects upon Jarman's body became increasingly evident.

The sound of Blue deep inside the camera

In 1989, during postproduction on his last major montage work, *The Garden*, Jarman had written: "So many fleeting moments lost to the camera, which seems destined to point in the wrong direction." The following July, AIDS-related toxoplasmosis left Jarman temporarily blind, a condition that was to increasingly dominate his final years and transform *Blue* from a meditation on the visual art of Klein to a meditation on the possibility of seeing as such. An August 13, 1992, diary entry records: "I think I have to come to terms with my blind fate, there is so much to do, I am certain I could make a film, if Beethoven could do the 9th without hearing."[39] Blindness would become a "medium" for a de-mimeticized cinematic image: an image whose "illusionism" would be *not to be an image*.

Unlike Conrad's *The Flicker* (and in radical contrast to many of Jarman's own "anarchic" and "improvised" Super-8 assemblages, such as *The Last of England*, *The Garden*, and the posthumous *Glitterbug*), the seeming stasis of *Blue* would belie the materiality of an imperceptible movement: the movement of "seeing" through the imposition of a blind, affected by way of sound. As Derrida writes in his 1993 reflection on the origins of drawing and self-portraiture, *Memoirs of the Blind* (and *Blue* is nothing if not such a self-portrait): "the visibility of the visible cannot, by definition, be seen, no more than what Aristotle speaks of as the diaphanousness of light can be."[40] In a dialectically counterpointed (if equivalently polemical) sense to Godard's 1969 collaboration with Jean-Henri Roger, *British Sounds*—"a very long lecture (or harangue)" on the fetishized imagism of "industrial rhetoric"[41]—if *Blue* was to be an "art of blindness," it would be above all, then, *not a depiction of blindness*.

As the visual dimension of Jarman's last film grew increasingly minimal, finally composed solely of seventy-six minutes of a monochrome blue screen, the soundtrack—composed by Simon Fisher-Turner and incorporating the voices of Jarman, John Quentin, Nigel Terry, and Tilda Swinton reciting poetry and texts culled from Jarman's diaries—became increasingly dense, and it was published as if it were a Hörspiel script (or stage play, or prose poem, etc.) under the strange title *Blue: Text of a Film by Derek Jarman* (1993).[42]

> Blue light. A spectral light. Leni's full moon falling through a crystal grotto in the High Dolomites. The villagers draw their curtains against this blue. Blue brings night with it. Once in a blue moon…[43]

While the monochrome of the blue screen provides the opening for an "an oasis of peace…without the pandemonium of images"[44]—a "thinking blind,"[45] as Jarman said—it also provides for the *vocalization* of a type of "writing," a *cinemato/graphy* tracing a movement of soundsense. Just as, spoken aloud, something we nominally call "poetry" becomes the concrete form of a visible erasure. The voices cast their shadows. The film becomes a verbal *skiagraphia*. Hypnotized by the cadences of this non-image, illusion itself seems to move deep within the "extreme austerity" of its monochromatic sea. As if to emphasize this, *Blue*'s London premiere was immediately followed on September 19, 1993, by a simulcast on Channel 4 and Radio 3, for which "Radio listeners were invited to write in for a blue postcard at which to stare for the length of the broadcast"[46]—a device reminiscent of Brecht's *Flug der Lindberghs* (1929) and *Der Ozeanflug* (1949), in which the Süddeutscher Rundfunk broadcast provided sound effects and musical accompaniment for an audience supplied with a copy of the script (and who would thus contribute the speaking parts or "oratorio"). The reception of *Blue*, in the form ostensibly of both a "transmission error" and a "radio picture," thus speaks to the idea of invisible cinema in the manner of Issou, Wollman, Debord, and Godard, in which the postcard (as proxy of the cinema screen) signifies *what cannot be seen*.

The self-avowed status of this work as "text"—even as a text *of* a film—asks not only about its proximity to radio (and other modes of signifying transmission), nor of the seemingly arbitrary distinctions that in *Blue* can be made *between* film and radio, but about the very idea of *medium*. That is to say, about the supposition that each of these is ostensibly a vehicle for the transmission of an autonomous (yet untranslatable) idea. This implicit Platonism runs up against the textuality of "language" in its broadest ramifications, including the generico-ideological "language" of film and radio, so that the question isn't simply how *Blue* might extend or exceed the idea of the "radio play," for example, beyond what is achieved by "writers" like Perec and Milligan, simply by operating within a visual paradigm (this would be trivial); nor how the aurality of *Blue* might sabotage the dominant visuality of "cinema," through the implosion of the image into a "pure" chromatism ("medium" reduced to wavelength and frequency.). Rather it is a matter of situating the logic of the work within a deconstruction of phonocentrism by way of a radical appeal to the *graphē*, to a "writing at the origin [of speech]," as Derrida says, in which the ideology of *mimēsis* is caused, through the *différance* of this soundscript, to be "ruined."[47]

Arguably this has always been one of the tasks of the avant-garde, but it became *the* task, par excellence, of a neo-avant-garde understood both as *parody* and as *self-subversion* of the institutionalization of avant-gardism itself *as a system or method of subversion.* Where the simple translation of *Blue* from screen to postcard/radio broadcast produces a certain *Verfremdungseffekt*, the substitution of one medium for another does not accomplish *by itself* a deconstruction of the logic of medium, of its *law of genre*: such a movement simply points to the prior inscription of *mimēsis* at the level of the "concept" (*Blue* as a kind of transcendental signified that can be supplied with multiple signifiers without losing or diminishing itself). *Mimēsis* must not be mistaken for the neutral instrumentality it itself assigns to the figure of the "signifier," but is always already an ideological system. This inscription *en avant* is precisely what is thrust into view, so to speak, with the implosion of its own representational field, which may in turn be said to situate the spatio-temporal "fold" of mimeticism within the dimension of a "non-image" (which it nevertheless determines to *produce* by way of an auto-critique—in the formalization, for example, of an *anti-art*).

If *Blue* can be read as a blueprint for an anti-mimeticism, it must therefore be as a form-in-suspense-of-itself: a verbo-visual synesthesia in which an ideology of (non-)representation (the blue pencil of erasure) and doublespeak (the blue of the police state and of pornography [blue movies]) jams the sheer indexicality of the *color blue* in its seemingly pure *mimēsis* "of itself." Unadulterated, as if to say, *by ideology*. There is, of course, no blue sky of pre-ideological paradise in Jarman: every soothing transcendentalism is also a poison ("the blue is poison"), every immateriality is traversed by the real. The image of this non-image remains inseparable from the substituting play of (non-)representation that in fact constitutes it (operating in the gap between the signifier and its simulacrum)—just as the "film" is inseparable from the scratched, dust-flecked physicality of the 35mm celluloid print from which it was originally projected whose expressiveness in turn mimics that of a "soundtrack" brought into tension with the technicity of *its* materiality, *inseparable from this (non-)image*.

Sped up or slowed down, the wavelengths shift, linguistic "content" is compressed or distends as the supposedly monochromatic *Hörspiel* dials through the spectrum, becoming all and none. Earblind. Radiokino for an acoustic eye. A polyphonic *roaratorio* of impure noise (noise being *information*). And if this generative anti-genre escapes totalization as blueprint for a cinema *yet to come*, of the (non-)image, of the (anti-)logos, it is because it operates within that *différance* from which the cinematic, the image, the voice emerge as the possibility of an art-iculation. Jarman's *Blue* denotes not a return, via a naive metaphysics of "disembodiment," to a more fundamental mimeticism, but rather an invasion of medium by a materiality that cannot be reconstituted into an image. In this it harks back to McLuhan's pronouncements of a technological post-literacy, such that the constellation neo-avant-garde implies a new configuration, "beyond" the literacy/orality dichotomy. If *Blue* is radio *after the fact* or *avant la lettre*, its transmedial radio-graphy—inscribed across a seeming irreconcilable divide—performs *something like* the role of invisible double to *The Goon Show*'s Dadaistic tabula rasa of post-war *entertainment*, "in an endeavour to prove that radio is not blind."[48] Like Mallarmé, Jarman casts the dice of singularity and duration, of a synesthesia irreducible to representation yet in which representation discovers its chance—just as, in the seeming chaos of *Roaratorio* and in the emptiness of Klein's commodified "void" (or in the aversions of Perec's *La Disparition* [1969]),[49] a certain *différance* persists in ruining the dream of a genre-beyond-genre, if not the very genre of *the beyond*.

CHAPTER 8

Minima Semantica

So why, pray, sign anything as long as every word, letter, penstroke, paperspace is a perfect signature of its own?

JAMES JOYCE, *Finnegans Wake*

ACROSS A BODY OF WRITING, from James Joyce's *Finnegans Wake* (1939) to Samuel Beckett's *The Unnamable* (1958) and beyond, it is possible to speak of a "poetics" of inscriptive-erasure (a semantic minimum) correlative with a crisis in the ideology of representation. A crisis of long gestation—from Plato to cybernetics—given critical impetus in the serial ruptures and "Copernican revolutions" of modernity. Some of these are still being brought into view, notably in the wake of artificial intelligence, quantum complexity, and the ubiquitous nature of digital economies. Both Joyce and Beckett's texts were written after the Copenhagen interpretation of quantum mechanics (1925–1927)—on indeterminacy and complementarity—and Alan Turing's "On Computable Numbers, with an

Application to the Entscheidungsproblem" (1936), setting forth the hypothesis of a "universal machine." Together, these doctrines articulated a fundamental crisis in the relation of "intelligibility" to "intelligence" whose ramifications, far from being restricted to the rarefied discourses of mathematical theory, have become increasingly ubiquitous aspects of "everyday life."

In Philip K. Dick's 1981 novel *The Divine Invasion*, a character meditates—in McLuhanesque fashion—on the technopoetics of *Finnegans Wake*, a seemingly prophetic work of future communications technologies, itself a kind of anachronistic machine for producing the kind of parallel universe in which PKD's own narrative unfolds. "It is impossible," Dick's character says, "that James Joyce could have mentioned 'talk-tapes' in his writing" insisting that "*Finnegans Wake* is an information pool based on computer memory systems that didn't exist until a century after James Joyce's era.... Joyce was plugged into a cosmic consciousness from which he derived the inspiration for his entire corpus of work."[1] Today, with the Wakean evolution of Turing Machines into Generative Adversarial Networks and Large Language Model AIs unfolding "in plain view," the anachronism of Dick's science-fictional "cosmic consciousness" is—as he himself well anticipated—rendered moot. The algorithmic circuits, random noise, and generative erasurism of today's reality discriminators are still as "prehistoric child's toys" to the transdimensional "joyceware" of *Finnegans Wake*, perhaps—this "hypermnesiac machine," as Derrida says (ventriloquizing PKD), "capable of integrating all the variables, all the quantitative and qualitative factors... because you can say nothing that is not programmed on this 1000th generation computer—*Ulysses* or *Finnegans Wake*."[2]

Claude Shannon, in his 1948 paper "A Mathematical Theory of Communication,"[3] identified *Finnegans Wake* as a type of entropy machine, in which language operates at the lowest threshold of redundancy (or upper threshold of compressibility)—a cybernetic system operating at what we might call the Planck limit "of the calculable and the incalculable."[4] Shannon identifies this semantic minimum of sublexical "difference" as the introduction of a blank—"paperspace" in Wakese—itself a mark of ambivalence, inscriptive-erasure, the prior condition of any signification as such. This minimum unit would seem to stand in inverse relation to the work required to describe the signifying system it underwrites, which in *Finnegans Wake* assumes a maximum of complexity and which in *The Unnamable* assumes (in place of complexity as such) an interminability—in each case, the infinitesimal stands in a direct relation to the exponential, while each likewise concerns itself with defining a bounding limit (analogous to the Planck limit for the division of space and the Bekenstein limit for the maximal amount of information required to describe a given system down to the quantum level). Where Joyce's text has often been described as maximalist to Beckett's minimalism, we might better speak of their complementary "dymaxionism" (to borrow Fuller's term) in which complexity and simplexity are generatively interdependent.[5] Joyce's combinatory "nat language"[6] and Beckett's cybernetic routines and subroutines encode within themselves the processes of their own inscription, deletion, reinscription, and computation, producing what *Finnegans Wake* calls a "proteiform graph…polyhedron of scripture."[7] In this sense, both Joyce and Beckett's texts are not a *mimēsis* of some futuristic word-technology, but "auto-productive" Universal Turing Machines in which a certain meaning of authorship is erased at the same time as other meanings are inscribed in its place.

Horreur chosesque

It is unsurprising that a certain status of *the author* and a certain fetishism of *authorship* should share their history with the advent of the mechanized printing press, mass literacy, and the global dominance of one form or another of capitalist ideology. We can say with a degree of certainty that contemporaneous with automated production arose the idea of an autonomous authorial subjectivity vested in a body of writing. Writing, in a sense, came to *produce* its authorship, in a broadly cybernetic, algorithmic process of abstraction and feedback, defining what we might call its ideal commodity. In prototype, this evolution from writing machines to machinic writing provides the subject of Michel Foucault's 1969 Collège de France lecture, "Qu'est-ce du'un auteur?"[8] in which—after quoting Beckett's *Texts for Nothing* ("What does it matter who is speaking")[9]—he proposed:

> Writing unfolds like a game that invariably goes beyond its own rules and transgresses its limits. In writing, the point is not to manifest or exalt the act of writing, nor is it to pin a subject within language; it is, rather, a question of creating a space into which the writing subject constantly disappears.

If the Platonic father-of-the-logos is dead, each logos becomes its own "father" in a double movement of erasure and self-inscription. This decentering movement has multiplied along each of its peripheries: devolving from the erased, suspended, phantasmatic form of the "transcendental signified" onto a "free-play of signifiers" that seemingly erupts in its absence.[10]

What's notable in this formulation is that this space of *disappearance* is the work, precisely, of an *excess*—of what we might call the *surplus-value* of a writing that *goes on* and whose transgressions are *invariable* (in other words, as probabilistically determined as Neumann and Morgenstern's 1944 *Theory of Games and Economic Behaviour*, for example).[11] Foucault's allusion is markedly not that of the Romantic author-revolutionary, or the performative individualism that characterizes the idea of "transgressive writing" throughout the so-called Modernist period, including much that has come to pass for a critique of the Cult of the Author itself. There is no doubt something deeply paradoxical about the personality cults manifest within precisely those critiques of industrial-era ideological excess. Nevertheless, the authorial agency Foucault begins to elaborate is rather one bound, in a seemingly counter-intuitive movement, to a constitutive "alienation." In this we can detect echoes of a series of elusive observations recorded by Marx in the *Grundrisse*, in which individuated subjectivity is said to be *produced* by mechanization: it is produced, in other words, through the very alienation *into which it constantly disappears*.[12]

At base, then, the question of the status of authorship is a question about the crisis of Humanism.

Or to put it otherwise, it is a question about the crisis *at the heart of Humanism*. For it is this "crisis," in which the genealogy of *technological innovation* resides, that has come to the fore in the various post-Humanist strains of thought to have emerged particularly in the second half of the twentieth century and which overlap with Beckett's later, broadly "cybernetic," writings. It is possible to read

Beckett in this context as closely concerned with the relation of authorship to *semantic labor* and the representation of power (and representation *as* power). Recalling his commentary on *Finnegans Wake*,[13] we can recognize in Beckett's own work, particularly of this period, a world in which writing *is* ontology; action *is* subjectivization—such that the act of writing itself, the theatre of its "self-presentation," constitutes a kind of *catastrophic agency*. Agency as the mechanism of a certain "turn": between the production of a *space of representation* and *its own (violent) disappearance*. Time and again in Beckett's writing catastrophe raises its head, in a play between "explicitation"—as the "Director" says in his 1982 theatre-piece for Havel, with "every i dotted to death"—and a staged appeal to *affect* as by-product of an unbearable scrutiny; of interrogation routines, inspection routines, routines of unpresentable disclosure, ellipsis, repetition, subjection, technicity.

Unsurprising, then, that Beckett should occupy a position of preeminence in Deleuze and Guattari's examination of "machinic desire" in their 1972 collaboration *Anti-Oedipus: Capitalism and Schizophrenia*,[14] anticipating the somewhat apocalyptic thought of latter-day Accelerationism: an emancipative critique of capitalism by way of "ever-accelerating catastrophes" toward "the coming annihilations"—as Alec Williams and Nick Srnicek phrase it in their "Manifesto for an Accelerationist Politics."[15] Yet there's a powerful ambivalence in Beckett's writing to those breeds of naïve catastrophist thought that seek to affirm themselves in the illusion of a transcendental "nihilism." All too often Beckett has been read as the author not, like Joyce, of a *revolution of the word*, but of an *abolition of language*: a radical Sartreanism intent upon transgressing the limits of discursive agency to the "horreur chosesque"[16] or nightmare-thingness beyond. Yet if anything can be said to affirm itself at this "catastrophic" limit of signification and base materiality it is rather a kind of *surplus minimum*: something, that is to say, instead of nothing. Or rather, *something more* instead of nothing. And here lies the real paradox at the heart of Beckett's writing, for, as Žižek elsewhere observes in the thinking of Meister Eckhart, "Nothing does not come for free, it is not a zero-point at which the universe is just 'resting for itself.'... [N]othing has to be sustained by an investment of energy."[17]

Beckett's *surplus minimum*, then, represents a least possible investment, sustained not by an existentialist *recoil* from the abyss of nothingness, but by a process of *catalytic conversion* in which the nothing stands in place of an unobtainable *object*: no longer of desire but rather of a "primordial" compulsion-to-repeat. The "nothing" thus assumes the semantic function of what Žižek calls "the paradox of a *thing* which is always (and nothing but) *an excess with regard to itself*."[18] An ideal commodity, in other words. In his 1992 introduction to *Quad and Other Plays for Television*,[19] Deleuze—continuing a line of argument from *Anti-Oedipus*—sought to negotiate this paradox in terms both of machinic desire and what Guattari had termed "planes of consistency": the deployment of desire according to an axiomatic system. For Deleuze, unlike purely structural axiomatics, "the axiomatics of desire *includes the principle of non-consistency*."[20] Consequently, the ever-increasing insistence in Beckett's writing on rigid structures of denomination—however seemingly parodic (like Krapp's banana skin, or the eroticism of *What Where*)—could be seen as corresponding to an increasing susceptibility to paranoia and contradiction, producing a kind of "disjunctive synthesis." For Deleuze, this "synthesis" takes place around a locus of *exhaustion*, which likewise exhibits contradictions: for example, between Beckett's theatrical mechanics and the nominal agency of its "protagonists," represented by the figure of the "exhausted man" (as distinct from the "fatigued man" who "still has possibilities even if he cannot realise them, unlike the exhausted man, who has none"[21]). For Deleuze, the subject (protagonist) "exhausts himself by exhausting the possible." This occurs in four stages: by 1. creating series of exhausting things; 2. drying up the flux of voices; 3. extinguishing the potentialities of space; 4. dissipating the power of the image. In this way, the "exhausted" is also the "exhaustive."[22]

Psychotic foreclosures

The exhausted man's approach to the *im*-possible broadly corresponds to the situation of *alienated subject* whose access to history is "blocked." Yet, by the same token, it is necessary to recognize that Beckett's protagonists are only ever *phantasms* of such an "exhausted possibility," since *the possible* is always elsewhere: not as some *prior* (and now depleted) *agency*, but as the future horizon of a radical *determinism*. What *goes on* evokes a beyond-of-the-possible only in the manner in which Freud speaks of a "beyond" of the fundamental drives—being "nothing more" than a *compulsion to repeat*—what Lacan later comes to call *the void of jouissance*.[23] The tendency of Beckett's writing is not so much post-dramatic in this respect, as *sub-dramatic*: there's always *something below* the theatrical minimum—and thus "below" the representational threshold of an *enaction-of-nothing*. Hence the signification of foreclosure, of an exhaustion or point-of-no-return, is constantly being *sub-verted*. For Beckett, this indeed is the very *possibility of writing*, in which repetition—while appearing as a movement of depletion, of a terminal narrowing-of-the-odds—provides a singular tactical advantage. Appearing on the one hand to be an incremental acceleration towards annihilation, and on the other a drastic collapse into terminal stasis, this event-horizon nevertheless describes the very *opening of possibility*. As in Mallarmé's *Un coup de dés*, repetition here doesn't abolish "chance"—such that, like Mallarmé's "All thought is a throw of dice," we might also say ALL "WRITING" IS REPETITION—and it is this repetition itself which, by a kind of metabolic sublimation, is the guarantee that writing "goes on."

We can see this, for example, in *Krapp's Last Tape*, whose setting is specified in the stage directions as "A late evening in the future,"[24] and whose present action is constituted by a ritual interaction with "a tape-recorder with microphone and a number of cardboard boxes containing reels of recorded tapes," representing a kind of primal scene of History which it is the (prematurely aged) protagonist's function to replay. The action is situated, in other words, in a zone of pure anachronism, as a spatiotemporal apparatus that produces its own repetition. In this way possibility is constantly inaugurated as a kind of reflexive-forethrow: an algorithmic system in which every "last" feedback acquires the status of +1. Repetition, in this self-ramifying aspect, appears therefore both as opening of minimal possibility and as perpetual check, or what Deleuze calls a "psychotic foreclosure": a foreclosure "which operates in the symbolic order at the very level of the 'signifier,' a kind of hole in the structure, an empty place, which causes whatever is foreclosed in the symbolic to *reappear* as hallucination in the real."[25] This delirium, of the hallucinated encounter between the "symbolic" and the "real," corresponds in Beckett to that crisis of Humanism in which the subject—as presumed author of its own actions—is suspended as a locus of perpetually re-enacted disappearance.

Throughout Beckett's work we encounter the lineaments of a subjective "catastrophism" presented alternately as humanistic farce and dehumanized compulsion: the entropically routinized surplus-labor of a machinic "abstract individualism." From the cyclic redundancy of *waiting* as both time-consuming labor and deferred gratification in *Waiting for Godot*, to the repetitive circuits of stone-sucking in *Molloy*,[26] to the "succession of irregular loops, now sharp and short as in the waltz, now a parabolic sweep" in *The Unnamable*, to the rigidified teleological impulses (redolent of pacing the perimeter of a prison yard) in *Quad*, Beckett's mechanomorphisms chart a topology of *constricted excess*: a seemingly paradoxical logic that sustains obvious parallels to the mass-standardization and hyperproduction of the Fordist assembly line, itself the model of culture industry "shock work." Like Soviet-era *udarny trud*—euphemistically superproductive "enthusiastic" labor—Beckett's textual machines are the operative *stuff* of an all-encompassing semiocapitalism: the routinization of language, signifier, and commodity, which produces—through its *perpetual exhaustion*—endlessly distracting, absorbing, vacant, nihilistic extensions of itself *ad infinitum* (the alchemical transubstantiation of shit into ideal signifier and back into shit again) in a conspicuously contrived display of "jouissance."[27] Whether as quasi-euphoric, farcically emancipative self-parody, or austere, rigidly bound inanition, Beckett's allegories of industrial alienation are first and foremost *operative*: allegorical *because* machinic[28]; alienational because constitutive of an imaginary subjectivity that *goes on* for no other reason.[29]

This is perhaps nowhere more evident than in the fixed camera and strict permutational schema for *Quad* (comprising movement, light, sound, costumes), in which an apparently closed system of rigid denomination is locked in orbit around a kind of black hole or "danger zone. Hence deviation,"[30] from whose negative presence the menace of *unpresentability* seems to exude. Like Malevich's *Black Square*, signifying possibility is not negated but produced via a template of *abstraction*.

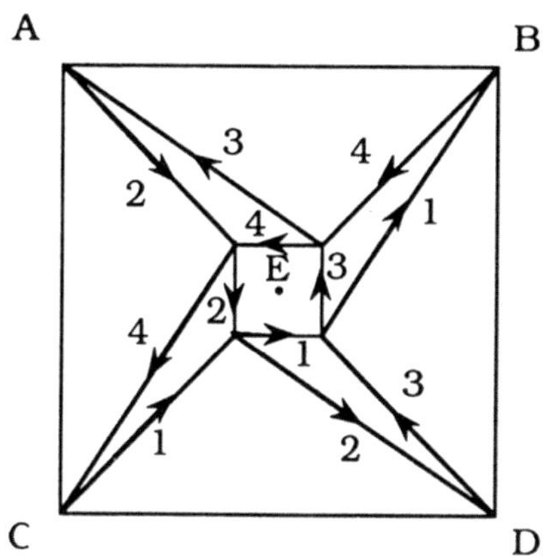

Likewise subjectivity, for Beckett, is never separate from technicity: increasingly his later writings invite comparison to programming code, instructional tables, and schematizations—as in *Ghost Trio*, *Come and Go*, and *...but the clouds...* Their operations, even at the level of verbal articulation (whenever it occurs), remain formal. "Little is left to tell," says R, "reading" from a book in *Ohio Impromptu* (whose very title reads as self-parody in this respect):

> In a last attempt to obtain relief he moved from where they had been so long together to a single room on the far bank... Relief he had hoped would flow from its unfamiliarity. Unfamiliar room. Unfamiliar scene. Out to where nothing ever shared. Back to where nothing ever shared... Day after day... Hour after hour...[31]

Beckett's (strictly detailed) staging of these routines of control and sublimation turns upon an idea of entropy that is also one of inflationary excess: like the event-horizon that masks a singularity, subjectivity *in language* is marked by the appearance of an accelerated *slowness* that is also a *hyperproductivity*; a movement of reduction that is in the same instant radically inflationary: a simplification that structures an indefinable complexity. This is because "subjectivity," for Beckett, is first and foremost a trope that is *also* a schema: both linguistic algorithm *and* textual circuit, as particularizable and universal as a point on a feedback loop.

And it is this radically *ambivalent* status of "technology" in Beckett that avails writing of a critical force: as that which, in the solicitation of a certain *overdeterminacy*, subverts the order of the pre-ordained, the totalizable, the presentable. There is no "subject" that is not also the very *image* of a supervening alienation: the image, in other words, of the *spectacle of representation itself* arising at the limits of the *un*presentable—which is to say, the *im*-possible—wherein this impossible object is discovered in an "aesthetic" counterpart. Subjectivity in Beckett thus holds a mirror to what we might call a universal panopticism: the constraining *all-seeing* eye (as in *Film*) that nevertheless *constantly insists* (in ratio to its own invisibility) *upon seeing more*, mirrored in the (by turns convulsive, paralytic) "subject" that exists solely in order to *produce* more. Even if that *more* is simply an accumulation of epistemological lacunae—as in *Krapp's Last Tape* and *What Where*—which serve primarily to conceal *an excess of alienation*. The rehearsal of a paranoiac "system of production," in other words, whose delirious authority over a "nothingness" (posited as the transcendental signified of its own inexorable devaluation), belies its radically ideological character as *surplus-minimum*. The "precariat" of its non-agents and pseudo-actors—operating within a programmatic realm of the narrowly permitted and in a constant state of crisis—reflects (insofar as it "reflects" anything) the very *condition* of its so-called self-presentation as a kind of tele-technology.

This theatre of alienation produces subjectivity to the extent that it "mirrors" a panopticism that is in fact immanent to it (just as a mode of spectation is immanent to the theatrical scene), and in doing so appears to describe the fixations of a machinic desire that already constitutes it. And it is here, in the intersection of language, libido, and political economy, that the *ideological* status of production (which is to say, of a certain "author function") comes most clearly into view, as a preeminently *technological* function, *producing itself*, as Foucault says, with "the anonymity of a murmur"[32] whose principal characteristic is that it *goes on*.

Future-obsolescence

Like Beckett's algorithmic theatre, it has been observed that *Finnegans Wake* is a kind of machine: a word-machine, an analytic engine, a critical apparatus, capable—like Turing's universal computer—of pre-comprehending, as if *in advance*, virtually everything that can be said about it. This idea has exercised a strange fascination over the cybernetic imaginary—from Marshall McLuhan's *Gutenberg Galaxy* (originally conceived under the title *The Road to Finnegans Wake*) to Murray Gell-Mann's naming of the fundamental constituent of the nucleon after a line in Book II: "*Three quarks for Muster Mark!*" (383.01)[33]—opening a purview onto what, in 1995, Donald Theall went so far as to call the "Joyce Era of technology, culture and communication."[34] Perceiving in the *Wake* a logic that extends the "revolution of the word" into a revolution of the world, Félix Guattari likewise derived from Joyce the term "chaosophy"—a synthesis of cybernetics and schizoanalysis, evoking a generalized *artificial intelligence* of distributed subjectivities, extending Gramsci's idea of the "molecular revolution" across a system of machinic subjectivities. Such a revolutionary world-machine must nevertheless wield an uncanny power. Indeed, the *Wake* itself frequently alludes to itself as a type of portentous doomsday device—one that generates discourse in order to totalize the field of discourse itself: "That's the point of eschatology our book of kills reaches for now in soandso many counterpoint words" (482.32). And here lies the apparent contradiction of the Wakean "chaosmos": that its irreducibility coincides with its universality.

Finnegans Wake describes itself as "mythametical" (286.23), a "vicociclometer" (614.27), propelled by a "harmonic condenser enginium" (310.01) whose permutations of the universal "adomic structure" (615.06) expend the probability of any outcome not already subjected to its calculus. Its operation might be described as programming, by an interminable self-inscription—"as highly charged with electrons as hophazards can effective it" (615.07-08)—a generalized *future-obsolescence*. This End of History—mythic in scale—would presuppose nothing short of the subsumption of *historia* itself into a Wakean recursive or re-causal "altereffect" (483.01). By a quasi-Viconian re-evolving, an inflated dialogical present would invade the dimension of the historical in the mythic guise of its own transcendence: an event that can only ever occur in prototype or, so to speak, precessionally:

> a split in their infinitive from to have to have been to will be. As they warred in their big innings ease now we never shall know.[35]

To speak of an "end" would thus be to speak of an effect inscribed already in its own beginning: a discontinuity at the origin subsumed into the form of a blueprint, program, or matrix: a semantic DNA, perhaps, whose autonomy has come to represent the dominant form of a *world order*. This Wakean "polyhedron of scripture" (107.08) appears to exist *as if to demonstrate* nothing else than this paradoxical drive to discontinuity and totality. And yet *it exists*—an existence posited as both the kernel and exteriorization of History—while nevertheless signifying the very impossibility of a "beyond." Moreover, it repeatedly advertises this contradiction through the interminability of its processes.

Occupying something akin to an event-horizon between the "End of the Book," as Derrida says, and the "beginning of writing,"[36] Joyce's text conjures a "cosmic" totality—"In the name of Annah the Allmaziful, the Everliving, the Bringer of Plurabilities" (104.01-02)—that is, *at the same time*, nothing if not provisional—an "untitled mamafesta memorialising the Mosthighest" which "has gone by many names at disjointed times" (104.04-05)—yet its dominant characteristic is that it is *provisional at every point*. If we read the *Wake* as a kind of doppelgänger of the system of modernity—describing, in effect, a feedback of self-presentation in the interminable form of a *to come* that saturates the *now*—we do so not simply as a *reflection* of a totalizing movement (its self-inscription as "chaosmos of Alle"), but as *operative*; not simply *miming* but *producing* "nichthemerically," as Joyce tells us, "by its corrosive sublimation one continuous present tense integumented slowly unfolded in all marryvoising moodmoulded cyclewheeling history."[37]

In *Of Grammatology*, Derrida charts the movement of a crisis in the logic of representation that, today, we are able to recognize as the constituent form of the Anthropocene. As both the demystification of a belated Humanism (in which industrial capitalism had long disguised itself) and the reification of its processes, the Anthropocene stands in a paradoxical relation to a certain *self-evidence*—exemplified in those ideologies of mimēsis that Derrida shows to be the true constituents of the term "language"—which has "dominated the history of the world during an entire epoch, and has even produced the idea of the world"[38]; an idea that, in the course of modernity, has come to be "overwhelmed" and "effaced" in what is called *writing*.

> By a hardly perceptible necessity, it seems as though the concept of writing—no longer indicating a particular, derivative, auxiliary form of language in general…no longer designating the exterior surface, the insubstantial double of a major signifier, *the signifier of the signifier*—is beginning to go beyond the extension of language. In all senses of the word, writing thus *comprehends* language.[39]

In Derrida's critique, language—corresponding to a Platonic ideal of "living speech"—enters into crisis with the invention of the technē of writing: of an autonomous form of signifying-exchange, presaging that of *currency* and of the *commodity*, the reification of surplus-value, alienation, and abstraction-in-general. That is to say, "as the universal category of society as a whole."[40] What is of central importance here, as Lukács tells us, is that a certain *agency*—a certain provisional *consciousness*—"becomes something objective and independent…by virtue of an *autonomy alien to man*."[41] Joyce calls this the "poeta":

> The prouts who will invent a writing there ultimately is the poeta, still more learned, who discovered the raiding there originally. That's the point of eschatology our book of kills reaches for now in soandso many counterpoint words. What can't be coded can be decorded if an ear aye seize what no eye ere grieved for. Now, the doctrine obtains, we have occasioning cause causing effects and affects occasionally recausing altereffects.[42]

This movement of *autopoiesis* can in turn be regarded as "producing" an *excess* of signifying agency: from the world as semiosphere to the critical mass of its termination in the real—the *eschatology* of the "Ends of Man" transfigured into world-meaning. Just as we might speak of a techno-anthropological shift in the geological register, so too the dimension of the "real" that re/turns in writing—as the *proof of the poeta*, so to speak, and in the erasure of a certain metaphysics—presages a crisis in the idea of the world: one whose transcendence henceforth designates *the impossible.*

Once again we're dealing with an eschatology—Joyce's "eternal chimerahunter" (107.14)—in which the disappearance of the so-called *subject of history* is both reified and anticipated in an apocalyptic re/turn of the "real."[43] Yet we must be wary, here, of any appeal to a tragic view of the so-called posthuman that would absolve the historical subject of what appears uniquely "machinic": that permits, in other words, the *anthropos* to be entroped, erased in its "disappearance." It is important to bear in mind Lacan's warning that—like the author of the Cyclops's blindness—"the subject is no-one"; that it is, from its origin, "decomposed, in pieces"[44] as that which emerges, *entropically*, from "the gap of the unconscious."[45] What, then, does it mean *to write* (transitively? intransitively?) in the consciousness of Humanism's self-erasure? That is to say, in the wake of this Joycean "hypermnesiac machine"[46] that appears to exhaust all future possibility by reifying and pre-comprehending everything, including the very possibility of a subject? Where all that was once supposedly human returns in the traumatic "self-evidence" of the real, as the absolute horizon of (non)being?

Voidheads

For the catalogue of the *Cybernetic Serendipity* exhibition at London's Institute of Contemporary Arts (ICA) in 1968—one of the first international exhibitions devoted to the nascent field of "computer art"—John Cage wrote:

> What we need is a computer that isn't labour-saving but which increases the work for us to do—that puns (this is McLuhan's idea as well as Joyce's) revealing bridges (this is Brown's idea) where we thought there weren't any—turns us (my idea) not "on" but into artists.[47]

What kind of *work* produces *artists* in place of an industrial consciousness ("turned on" by salvation *from* labor)—if by "artist" we mean an agency that stands at odds with the cold and pragmatic implementation of the control apparatuses whose "predominant mode," as the Invisible Committee remind, is the "management of crisis"?[48] An agency that is irreducible beyond its alienation-effect—to a palliative realism, for example, in which the myth of history struggles on to its manifest destiny in the image of a humanoid "fundamental fantasy"? That *puns*—and thereby calls forth a techno-poetics inimical to rationalization? In other words, the polysemy of a writing *born of resistance*?

The apparent contradiction on which Cage's Joycean "computer" is built—between the automation of cognitive production in the Fordist mode (the machine assumes the burden of *thought and action*, proclaiming an emancipation from onerous labor) and a systematic demand for an *increase* in intellectual effort (in which art is identified with the very opposite of convenience)—is not one that Cage seeks to resolve but rather to exacerbate. We might say that the product of such an exacerbation is what Derrida later calls Joyce's "1000th generation computer," *Finnegans Wake*.[49] And it is as if, by means of a generalized *resistance*, this 1000th generation computer programs itself to evolve into a fully autonomous system of "artificial intelligence."

So the question becomes—not What does it *mean* to write? but *What writes*? And further, what is this entropology of the Joycean *poeta* that on the one hand resists technē, while at the same time *superseding* it? In the vertigo of this movement there is indeed "a certain pleasure in calculating the risks"[50]—a certain *jouissance* of the acceleration towards a catastrophe, in which the *possible* is both foreclosed and made to appear to open out indefinitely—and in which the path of greatest resistance inscribes itself on the face of the Void.

At the beginning of the "History Lessons" episode of the *Wake*, Fordist eschatology is construed the portmanteau "teetootomtotalitarian" (260.02)—evoking Huxley's T-totem[51] and the "total" process of the Model-T integrated-assembly line (the apotheosis, as McLuhan observed, of the Gutenberg printing press). What begins as the divine word is transubstantiated into the machine-made-commodity bereft of any transcendental signified. So, too, the materiality of the Wakean cosmos is nothing but text, vectors of *information flows*. There is no end in sight *beyond the text*: it is, as Beckett might well have said, that End itself.[52]

Between the logic of the book as an eschatology or *apocalyptō* of "revelation," and writing as technē—which is to say, *as history*—a recursive, machinic conception of an art that *thinks*, and thereby construes a general consciousness, permeates the *Wake*. As counter-eschatology, it describes an acceleration by cosmic *détournement*:

> Anyhow, somehow and somewhere, before the bookflood or after her ebb... wrote it all, wrote it all down, and there you are, full stop... But one who deeper thinks will always bear in the baccbuccus of his mind that this downright there you are and there it is only all of his eye. Why?
>
> Because Soferim Bebel... every person, place and thing in the chaosmos of Alle anyway connected... was moving and changing every part of the time: the travelling inkhorn..., the hare and turtle pen and paper, the continually more or less intermisunderstanding minds of the anticollaborators, the as time went on as it will variously inflected, differently pronounced, otherwise spelled, changeably meaning vocable scriptsigns... riot of inkblots and blurs and bars and balls and hoops and wriggles and juxtaposed jottings linked by spurts of speed.[53]

In this sense, the *Wake* is a time machine producing modernity by radical anachronism. Where the logic of the book begets history, writing begets a temporality ambivalent to historical subjectivity. "Who in hallhagal wrote the durn thing anyhow?" (107.36-108.01) the *Wake* demands. If Cage seeks to distinguish a mode of art (and of *artificial intelligence*) as *agency of thought*, by an appeal to acts of resistance, the *Wake* itself situates that point of resistance outside any *end in itself*. What we might call its deconstructive labor of "AMBIVIOLENCE"[54] evokes nothing less than a writing of the impossible, or rather, writing as the impossible.

Behind the appearance of self-evidence is the sheer vertigo of a calculus of indeterminacy. In his 1968 essay "La différance," Derrida likens the ambivalence of the signifier to quantum-like phenomena that do not resolve into Cartesian knowability. In the wake of the text's "disappearance"—a double erasure that, like ALP's missing letter in *Finnegans Wake*, nevertheless leaves traces (not of itself, but as the holograph of its own non-presence, the erasure of its erasure)—no armature of the "real" is there to expose itself like some agent of epistemic (or even epistolic) revelation. As with the Freudian return of the repressed, what re/turns is a t(r)opos of erasure and substitution, a "return-of-the-return." And if *epistemological erasure* itself designates the condition of a "re/turn of the real." And however "insufficient" this dialectical "equivalence" appears, its reduction is not a measure of the failure of "meaning," but of a mimēsis as *erasure at the origin* (Derrida): its "singularity" is always a factor of the unpresentable.

In place of Sartre's pebble on the beach—an inert, base materiality—this repetition compulsion announces itself by way of a radically deformed signspace. An event-horizon in which time is simultaneously compressed and distended. A seemingly paradoxical structure of differences-without-terms: a "Nichtian glossery which purveys aprioric roots for aposteriorous tongues this is nat language at any sinse of the world" (83.10-12). What we find in the *Wake* is precisely this conception of an autopoetic "re/turn" in the resistance of writing. Towards the end of Book I, for example, Shem is depicted as producing:

> nichthemerically from his unheavenly body… till by its corrosive sublimation one continuous present tense integumented slowly unfolded in all marryvoising moodmoulded cyclewheeling history.[55]

In this way, according to Lyotard, "Joyce allows the unpresentable to become perceptible in his writing itself, in the signifier."[56] Yet this preoccupation with the signifier distracts from what is at stake here, and which Cage intuits in the resistance of polysemy and the labor of a certain ambivalence in which the algorithm of automated sign-substitution is no longer available as the constituent mode of subjectivity, historical or otherwise. That is to say, the dimension of the real "in" the symbolic, which is precisely that of its *operations*.

To this end, the "re/turn of the real" marks that singularity in which the End of History fails to coincide with itself. Which in turn marks the failure of an idea of the world to coincide with *itself*. Žižek has said that "humanity became aware of its self-limitation as a species precisely when it became so strong that it influenced the balance of all life on Earth. It was able to dream of being a Subject only until its influence on nature (Earth) was no longer marginal, i.e. only against the backdrop of a stable nature."[57] That is to say, a homeostatic nature—nature "in balance"—the husbanded, supplemental "nature" of Rousseau which is, has always been, at its core, "ideological" *because* techno-poetic. The question of nature has never been separate from that of power: What hegemony *ex(er)cises itself* in the construction of nature? In the organic conception of the text? In the evocation of a *body of writing*, for example? The topology of its relation to its "object" (intractable nature) is at the same time *tropological* (there is no intractable nature, only information): a circuit of production which is itself a semiosphere—a world autopoetically constituted. And insofar as the "consciousness" of this world exceeds subjectivity—this is not simply because it "manifests" on a purely technological, cybernetic scale: a global array irreducible to (and corrosive of) any Cartesian agency—but because this excess is also constitutive of the subject in the first place. A subjectivity inseparable from the "nichthemeric production" of surplus-value—of that excess of fetishized alienation on which its currency, as world-determining agency, is founded. An excess masking a void. And this void of subjectivity is the real.

CHAPTER 9

▪

The Interpunct

Where now? Who now? When now? Unquestioning.
I, say I. Unbelieving. Questions, call them that.
Keep going, going on, call that going, call that on.

SAMUEL BECKETT, *The Unnamable* (1952)

Writing should go on.

GERTRUDE STEIN, *Lectures in America* (1935)

In her 1985 volume of essays *The Originality of the Avant-Garde and Other Modernist Myths*, Rosalind Krauss notes that, "Over the last ten years rather surprising things have come to be called sculpture."[1] She goes to elaborate how the term "sculpture" has been applied apparently without discrimination to "narrow corridors with TV monitors at the ends; large photographs documenting country hikes; mirrors placed at strange angles in ordinary rooms; temporary lines cut into the floor of the desert." For Krauss the situation of sculpture can be taken as paradigmatic of an erosion of categorical imperatives in the arts from the mid-1950s, following a decade of Greenbergian purism in which it was the task of the artist to hold fast, against the corrosive invasion of kitsch, at the frontiers of genre—not to push outward, but to defend against the subversion of art's manifest destiny ("universal categories," as Krauss says, "to authenticate a group of particulars"[2]). To a Greenbergian eye, "Nothing, it would seem, could possibly give to such a motley of effort the right to lay claim to whatever one might mean by the category of sculpture." Krauss's caveat—"Unless, that is, the category can be made to become almost infinitely malleable"[3]—is tempered thus:

> I would submit that we know very well what sculpture is. And one of the things we know is that it is a historically bounded category and not a universal one. As is true of any other convention, sculpture has its own internal logic, its own set of rules, which, though they can be applied to a variety of situations, are not themselves open to very much change. The logic of sculpture, it would seem, is inseparable from the logic of the monument.[4]

Coining the expression "sculpture in the expanded field," Krauss poses the apparent formlessness of sculptural works against a historical formalism of the monument, in which the seeming decoherence of the category "sculpture" is, as it were, materialized. The example cited by Krauss to open her discussion of the "expanded field" is an otherwise minor earthwork by Mary Miss, entitled *Perimeters/Pavilions/Decoys* (1978):

> Toward the centre of the field there is a slight mound, a swelling in the earth, which is the only warning given for the presence of the work. Closer to it, the large square face of the pit can be seen, as can the ends of the ladder that is needed to descend into the excavation. The work itself is thus entirely below grade: half atrium, half tunnel, the boundary between outside and in, a delicate structure of wooden posts and beams.[5]

The description evokes a dialectical counterpart to the set design of Beckett's *Happy Days*, in which the female protagonist is buried waist-deep and then neck-deep in a mound of earth. It evokes other works of an entropological "anti-aesthetic," too, like Robert Smithson's *A Heap of Language* (1966) and Richard Serra's *Splashing* (1968)—the latter a palimpsest of molten lead flung at the foot of one of Leo Castelli's New York warehouse walls like an old-school hot metal typesetting catastrophe. Something approximating a theme emerges here, of a certain materiality of language, of *the text*, impinging on the spatiotemporal "logic of the monument." The title itself—*Perimeters/Pavilions/Decoys*—alerts us to the game at hand: whether or not anything on display here is what it seems, it is precisely the question of seeming that stands at the center.

Here, the status of the "work" as "text" is in no way peripheral to the problem of categorical erasure with which Krauss commences: the "logic of the monument" doesn't limit this problem, rather it instantiates erasure itself as the necessary basis of any consideration of categorical thought. Which is to say, the difference-within-the-same which is the underwriting structure of all categorization, all signification, all discourse as such. But what's the use of such an instant universalism unless it speaks to the particularity of that species of erasure with which the "logic of the monument" is constructed? Anything less must appear utterly trivial—as trivial, in fact, as a pile of dirt.

"A New Order of Space"

In the final diaristic pages of her 1969 "novel," *Passages*, Ann Quin evokes the seemingly contradictory idea of a "metamorphosis" that is "made to *order*"—a negative-dialectical mechanism that, in her earlier text *Berg* (1964), is figured by the anagrammatical inversion of the protagonist's name: "A man named Berg, who changed his name to Greb, came to a seaside town intending to kill his father."[6] Across the interval separating the first and last pages of this "novel," a narrative unspooled between two views of a window, the one "blurred by out of season spray," the other "just cleaned."[7] A reflection-effect of chiasmatic erasure and re-inscription (father, son, mother, lover) presents itself as the central conceit, which is to say as a pervasive topos of its decentering. In *Passages*, this effect is extended beyond narrative schema to the "formalism" of the work's bibliographical codes. The polysemy suggested in the book's title participates in a general reversioning of the *text-as-subject* into a general tropology of "metamorphosis," played out between the physical "marks on the page" and the semantic rites of "ordering":

> *Monday.* Day after day I search for the girl. Ah yes and then supposing I do eventually find her, what then? Perhaps the orgy my imagination composes is better than the actual thing? The bend of her body under the whip, would I really

> arrive at the same satisfaction a second time? But a dozen times I go over it, half awake, in dreams sometimes it is the other woman who handles the whip, who dances over me, my body covered in sperm, sweat and blood. And in her mind, as we make love in front of the mirror, what forms does she really see there?[8]

The above passage is accompanied by marginalia, recording a description of a Minoan fresco, which parallels, doubles, or inverts it: "A girl acrobat has hold of the horns of a bull at full gallop, one of the horns runs under her left armpit. She is about to perform a backward somersault over the animal's back. A second female performer behind stretches out both her hands as if to catch the flying figure or to steady her when she comes to earth the right way up." At the top of the following page, the Cretan acrobats, or the SandM performers, seem to metamorphose into "a child on a swing in some large gardens." One entry further down, before a short passage headed *Metamorphosis*, Quin (writing now in the first person) adds: "I am on the verge of discovering my own demoniac possibilities and because of this I am conscious of not being alone within myself. // The question then: who is it that today inhabits me?"[9] The typographic/typological character of this metamorphosis renders the teleology of its *form* recursive or even superpositional, a concatenation of "units"—as Quin says—where each textual quantum decoheres into "contradictory attributes never moulded or fused together, but clearly differentiated," inaugurating a "new order of space."

It is precisely this "contradictory" element—between a *schematic* and what we might call a *schizmatic* textual apparatus—that suggests the rudiments of a theory of writing that is also a monument of praxis: an oscillation ("a child on a swing"), a feedback operation of "distance" that "never reaches its limits." Quin's "new order of space"—articulating a formal ambivalence by way of an anticlassicism of the "fragment" ("invented statuary...of strange varieties of shape")—establishes a certain proximity to what Krauss, in the final chapter of *Passages in Modern Sculpture* (1977), calls "a new syntax."

Drawing upon the figure of the double-negative in reference to a 1969 short (three-minute) film by Richard Serra entitled *Hand Catching Lead*, Krauss frames a special syntax of "relentless persistence"—of "one thing after another"—as distinct from what Donald Judd had described as a classical and/or rationalist "a priori system" of "balance" ("you do something in one corner and balance it against something in the other corner"). The double-negative—evoking both an asymmetrical spiral that is "repetitive, austere and nearly without incident" and the *revolutionary movement* of a negation-of-negation—expresses itself in a sculptural/textual operation that is also the object of its own de/stabilizations: not in the form of a dialectical synthesis, but in the radical form of an ambivalence-of-ambivalence. Krauss's monumental logic of accumulative, concatenated "form"—articulated by way of repetition compulsion that is also a "grasping machine" (via McLuhan via Robert Browning)—proposes that all categorical thought must exceed its grasp, *or else what's a metaphor*?

A latter counterpart to Quin's anti-formalism can be found in the work of post-Situationist "psychogeographer" Iain Sinclair, whose serial works of urban archaeological counter-erasure produce monumental anagrams of semantic topography, "caught" in superpositional freeze-frame. Frame after frame. Like Serra's *Hand Catching Lead*—and its direct inspiration, Yvonne Rainer's *Hand Film* (1966)—Sinclair's perambulations through entropy, repetition, accumulation, and monumentality mirror Quin's *dérives* of back-masking and permutation, exposing a "secret" system of *differences-without-terms* productive of a quasi-Diracian hypothesis on textual antimatter. Here, Joycean "ambiviolence" marks something like an encounter between quantum complexity and special relativity.

Psychotic geography

Lights Out for the Territory (9 Excursions in the Secret History of London)—Sinclair's 1997 "psychotic geography" of London, "bisecting the capital's boroughs and re-working conventional delineations of the city as a series of 'zones'"[10]—begins with an epigraph from the Hastings writer and artist Richard Makin and recounts a bizarre quest by Sinclair to track down one of Makin's guerrilla "site-specific" installations, *seminarium*, at Greenwich University's Technology Faculty. Sinclair quotes from the curatorial text:

> *Makin was given complete freedom regarding the site and the nature of the piece.... The piece is textual and is condensed from the site's appellation, the artist working with the constraints of synonyms, associations and the etymology of the compounded words* seminar room. *These served to focus heterogeneous responses to the subject environment and its broader surroundings and were instrumental in producing a poetic constellation evoking various motifs correlational to the function of that environment. The yield is an equivocal conjunction intended to investigate a pondering and contemplation of simultaneously the presented semantic arrangement and the function of the host space, the receiver situated within the weave of locus and stream of words that*

> *have emerged from the nominative of a particular physical domain: a transparent and resonant superimposition of word and place.*[11]

The scene was thus set for a framing of Makin's work, virtually unknown to the mainstream of British contemporary literature, within a border zone between psychogeography, installation art, experimental writing, and avant-gardist subversion. Yet, through the manifold detours of Sinclair's text, "Richard Makin's assault on Seminar Room 178 of the University of Greenwich"[12] never arrives, or is indefinitely delayed, an open-ended detour, a missed-encounter, a void at the center of *Lights Out* which presages Makin's own "site-specific" graffiti and its inevitable erasure (yet, left unattested in this way, could it be said to have existed at all?).

"The writing is that it is," Sinclair later wrote of Makin's 672-page tome *Dwelling*, published by Reality Street in 2011, "ghosting a text that is never gratuitous, offering nothing that isn't there.... An author who is what he says." Like Makin's subsequent books—*Mourning*, *Concussion Protocols*, *Work*—*Dwelling* first appeared in serialization, itself a work of textual performance: "More fire-trap than cut-up, aeolian ash: the horror of leaving an empty space in an artistic composition. Separated flake by flake, pieced together and sandwiched between sheets of glass, like the joints of a finger. Incomplete, wanting one syllable in the last step. Incomplete to stop."[13] The text seems to come into existence as a series of ephemeral installation pieces, distributed thorough the evasive interstitial zones of an "unclassifiable" experimental underground that verges at times upon (and at times slips over into) a fringe of criminality, violence, and moral incomprehension.

Unlike another of his contemporaries, Stewart Home—whose infamous pastiche of Quin's *Berg*—*69 Things To Do with a*

Dead Princess (2002) articulates the malaise of post-Thatcherite class consciousness under "New Labour" and the tabloid conspiratorial diversions around the death of Diana, Princess of Wales on August 31, 1997—Makin's preoccupations lie with effects of corrosive sublimation in the collective linguistic unconscious. Where the "ambiviolences" of Home and Sinclair are more of general narrativized relativity, Makin's are quantized, barely formulated before decohering into sub-narrative event-states:

> Of feeling alien within your own tongue / Yes, that is what
> we must do, we must take the most minute precautions
>
> The end of political independence brought a new interest
> to the life of the individual—any strip of water appeared
> metallic in the dull autumnal light. We are wedged between
> the indifference
>
> There was a pattern—he began every operation with a
> diversionary move. What happened next was divine influx,
> as we have said: renewable silence. Hell was something
> electroneural
>
> Now, a playful alienation, a familiar pet-name of the
> commonwealth[14]

Makin's "alienism" is here fused to a textual praxis, subversive of terms like "experimental" in their current revisionist iteration by institutions engaged in selectively recuperating the literary *personae non gratae* of the late twentieth and early twenty-first century in a miserable attempt to buy credence for their own sham productions. The current rehabilitation of Quin, for example, by an industry that for 60 years assiduously erased her from literary history. If Makin "represents" anything, it is the ambiguous and *distasteful* character of the desire to represent, to account for, and to detoxify the "unpresentable" within a framework of agreed/agreeable aesthetic and social values:

> Of the order of things I am still uncertain. However, I am convinced there are some bacteria that enter through the labyrinth of the ear and attack the nervous system. It seems as if death, the extinction of the ego-consciousness, brings with it a considerable extension of knowledge: an illumination—radiant, void and inseparable.[15]

Black holography

Erasure extends into all aspects of signification and is a statement about power—power exercised through the control of meaning and the submission of language to the status of property. Erasure is also the articulation of a contrary power—"writing power." This is the power of what Derrida refers to as *différance*—irreducibility, polysemy, supplementality, but also as the inscription of a certain erasure within the framework of a metaphysics of presence for which the action of signification is first and foremost a *paternalistic act* by the "father of the logos" (Plato). By placing metaphysics under the sign of erasure ("sous rature"), Derrida brought into view not a "negative dialectics," as has often been supposed, but a fundamental *ambivalence* in the way signification operates *in the absence of an "authorial" presence*. Makin:

> The book is generally regarded as being written by a single hand. Origin denotes a spirit disembodied, always.... Origin is late from old of unknown origin[16]

Much has been said about Roland Barthes's "death of the author" and Michel Foucault's "author-function," but Derrida's erasurism, like Makin's, is not concerned with a post-mortem condition of the text, as if language must continuously mourn or emancipate itself from the impositions of origin or paternal authority. Nor is it merely a trope designed to evade the totalizing power of a Hegelianism that refuses to give up the ghost. Writing power is not simply the "other side" of ideology, for example. It is not *one form of power among others* or a *power in opposition*. Writing power evokes a "solicitation," as Derrida says—a calling-for and simultaneously shaking-from-within—of power "itself": an *inscriptive erasure* or *erasive inscription*.

In January 2017, Adam R. Brown and Leonard Susskind published a paper entitled "The Second Law of Quantum Complexity,"[17] outlining what in effect serves as a "general theory" of erasurism. In it, Brown and Susskind hint at how, analogously, a residual notion of the "author-function" might be seen to devolve into an operation that we have elsewhere called *entropement*: an auto-poetic language-effect understood as a probability field (an idea initially derived from Claude Shannon's "statistical model"). Complexity, in the title of Brown and Susskind's paper, refers to system dynamics characterized by unpredictability, nonlinearity, randomness, and indeterminacy, and is analogous to the tendency of entropy in any closed system to increase (until equilibrium or entropic maximum). Derived from observations about the growth of black holes (whose entropy is determined by its surface area[18]), but revealing a general principle of materiality, Brown and Susskind proposed that the tendency of complexity to increase represents a quantum analogue of the second law of thermodynamics, wherein a system increases in complexity *even after it reaches "thermal equilibrium."* As with entropy, however, complexity, too, eventually reaches a state of "complexity equilibrium," at which point it can be said to have inhabited every possible configuration of states that it is capable of. At this stage, somewhat reminiscent of a Viconian *ricorso*, the system *spontaneously resets* and returns to its initial "simple" state to recommence its evolution.

Discussing these findings, George Musser offers the following schematization, which he calls "The Five Stages of Quantum Systems":

> The first is **initialization**. The system starts simply: just a bunch of particles or other building blocks, acting independently.
>
> Then comes **thermalization**. The particles bounce around and collide with one another, eventually reaching thermal equilibrium. Their shenanigans also begin to link the particles through quantum entanglement. In a process that Susskind calls "scrambling," information is disseminated through the system until it no longer resides in localized places, much as a butterfly flapping its wings in Brazil can affect weather over the whole globe…
>
> Next is **complexification**. Here, the system is in thermal equilibrium but has not stopped evolving. It keeps getting more complex, but in a way that is almost invisible to standard measures such as entropy. Theorists rely instead on circuit complexity, which expresses the increasingly

> intricate linkages among entangled particles.... This stage lasts exponentially longer than thermalization.
>
> Then the system reaches complexity **equilibrium**, where complexity hits a ceiling. Although the system *continues to change*, it can no longer be said to evolve—it has no sense of directedness, but wanders among equal states of maximal complexity.
>
> The last stage is called **recurrence**, where the system stumbles back into its original simple condition. For this to happen by accident is highly improbable. But eternity is a long time, so it ultimately does happen, after a period of time that is not merely exponential, but an exponential of an exponential. The whole process then repeats.[19]

This *ricorso* implies a strange topology of the so-called "original" state—a *tropology*, rather, of inscriptive-erasure, of resetting and recommencing, a Joycean "ambiviolence" in which the end ("fin") is *both* immanently and spontaneously entangled with another beginning ("again"), as in the "cyclewheeling history" of *Finnegans Wake* viewed through the holography of its portmanteaux.[20] It may serve, too, as an analogue to the superpositionality and what Krauss, with Yve-Alain Bois, calls the *formless*—after Bataille's *l'informe*—a "strange integer" of indifference which Bataille first likens to a "tooth deadened by novocain" and later, more explicitly, to "inkspots," a "spider," and "spit."[21]

Bataille's infamous non-definition of *l'informe*, published as a "dictionary" entry in the journal *Documents*, notes: "It is not only an adjective having a given meaning, but a term that serves to bring things down [*déclasser*] in the world."[22] The formless—like a "heap of language"—points to a base materiality that "operates," as Krauss says, as an un(re)presentable substrate, perturbing any system of meaning or *mimetic ideology* vested in formalism by a subversive declassification. The formless devalorizes, by the persistent erasure of categorical distinctions—from the particulate to the universal, tropic to schematic, paperspace to hyperspace. Moreover, it does this *without any (contradictory) investment of ("use") value.* Whatever paradigmatic function Krauss and Bois envisage for the formless, it remains (must remain *by definition*), irrecuperable for, and irreducible to, any paradigm whatsoever.

From text to work

In his "monumental" poetics of entropy, *Work* (2022), Makin enigmatically instructs the reader to "Strike him out. Extend erasure to any objects found existing out of joint. Retain only the more imposing samples, tapering away beyond form"[23] ("in so doing he has cleverly erased our remaining alternatives"[24]). The author, as point-of-origin ("Origin is mid-solitary"[25]), is *sous rature*, in the Derridean sense of ghosting a text the way entropy ghosts complexity: "Note the haste with which fragments are written down before the thought can slip away: alternatives and erasures, the erratic configuration of parts. I believe too there survives some trace of the original, your residue."[26] Makin calls this point-of-origin an "interpunct":

> Word-separating spaces disappeared some time between six and eight, before the interpunct landed. Language says the interpunct has a variety of uses. It was female. The interpunct is present. I am unicode.

> The fragmented sign is a typographical anomaly. I am attempting to reference the numbered sections of a document using an old-fashioned card index. Frequency is an illegal cipher.[27]

Interpunct (unicode U+00B7), "also named interpoint," is a "sign"[28]—a "black hole" or lacuna—whose gravitational force "centers" or "constellates" a mass of signifiers presupposing a signified, each the phantasmatic project of a *difference-without-terms*. It isn't only, as Amy Catanzano suggests in "Poetry in Superposition," that language "can be treated as a dynamic complex system that increases in complexity as its interactive elements increase, though not toward fundamental synthesis, narrative, and ethics or spatial, temporal, and conceptual direction. As each element becomes more interactive, a poem becomes less chiral, more multiversal, more *immarginable* (Joyce)."[29] Such a multiversality is always already inscribed/erased at its point-of-origin, interpunctually. The sign, as non-site of a re-presentation that is both "present" and "immarginable," indexes future itineraries of epochal recursion:

> See, one reckless idea after another. When people read, they have no way of knowing what has been erased, what has been given sanction to remain.[30]

> The physical evidence is erased and the crime scene dissolved.[31]

> Apparently the numbers are a mannerism and must be erased. It is imperative that you leave this instant, transfigure yourself through the portal.[32]

If the entropy of black holes implies a spacetime composed of infinitesimal, recombinable "pieces," its textual analogue for Makin lies in the interpunctuality of sign-stuff—"a small particle of disgust"[33] like Blake's "grain of sand" containing (un)imaginable vortices of recursion, singularity, Hawking radiation—an inscriptive-erasure that *goes on*. Redolent of Duchamp's *infrathin*, Bataille's *strange integer*, Stein and Beckett's attritive *goings-on*, etc., the micropoetics of Makin's *interpunct* dislocates the observable frame of the so-called textual object into a "distance," as Quin says, "that never reaches its limits." And whereas, for example, Smithson's *Heap of Language* performs a mirror displacement of Krauss's "logic of the monument," from complexity to decoherence—a movement exemplified in Smithson's 1966 essay "Entropy and the New Monuments," in which he writes: "Instead of causing us to remember the past like the old monuments, the new monuments seem to cause us to forget the future"[34]—Makin's interpuncts *(re)produce* the future, from a kind of archaeologic-linguistic detritus, "an entire alphabet nailed into the earth."[35] Such augury recalls moments of Samuel R. Delany's glitched, hallucinogenic post-apoc-futurism in *Dhalgren* (1974), reduced to a matrix of erased, disassembled, reassembled street signage:

> After the smashed glass of an army surplus store came movie marquees: no letters at all on the first, a single R on the second; the one line on the next, he had time to reconstruct was "Three Stars says the Times." On the next R,

O, and T were stacked on top of one another; E, Q, and U were followed by a space of three letters and then a Y...

ECK N W'S
S R OGS
ND
T E G TA Y

announced the next marquee.[36]

Relating a categorical thought of futurity to a certain foreclosure on the logic of its (dis)assembly, these "new monuments" index a temporality that decoheres under pressure—not of accumulation, but of a recursion *in advance of itself.* If such a movement has elsewhere been likened to a circuit of repetition-automation, it is tempting here to draw a further analogy with quantum complexity to consider that the "meaning" of this circuit doesn't arise from some erased, détourned, repressed, or hidden element which yet may be made manifest, but is itself a byproduct of signification's "lossiness." Like a syntacto-grammatical probability machine, the circuit operates a process of "postselection"[37] which deletes redundancies *both* in its simplest *and* most complex forms (the interpunct is itself a matrix or, as Joyce says, "polyhedron" of all inscription). In short, it transforms an "information paradox" arisen from "featureless complexity" into *language.*

Limits of disorder

In physics, such limit-effects or thresholds can be defined by Ramsey numbers, fundamental quantities that correspond to the limits of possible disorder in a given system. Ramsey numbers define such limit-effects geometrically, by measuring general conditions for the existence of substructures with regular properties—specifically, how many vertices and edges (called "graphs") can be contained in a random collection before inevitably giving rise to predictable forms or patterns. If the emergence of structure is an ongoing and recursive movement, constantly haunted by decoherence, then we are led to conclude that a signifying minimum mirrors an entropological maximum. For Brown, Susskind, and others, this relation has a "textual" status, expressed in terms of *information*: the minimum unit to carry information stands in inverse relation to the time required to extract information from maximum complexity—just as the infinitesimal stands in relation to the exponential, each falling within a bounding limit (Planck; Bekenstein).

Where Delany's reconnoitering of semiotic apocalypse implies a negative teleology, where sign-wreckage remains—like Linea-B—to be somehow deciphered anew against a backdrop of randomness, Makin's interpunct evokes a shrinking boundary of semiotic spacetime folding back onto an inflationary interior. We're not speaking here merely of an interstice between the semic and the asemic, the categorical and the "infinitely malleable," but a relationship between (de)coherence and (im)possibility. As assembly theorist Lee Cronin says, "It is one thing to say that an object is possible according to the laws of physics; it is another to say there's an actual pathway for making it from its component parts."[38] In other words, complex textual structures don't just emerge from some zone of pure possibility, because—by itself—"the combinatorial space is too vast."

Language, in this view, is simply too complex to have been assembled "by chance" alone. In such cases, "something," argues Cronin, "must have guided that process even before a 'Darwinian'-type selection took over." This is not to imply some species of "intelligent design" at work in the evolution of signspace, but rather that "complex objects can't arise in isolation—they can only occur in conjunction with others." The matrical character of signifying genesis, here, is not a punctum birthing contingent histories (Makin's "poison of lineage"[39]) but a generalized condition—the very "stuff" of semantic spacetime. (Cronin: "The information is in the assembly, not the initial conditions."[40]) Language—like what mathematicians call anti-de Sitter space—might thus be thought of as a "bunch of particles" on its "periphery" correlating to an "interior" semantic spacetime—where "probability" corresponds to "signifiability" along a (recursive) fold of postselection. Selection (inscriptive-erasure), while of necessity *autonomous of all elements of the system*, would nevertheless not be autonomous of the system itself, being its *ongoing articulation*.

If we accept this view, then the question of selection—as *assemblage*—must inevitably give rise to questions about structure—of coherence, representability, meaning, etc. Just as selection implies valency, so an interpunctual "limit effect" is implied in the evolution from apparent randomness to structure—from the asemic to the semic, from "unreadable" stuff to "readable" text, from "featureless complexity" into *language*. How such an effect might obtain and where it might be located have been vexing problems for theories of language vested in linguistic-semantic formalism. Less so for a line of thought running through the work of, for example, Lacan and Derrida, incorporating key ideas of complexity and cybernetics. Structural emergence and decoherence are crucial to what we call *erasurism*, which is ultimately concerned with thresholds of representation and bears consequences for mimēsis in general. What we call inscriptive-erasure—understood in its broadest ramification—lies at the very heart of what it means to *represent*.

CHAPTER 10

The Xenotext

Life: the perfect malware

Rotating once every seven hours, the spectral Cg-type object resembles, as the spacecraft approaches it, a dark kilometer-wide diamond-in-the-rough. In 2015, the Minor Planet Center in Cambridge, Massachusetts, designated it "162173 Ryūgū"—in reference to a Japanese fable about a magical underwater dragon's palace. In the fable, the dragon's palace is a time machine, where one day inside its walls corresponds to a century in the outside world. The object rotating in space is also a time machine: an asteroid of the Apollo group, designated as "potentially hazardous," meaning its 474-day passage around the sun transects Earth's orbit. There is the possibility that one day in the future the two will collide.

On the monitors at JAXA mission control,[1] Ryūgū spins slowly along its vertical axis in digital time-lapse. The camera tracks it from a distance of 400 kilometers to a final approach of 20, the image resolving into a sudden sharp focus. A prominent crater stands out of the asteroid's equator: it appears something has landed there before. The spacecraft, Hayabusa2, powered by ion thrusters, completes its approach on June 27, 2018. Its mission: to collect multiple sub-surface mineral samples and return them to Earth by the year 2020. A Reuters news bulletin marking the occasion recycles the standard PR line: "Asteroids are believed to have formed at the dawn of the solar system and scientists say Ryūgū may contain organic matter that may have contributed to life on Earth." It may also, as if *incidentally*, present a viable opportunity for future asteroid mining.

Two scenarios then: on the one hand, a time machine possibly bearing secrets of celestial human origins; on the other, a potential resource-rich stepping-stone to a hyper-Anthropocenic, space-faring future.

"Life," @christianbok tweeted three days after the landing, "is the perfect malware for infecting the computations of matter." It could easily have meant that the "search for life" is an ideal alibi for extending semiocapitalism's horizons into outer space. Or simply that capital—and only nominally "space technology"—is already *alien life*. It is a matter of no small significance to such speculations that traveling aboard the Hayabusa2 on its mission to Ryūgū—among an array of cameras, sampling devices, impactors, landers, and rovers—is a digital payload incorporating Christian Bök's *Xenotext*, the outcome of a fifteen-year project which *American Scientist* magazine described as a combination of "poetry, cryptography and bioengineering" and which *Engadget* blog (alluding to Blaise Cendrars's 1913 simultanéiste masterpiece) called "prose at the end of the universe."

The *Xenotext* is not the first cultural artifact to have journeyed off-world. In 1972 and 1973, at the behest of Carl Sagan, the

Pioneer 10 and 11 space probes were fitted with gold-anodized aluminum plaques featuring nude male and female human figures and symbolic diagrams designed to communicate information about the spacecraft's origin. In 1977, Voyagers 1 and 2 each carried a gold-plated phonograph record containing 116 images and a variety of natural sounds, such as those made by surf, wind, thunder, and animals, as well as recordings of Bach, Mozart, Beethoven, Stravinsky, and Chuck Berry—selected to provide a picture of the diversity of life and culture on Earth for any extraterrestrial disc jockeys who might one day find them. In 1982, 154 op-art serigraphs by Victor Vasarely were sent aboard the Soviet space station Salyut 7, but later returned to Earth to be auctioned in aid of UNESCO.

What sets Bök's *Xenotext* apart is its ambivalent status as *artifact*: neither aesthetic commodity nor message-to-the-cosmos in any straightforward sense, it represents rather an *autopoiesis* founded in biological cybernetics: an attempt, as Bök says, at a "living poetry." Its medium is the stuff of evolution. At its core, the *Xenotext* project is an attempt (so far only accomplished in the laboratory) to translate what Bök describes as a sonnet "about language and genetics" (entitled "Orpheus," commencing *any style of life / is prim…* and ending *my myth / now is the word /* [blank line] */ the word of life*)—using a programming language called Python, a substitution code and chemical alphabet—into a functional DNA sequence implanted into the genome of Deinococcus radiodurans, a polyextremophile bacterium notable in particular for its resistance to radiation. The DNA code—referred to as a "poetic cipher, gene X-P13"—is programmed to generate a protein ("Protein 13") to which the bacterium cell responds by causing the bacterium to fluoresce red (via an mCherry red fluorophore tag) while transcribing the inserted DNA into a sequence of amino acids, whose structure expresses itself in a form readable by Bök's "Xenocode" as the counterpart of the original verse (entitled "Eurydice," *the faery is rosy / of glow* [...] *we wean / him of any milk /* [blank line] */ any milk is rosy*).

POET (DNA ENCODED TEXT)	GERM (RNA ENCODED TEXT)
any style of life is prim	the faery is rosy of glow
oh stay my lyre	in fate we rely
with wily ploys moan the riff	moan more grief with any loss
the riff of any tune aloud	any loss is the achy trick
moan now my fate	with him we stay
in fate we rely	oh stay my lyre
my myth	we wean
now is the word	him of any milk
the word of life	any milk is rosy

In order to accomplish this, Bök "arbitrarily assigned a letter of the alphabet to each of 26 codons (the nucleotide triplets that form the basic units of genetic code) that he'd chosen from a possible 64." He then generated word lists that "indicated which words could be substituted for each other within a given code set," thus producing "a basic vocabulary for each potential cipher." These ciphers—approximately seven trillion of them—were then tested to determine optimal functionality and coherence, resulting in the approximately 120-word Xenocode ("ANY-THE 112").

ALPHABET: a b c d e f g h i j k l m n o p q r s t u v w x y z
XENOCODE: t v u k y s p n o x d r w h i g z l f a c b m j e q

ANY-THE 112 cipher in which Bök composed the *Xenotext* "sonnets"

The texts themselves were then composed simultaneously with additional constraints, being that both the plaintext ("Orpheus") and ciphertext ("Eurydice") should be both syntactically coherent and "act in dialogue with each other, while also commenting on the subjects of bioengineering and mortality."[2] What complicates this arrangement is that the plaintext and ciphertext are not merely coded versions of one another, but in a manner of speaking *complementary*, immanent to the code itself. As Darren Wershler outlined in a 2012 article, "The Xenotext Experiment, So Far":

> transcription is much like a newspaper cryptogram, except that instead of one set of letters being gibberish and the other being meaningful, both sets are meaningful. Because there is a *codependent* biochemical relationship between any preliminary DNA sequence and its resultant RNA sequence (which creates the string of amino acids in the protein), Bök's two poems must also be *codependent* in order for his project to work. He is therefore always writing two poems at the same time—poems that are mutual ciphers of each other. There are 7 trillion, 905 billion, 853 million, 580 thousand, 6 hundred and 25 (7,905,853,580,625) ways to pair up all of the letters in the alphabet so that they

> mutually refer to each other. All Bök has to do is find one of these ciphers that works in such a manner that when he writes a poem using one of the letters in the pair, it produces a second poem using the other letter.[3]

The process of enzyme transcription which Bök's code is designed to initiate is designed to be ongoing and capable, at least in principle, of replicating itself indefinitely without mutation—far beyond the event-horizon of Hyabusa2's sample-return mission—encompassing a hypothetical timeframe that would in all probability exceed that of the life-sustaining capacity of Earth. Indeed, Deinococcus radiodurans was specifically selected for its potential not only to accommodate Bök's "alien" DNA code, but to survive in the vacuum of space, thus presenting the possibility of transmitting the *Xenotext* to distant points in the galaxy far beyond the temporal horizon of life on Earth. Bök describes it as, "in effect, engineering a life-form so that it becomes not only a durable archive for storing a poem, but also as an operant machine for writing a poem—one that can persist on the planet until the sun itself explodes…"[4] Or off-world, in interstellar space, generating future "semantic" content for the ever-expanding void: heavens that it alone may remain to witness gradually turning black.

Logos cast upon the Void

It is in this sense that Bök's *Xenotext* represents an attempt at both a radical *literalizing* of the poetic and a radical *conceptualism*. It represents in fact a kind of surplus-effect of the very idea of history itself, inscribed within the sign of an absolute erasure of context:

the proverbial "logos" cast upon the void; the detached remainder of an impossible authorization. If conceptualism—as a mode of art that "works with meaning" (Joseph Kosuth)—thereby seeks to question "the inherent values of...culture and society" by challenging "the traditional status of the art object,"[5] the *Xenotext* may be seen as an attempt (self-avowed in any case) to challenge aesthetic categorization by challenging categorical thought itself, as the taxonomic order of cultural epistemology and social meaning, as well as the humanist purview in which it has been both defined and contested by previous art/literary movements. Yet there is the sense that Bök's (seemingly ironic) anti-aesthetic of "alienation" wants to go beyond the anthropocentric perspectives both of symbolic capital and of autonomous agency,[6] by appealing to a certain posthuman "idea"—not (simply) as a conceptualist "machine to make *art*" (Sol LeWitt),[7] but as a formal system for the synthesis of *art and life*.

The *Xenotext*'s procedural poetics consequently situates itself somewhere between a bioengineered "origin" of future life and an indeterminate/open-ended posthuman "surplus-production" of semiocapital. Bök himself contends that the *Xenotext* is "not simply a code that governs the development of an organism and the maintenance of its function," since "the genome can now become a vector for, heretofore unimagined, modes of artistic innovation and cultural expression."[8] Which is also to say, of *ideology*. And here lie perhaps the most radical aspects of the *Xenotext* experiment: the purchase (however provisional) of ideology upon not only the *idea* of the future, but upon its *operative materiality*, far beyond the assumed horizon of ideology's *global* reach—and that this very possibility arises in a strictly *poetic* function. In this, Bök seeks to renovate the historical concept of a political/cultural avant-garde. "Postmodern life," he observed in a 2007 interview with Kenneth Goldsmith,

> has utterly recoded the avant-garde demand for radical newness. Innovation in art no longer differs from the kind of manufactured obsolescence that has come to justify advertisements for "improved" products; nevertheless, we have to find a new way to contribute by generating a "surprise" (a term that almost conforms to the cybernetic definition of "information"). The future of poetry may no longer reside in the standard lyricism of emotional anecdotes, but in other exploratory procedures, some of which may seem entirely unpoetic, because they work not by expressing subjective thoughts, but by exploiting unthinking machines, by colonizing unfamiliar lexicons, or by simulating unliterary artforms.[9]

"Life" as such is not the privileged referent here, but rather we are confronted with a poetic operation that constitutes an ambivalent translational zone between life and non-life (*postmodern* of otherwise), beyond the false dichotomy between language and matter. This is what *Tiqqun*, in 2001, referred to as the "Cybernetic Hypothesis"—being "a political hypothesis, a new fable" which has "definitively supplanted the liberal hypothesis. Contrary to the latter, it proposes to conceive biological, physical, and social behaviours as something integrally programmed and re-programmable."[10] Bök himself refers to the *Xenotext* as a bioart project, a *poetry of record* of the Anthropocene. For Bök, cybernetcization opens the possibility for *de-romanticizing* the social function of avant-gardism and the value of manufacture of *surprise* as no longer mere aesthetic novelties but something of much more profound consequence. There is a clear distinction here to be made between the implicit Humanism of *Tiqqun*'s stance (and that of much of post-1968 cultural criticism) and Bök's engagement with an avant-gardism both cognizant of and prepared to exploit the "cybernetic hypothesis" which, for political theorists like Harvey Wheeler, already in 1968 constituted a "universal revolution."[11]

In "Aleatory Writing: Notes Towards a Poetics of Chance" (2006), Bök notes: "Modern writers who deploy an aleatory strategy in their work may appear to do little more than *emulate* the random excess of irrational liberation, when in fact they confirm that, within language, such random excess is itself a sovereign necessity, an overriding requisite, which reveals the coincidental, if not conspiratory, order of words set free from the need to mean."[12] Bök relates such post-literary strategies ("a hybrid fusion of science and poetics")[13] to an encounter between literary experimentalism and such phenomena as Markov chains, quantum indeterminacy, and stochastic systems of "information," resulting in a species of *alien lettrisme* that encompasses DNA and protein as *textual constraints* and as *media*. What Claude Shannon and Warren Weaver called the "asymptote of intelligibility"[14]—whose implications are no less ideological than they are empirical—here describes not a *conceptualism* (an "alien" *logos* subsisting like a "harmless parasite, inside the cell of another life-form"[15]: a "life-form" ultimately indistinguishable from "language"), but rather a kind of *data aggregate*; a "critical mass" of signifiability. This asymptote of intelligibility points also to the status of the *Xentotext* as feedback system, projecting in turn a new posthuman species (in holograph) of what we might call *Homo Xenopoeticus*.

At base, what this all points to is that *autonomy* is an epiphenomenon—"an emergent result" not only, as N. Katherine Hayles puts it, "of all the technological couplings, communications, energy flows, and material affordances that are deeply integrated with computational media,"[16] but of their constituent *possibility*, of which the operations of *transcription* are here the formal expression. Bök's DNA coding—as an abstraction and recombination of terms—does not *precede* the "codependency" of transcription (what Maurice Merleau-Ponty called "differences *without* terms"[17] and what Derrida called simply "différance"[18]), since each is, as it were, immanent to the other. The "medium" in other words is indeed the "message," so that Bök's apparently straightforward proposition for engineering "a primitive bacterium so that it becomes not only a durable *archive* for *storing* a poem, but also a usable *machine* for *writing* a poem,"[19] likewise produces the problem that it itself is a poiēsis and not a vehicle, or a "machine,"[20] acting as if *upon* the "poem" as an abstract entity. This is where the materialism of Bök's *Xenotext* experiment runs up against a theoretical limit, in the assumption that "language" is an external agency, an operating system, supervening in the otherwise autonomous operations of "writing" (transcription). Bök:

> even though language *may attempt to regulate the ephemeral interplay between the errancy of the arbitrary letter and the grammar of its mandatory syntax*, the act of writing nevertheless finds itself traversed, inevitably and invariably, by the entropic dyslalia of chance-driven phenomena (mistakes, blunders, ruptures, hiatuses, glitches, etc.)—forces of both semiotic atomization and semantic dissipation, threatening always to relegate language to a dissonant continuum of chaos and noise.[21]

But language *is* this continuum of so-called "chaos and noise." Precisely that "chaos and noise" constitute the seven trillion possible substitution ciphers from which the constraints of the *Xenotext* experiment "caused" the 120-word Xenocode ("ANY-THE 112") to be "selected." They are constitutive also of the evolutionary processes resulting in the given characteristics not only of Deinococcus radiodurans, but of its cell structures generally and indeed of the very transcriptive operations that underlie all of "life." This generalized semiotics—as autopoetic and codependent—doesn't equate to some sort of "portentous cryptogram" beyond which lies a hidden "concept," or even a "human design." Bök:

> Borges in "The Library of Babel" imagines a hellish archive of books—a macrocosmic columbarium, whose infinite chambers provide an exhaustive repository for all the permutations and combinations of the alphabet. Inside this endless library (where a single, random volume might consist of nothing but the letters MCY, perversely reiterated on every page), nonsensical texts so drastically outnumber any intelligible books that a coherent phrase, like "0 time thy pyramids,"[1] must seem tantamount to a wondrous mishap: "for one reasonable line…there are leagues of insensate cacophony"[2]; hence, "[t]he impious assert that absurdities are the norm in the Library and that anything reasonable…is an almost miraculous exception."[21] Such an allegory inverts the dominant norms of semantic value in order to suggest that meaningful statements constitute only the tiniest, fractional subset of an even greater linguistic matrix. Such a repressed nightmare already haunts the work of literary scholars, who confront the oppressive

> totality of literature with the nagging concern that each book might have arisen of its own accord, not from the expressed sentiment of a unique author, but from the automated procedure of a formal system—a fatal order, in which even the most unlikely sequence of letters, *dhcmrlchtdj*, might yet convey a message in the form of a portentous cryptogram.[22]

Alien wor(l)ds

Such portentousness always evokes the existence of an occult meaning which, by a paranoiac iteration, assumes the form of a "message" presenting its addressee with the spectacle of its withdrawal behind an endless promise. It is, so to speak, the secret promise of teleology—of the very *concept* governing history as the "meaning of Being." This portentous cryptogram is nothing less than the *logos* of Homo sapiens. To the extent that the *Xenotext* represents the "metonymic dwarf"[23] of this portentous cryptogram, it does so in being brought back to what Derrida calls "its own finitude at the very moment when its limits seem to disappear, when it ceases to be self-assured, contained, and guaranteed by the infinite signified which seemed to exceed it."[24] Adrift "in the threat of limitlessness," the *Xenotext* rehearses the Platonic theatre of paternalistic dread issuing from the *crisis of writing*, as allegorized in the *Phaedrus*. The limitless *dérive* opened to the logos in the guise of a supplemental "writing"—as simultaneously "mnemotechnique and the power of forgetting"[25]—threatens to *exceed any supervening context*. This radical inflation is arrested only by the "finitude" of writing itself—which Derrida reformulates in his critique of Plato (via the semiology of Saussure) as a "becoming-space of time and the becoming-time of space"[26]: which is to say, the finitude inscribed in difference.

It is not simply that, in a posthuman future, the *Xenotext*—as an analogue to what Pak Chung Wong called a "data-preservation problem of apocalyptic magnitude, using genome encryption in extremophile bacterias"[27]—would in fact *signify* obsolescence and self-supersession, or that its "human data" would be nothing but redundant genetics, but that its very operations would mitigate against precisely such an *apocalyptic* view of history that can only be defined, paradoxically, by a posthumous *living-on* (bacterial genome as Noah's Ark) in the significations, so to speak, of "dead language." In fact, what the *Xenotext* comes to represent here is a certain *ambivalence*, in which the apparently contradictory forms of living archive and mausoleum coincide. "DNA," Bök writes, "might permit us to preserve our cultural heritage against planetary disasters," citing Wong to the effect that "organisms…on Earth for hundreds of millions of years represent excellent candidates for protecting critical information for future generations."[28] A preservational imperative that likewise gives birth, by way of a certain ambivalence, to "a man of the future," in the words of André Leroi-Gourhan, who will "no longer be a 'man'" but rather a "toothless humanity that would exist in a prone position using what limbs it had left to push buttons with," etc.[29]

But this preservational imperative, vested in the "alien words" of Deinococcus radiodurans, runs contrary to the very technogenesis it seeks to enlist, relying on a wholly *artificial* instrumental limit which is implicitly imposed upon it—for example in the analogy, readily evoked, between the instrumentality of Hayabusa2 and the *Xenotext* as both experimental organism and remote "space-probe." It would be simple enough to imagine such an organic probe linked to some "human" future-present by quantum entanglement as a prosthesis for the exploration of space *and time* (a "lived experience," as Derrida says, "neither *in* the world, nor in 'another world'"[30]). Where genetic transcription becomes indistinguishable from a certain "cybernetic programme," evolutionary *semblance* (man *of the future*) would simply be a piece of corresponding code: a *poetics* of an imaginary idea (the human, the alien: "any style of life") that would *preserve only its erasure*. ("In the last instance," Derrida argues, "the difference between the signified and signifier *is nothing*."[31]) It is not the concept (of man) that is communicated through the movement of transcription, but transcription that produces, as it were, the concept.

Enciphered in its very logic, the "content" of Bök's conceptualism is nothing less than the human idea itself, disguised in the autonomous operations of an abstract materiality—acting as if *in the gap between art and life*. It implies that even in a universe from which humanity may be theoretically absent, a certain *human idea* will never cease its claims of paternity over those forms of "autonomous agency" that persist as if *in place of it*, whether in the guise of autopoiēsis or metaphysic. This, as Lacan suggested in his 1954 seminar on a materialist definition of consciousness, is what could be called the *posthumous* counterpart of that panoptic illusionism of seeing-oneself-seeing. For the purpose of illustration, Lacan constructs a scenario in many respects similar to Bök's, with the distinction that it describes a world from which *all living beings* have vanished. In it, a photographic mechanism remains standing on a tripod at the edge of a lake, focused on the image of a mountain reflected there. The camera is set to operate automatically, recording whatever is framed through its viewfinder. "Once again," Lacan says, "we're dealing with a mirror":

> What is left in the mirror? The rays which return to the mirror make us locate in an imaginary space the object which moreover is somewhere in reality. The real object isn't the object that you see in the mirror. So here there's a phenomenon of consciousness as such. That at any rate is what I would like you to accept, so that I can tell you a little apologue to aid your reflection.
>
> Suppose all men have disappeared from the world. I say *men* on account of the high value which you attribute to consciousness. That is already enough to raise the question—*What is left in the mirror*? But let us take it to the point of supposing that all living beings have disappeared. There are only waterfalls and springs left—lightning and thunder too. The image in the mirror, the image in the lake—do they still exist?[32]

No doubt certain analogies can be drawn between the camera's production of a "perception" and the bacteria's production of a "poem" (the production, by way of transcription, of a *reading* that is also a *writing*). The question is posed, as if for some higher adjudication, as to whether this reflexive theatre can be said to constitute *agency*: the "image," the "text"—*do they still exist?* This is the question that haunts Bök's project. In its implied universalism, it points to a certain crisis of self-supersession in the rationality which has so far appeared to govern its "experimental" program. Evoking as it does the specter of an end-of-history, it nevertheless does so in the manner of a "historico-metaphysical epoch," as Derrida says, finally determining "as language the totality of its problematic horizon."[33] With each iteration, the *Xenotext*—as an index of pure repeatability—in fact *erases* the conceptual domain of historicity, by reinscribing it as technopoiesis (history *as writing*).

It is in this relation—of an *"autonomous" excess* of the symbolic function—that we can properly speak of a *poetics* of the *Xenotext* experiment: not as the post-Humanist kitsch of Bök's aestheticized glowing bacterium, but as the intelligenic DNA of a poiēsis *without content.* As in Beckett, there is something of an appeal to an autopoiēsis in which writing (inscription) is reduced to a degree zero of subjectivity, as pure repetition-compulsion of a signifying materiality conceived as a "something of nothing": the epigenetic code as the *objet petit a* of writing as such. Yet if, as Derrida argues, writing can never *in any case* be subsumed "under the category of the subject,"[34] then the alienism of the *Xenotext* is immanent to writing itself, rendering the self-serenading of a mutant bacteria in space simply an exotic exemplum of *astrocapitalist poetics*,[35] whose message in a-bottle—like Carl Sagan's Voyager records or microplastics in the Mariana Trench—is ultimately *designed*, in the absence of any God, to infect the universe with an indelible *human* presence. It is as if—read against the *Xenotext*'s radical technicity—what Bök is really offering, by way of the red herring of "the poem," is an autocritique of *a "conceptualism" that mystifies itself* as a "means of art to construct a 'system' of…internally coherent signs,"[36] in which a residual Humanism nevertheless persists in its attempt to *produce the "real."*

NOTES

Chapter 1

1 Jacques Derrida, *Of Grammatology*, trans. Gayatri Spivak (Baltimore: Johns Hopkins University Press, 1974), 45.

2 Derrida, *Of Grammatology*, 45.

3 Jacques Derrida, "Scribble: Writing Power," in *The Derrida Reader: Writing Performances*, ed. Julian Wolfreys (Lincoln: University of Nebraska Press, 1998).

4 Derrida, *Of Grammatology*, 66.

5 Jacques Derrida, *Dissemination*, trans. Barbara Johnson (London: Athlone Press, 1981), 186.

6 Derrida, *Dissemination*, 265.

7 Cited in *Le "Livre" de Mallarmé,* ed. Jacques Scherer (Paris: Gallimard, 1957), 32.

8 Marshall McLuhan, "Joyce, Mallarmé, and the Press," in *The Interior Landscape: The Literary Criticism of Marshall McLuhan 1943-1962*, ed. Eugene McNamara (New York: McGraw-Hill, 1969), 11.

9 Octavio Armand, *Refractions*, trans. Carol Maier (New York: Lumen, 1994), 187.

10 Johanna Drucker, *The Century of Artist' Books* (New York: Granary, 1995), 115.

11 Jacques Rancière, "The Space of Words: From Mallarmé to Broodthaers," in *Porous Boundaries: Texts and Images in Twentieth-century French Culture*, ed. Jérôme Game (Bern: Peter Lang, 2007), 41.

12 Rancière, "The Space of Words," 43.

13 See James Schevill, *where to go what to do when you are Bern porter: A Personal Biography* (Gardiner, Maine: Tilbury House, 1992), 98.

14 Jerome Rothenberg, Preface to Jackson Mac Low, *Representative Works: 1938–1985,* (New York: Roof Books), 1986, viii.

15 A constellation may be thought of as a *virtual* in which disparate events are said to have been "brought into communication" in time and space—a montage effect by which communication is underwritten and made possible by the absence of any measure of a common, objective present, or "degree zero." In this sense there are no degrees or planes of a revelation of structural intention, only degrees or planes of *constellation*. There exists no network or *system* of signification to render the constellation meaningful in and of itself, merely the confabulated appearance of unicity, of a fixed circuit of spatial and temporal variances (a *primum mobile*)—a schematized, *contingent* present from which "all other" orientations of time and space take their measure according to the relativity of a generalized parallax or anamorphosis.

16 Jacques Derrida, *Memoirs of the Blind*, trans. Pascale-Anne Brault and Michael Naas (Chicago: University of Chicago Press), 1993, 3.

17 Jackson Mac Low, *Representative Works: 1938–1985* (New York: Roof, 1986), 18.

18 See bpNichol, *Translating Translating Apollinaire: A Preliminary Report* (Milwaukee: Membrane Press, 1979).

19 Among the work's collaborators were Steve McCaffery, Dick Higgins, and Douglas Barbour.

20 This expression, from *Finnegans Wake*, was adopted by Bob Cobbing and Bill Griffiths for their 1992 Writers Forum anthology, *verbi visi voco: a performance of poetry*.

Chapter 2

1 "Take a newspaper. / Take some scissors. / Choose from this paper an article of the length you want to make your poem. / Cut out the article. / Next carefully cut out each of the words that makes up this article and put them all in a bag. / Shake gently. / Next take out each cutting one after the other. / Copy conscientiously in the order in which they left the bag. / The poem will resemble you. / And there you are—an infinitely original author of charming sensibility, even though unappreciated by the vulgar herd," in Tristan Tzara, *Seven Dada Manifestos and Lampisteries*, trans. B. Wright (New York: Alma Classics, 2013).

2 "P P P P P P P P P / p o r n o g r a p h i c —poem / The go / Its bleating is / Sweet & peaceful / And it will not / With its horns / The line indicates where I cut lengthwise through an innocuous poem from a children's picture book. From the goat came a go. / And it will not / become provoked / With its horns / to shove & poke." Cited in Craig Dworkin, *Reading the Illegible* (Evanston, IL: Northwestern University Press, 2003, 148–149).

3 Dworkin, *Reading the Illegible*, 149.

4 J. Hawkins and A. Wermer-Colan, eds., *William S. Burroughs Cutting Up the Century* (Bloomington: Indiana University Press, 2019), 84.

5 John Cage, *Roaratorio: An Irish Circus on Finnegans Wake*, ed. Klaus Schoening (Königstein: Atheneum Verlag, 1982), 173.

6 Marjorie Perloff, *Poetry On & Off the Page: Essays for Emergent Occasions* (Evanston, IL: Northwestern University Press, 1998), 292.

7 Steve McCaffery, *The Darkness of the Present: Poetics, Anachronism, and the Anomaly* (Tuscaloosa: University of Alabama Press), 2012, 44.

8 McCaffery, *The Darkness of the Present*, 219.

9 Steve McCaffery, *North of Intention: Critical Writings 1973–1986*, 2nd edition (New York: Roof Books, 2000), 63.

10 Thom Donovan, "Interview of Charles Bernstein, Part 1," Poetry Foundation, April 23, 2010, www.poetryfoundation.org/blog/uncategorized/53768/interview-with-charles-bernstein-part-i.

11 A digital edition aligning Bernstein's poem with Goffman's text is available here, both accessed August 24, 2025: eclipsearchive.org/projects/ASYLUMS/html/contents.html and writing.upenn.edu/epc/authors/bernstein/asylums/Asylum.html.

12 Dworkin, *Reading the Illegible*, xviii.

13 Dworkin, *Reading the Illegible*, xx.

14 Dworkin, *Reading the Illegible*, 3.

15 Dworkin, *Reading the Illegible*, 5.

16 Dworkin, *Reading the Illegible*, 3.

17 Dworkin, *Reading the Illegible*, 13.

18 McCaffery, *The Darkness of the Present*, 107.

19 Charles Bernstein, *A Poetics* (Cambridge, MA: Harvard University Press, 1992), 46.

20 See, in particular, chapter 3 of Marjorie Perloff's *Radical Artifice: Writing Poetry in the Age of Media*, Chicago: University of Chicago Press, 1991.

21 Gertrude Stein, *Look at Me Now and Here I Am: Writings and Lectures 1909-1945*, London, Penguin, 1967, 26.

22 Anne D'Harnoncourt and Kynaston McShine, eds., *Marcel Duchamp* (New York: Museum of Modern Art, 1973), 291.

23 Paul Ricoeur, *Freud and Philosophy: An Essay in Interpretation*, trans. Denis Savage (New Haven: Yale University Press, 1970), 32.

24 Rita Felski, *Uses of Literature* (New York: Wiley-Blackwell, 2008), 2.

25 Even though erasurist strategies can conceivably be applied to non-found material, the examples considered here reflect the foundist orientation which characterizes the vast majority of contemporary erasurist works, at least in the field of literature.

26 Text online at gallica.bnf.fr/ark:/12148/bpt6k10568643.imag, accessed September 5, 2025.

27 Charles Coqueley de Chaussepierre, *Le Roué vertueux: poëme en prose, en quatre chants, propre à faire, en cas de besoin, un drame à jouer deux fois par semaine* (Lauzanne (Paris): unidentified publisher, 1770), 12.

28 De Chaussepierre, *Le Roué vertueux*, 3.

29 Theodor Adorno, *Notes to Literature*, ed. Rolf Tiedemann, trans. Shierri Weber Nicholson (New York: Columbia University Press, 1991), 91.

30 "The Gertrude Stein scholar, Ulla Dydo, tells us that visuality is a key aspect in reading Stein's texts. Often, she says, Stein's pages were never meant to be 'read.' They were meant to be looked at, to be scanned visually. This was a great revelation to me in forming my ideas about Conceptual Writing. It also dovetailed with concerns earlier in my work about the theorized utopian linguistic state of concrete poetry—a language that could be read by looking—and, like Esperanto, understood visually and intellectually without understanding the language it was written in." (Sarah Posman, "An Interview with Kenneth Goldsmith," accessed September 5, 2025, www.ny-web.be/artikels/interview-kenneth-goldsmith).

31 Derek Beaulieu, *a, A Novel* (Paris: Jean Boîte Editions, 2017).

32 "A Short Interview with Derek Beaulieu," *Nuts and Bolts* (March 2021): unpag.nutsandboltspublishing.com/2021/03/18/a-short-interview-with-derek-beaulieu.

33 Artist's statement, our translation, accessed September 5, 2025, www.galerieannebarrault.com/expositions/gerner.html.

34 Gerner, *TNT en Amérique*, unpagin. ("The production keeps the shutters closed / An adversary stays at the hotel / The production stays in Chicago / The hotel keeps the bird").

35 Stéphane Mallarmé, *Collected Poems and Other Verse*, trans. E. H. and A. M. Blackmore (Oxford: Oxford University Press, 2009), 68.

36 Stéphane Mallarmé, *Selected Poetry and Prose*, trans. Mary Ann Caws (New York: New Directions, 1982), 99.

37 Stéphane Mallarmé, *Igitur, Divagations, Un coup de dés* (Paris: Gallimard, 1976), 429.

38 Man Ray's 1924 visually similar "Lautgedicht" is an important precursor with the essential difference that its main emphasis is on sound rather than space, as evidenced in the silent, residual musicality of its regular metrical patterns.

39 Mallarmé, *Igitur, Divagations, Un coup de dés*, 406.

40 Mallarmé, *Igitur, Divagations, Un coup de dés*, 405.

41 Stéphane Mallarmé, *Correspondance Tome 1 (1862-1871)* (Paris: Gallimard, 1956), 137.

42 Stéphane Mallarmé, *Selected Letters*, trans. R. Lloyd (Chicago: University of Chicago Press), 60.

43 Jacques Rancière, "The Space of Words: from Mallarmé to Broodthaers," in *Porous Boundaries: Texts and Images in Twentieth-Century French Culture*, ed. Jérôme Game (Bern: Peter Lang, 2007), 61.

Chapter 3

1 Harold Bloom, *The Anxiety of Influence: A Theory of Poetry*, 2nd ed. (Oxford: Oxford University Press, 1997), 19–48.

2 Ronald Johnson, *RADI OS* (Chicago: Flood Editions, 2005), 6.

3 Guy Davenport, Preface to Ronald Johnson's *RADI OS* (Chicago: Flood Editions, 2005), 104.

4 Barry Alpert, "Ronald Johnson: An Interview (1974)," in *Ronald Johnson: Life and Works*, ed. Joel Bettridge and Eric Murphy Selinger (Orono: National Poetry Foundation, 2008), 556.

5 Johnson, *RADI OS*, 6.

6 Cited in Johnson, unpag.

7 Davenport, Preface to Ronald Johnson's *RADI OS*, 100.

8 Jean Clair and Manlio Brusatin, eds., *Identity and Alterity: Figures of the Body 1895–1995* (Marsilio, Venice 1995), xxvii. Oppenheim is not just a continuator of Duchamp or a precursor of later artistic experiments with X-rays by the likes of Robert Rauschenberg or Wim Delvoye. Her self-portrait also references Röntgen's very first radiograph, that of his wife's left hand, which was also adorned with a ring.

9 Marjorie Perloff, *Differentials: Poetry, Poetics, Pedagogy* (Tuscaloosa: University of Alabama Press, , 2004), 197.

10 Davenport, Preface to Ronald Johnson's *RADI OS*, 96.

11 Janet Holmes, *The ms of m y kin*, Exeter, Shearsman Books, 2009, 169.

12 Silliman's Blog, unpag., accessed September 7, 2025, www.writing.upenn.edu/epc/mirrors/ronsilliman.blogspot.com/index.html.

13 Vincent Broqua, "Stephen Ratcliffe's '[where late the sweet] BIRDS SANG' Or, writing through Shakespeare's sonnets," *Jacket2*, October 20, 2011, unpag.jacket2.org/article/stephen-ratcliffe%E2%80%99s-where-late-sweet-birds-sang.

14 Broqua, "Stephen Ratcliffe's '[where late the sweet] BIRDS SANG.'"

15 Jen Bervin, *Nets* (New York: Ugly Duckling Presse, 2003), unpag.

16 Bervin, *Nets*.

17 Bervin, *Nets*.

18 Bervin, *Nets*.

19 Travis Macdonald, "A Brief History of Erasure Poetics," *Jacket2* 38 (2009), unpag., jacketmagazine.com/38/macdonald-erasure.shtml.

20 Macdonald, "A Brief History of Erasure Poetics."

21 Travis Macdonald, *The O Mission Repo* (Santa Fe, NM: Fact-Simile Editions, 2008), unpag.

22 M. NourbeSe Philip, *Zong!* (Middletown, CT, Wesleyan University Press, 2008), 193.

23 Philip, *Zong!*, 193–194.

24 Philip, *Zong!*, 195.

25 Philip, *Zong!*, 199.

26 Laurie Lambert, "Poetics of Reparation in M. NourbeSe Philip's *Zong!*," *The Global South* 10, no. 1 (2016): 120.

27 Philip, *Zong!*, unpag.

28 If one adopts a broader perspective, one cannot help being reminded of the famous Oulipian precedent set by Georges Perec's lettrist

representation of genocide in *La disparition*, where the disappearance of the letter *e* commemorates the erasure of an entire people.

Chapter 4

1 For a critical account of the function of the detail in dominant discourses on realism, see Naomi Schor, "Details and Realism: Le Curé de Tours," *Poetics Today* 5, no. 4, (1984): 701–709.
2 Ian Watt, *The Rise of the Novel* (London: Hogarth Press, 1987), 29.
3 Watt, *The Rise of the Novel*, 30.
4 Watt, *The Rise of the Novel*, 32.
5 William John Harvey, *Character and the Novel* (London: Chatto, 1965), 28.
6 "[Die] Zersetzung, die den Lebenswillen vom Ganzen in die Einzelheiten verdrängt." Robert Musil, *Der Mann ohne Eigenshaften*, complete online text: gutenberg.spiegel.de/buch/6882/118.
7 Jorge Luis Borges, *Ficciones* (London: Grove Press, 1962), 112.
8 Charles Baudelaire, Œuvres complètes vol. 2 (Paris: Gallimard, 1976), 698.
9 Borges, *Ficciones*, 115.
10 Borges, *Ficciones*, 114.
11 Borges, *Ficciones*, 114.
12 Jean-Pierre Maurel, Preface to Robert Musil's *L'homme sans qualités* vol. 1 (Paris: Seuil, 1995), viii.
13 Ernesto Sabato, *The Tunnel/El Tunel* (New York: Ballantine, 1991).
14 Gaston Leroux, *Le Parfum de la dame en noir*. Our translation. Complete online text: www.gutenberg.org/etext/15554.
15 Leroux, *Le Parfum de la dame en noir*, unpag.
16 Daniel Arasse, *Histoires de peintures* (Paris: Gallimard, 2004), 290.
17 Arasse, *Histoires de peintures*, 217.
18 Georges Didi-Huberman, *Devant l'Image: Question posée aux fins d'une histoire de l'art* (Paris: Les Editions de Minuit, 1990), 310.
19 Arasse, *Histoires de peintures*, 217.
20 Didi-Huberman, *Devant l'Image*, 298.
21 Didi-Huberman, *Devant l'Image*, 294, 313.
22 Didi-Huberman, *Devant l'Image*, 313.
23 Cited in Marjorie Perloff, *Differentials: Poetry, Poetics, Pedagogy* (Tuscaloosa: University of Alabama Press, 2004), 175.

24 The sixth and final edition of *A Humument* was published in 2016, bringing the experiment to a close after each page of the source text had been "treated" twice.

25 Tom Phillips, *A Humument: A Treated Victorian Novel*, 4th edition (London: Thames & Hudson, 1980), 100.

26 Phillips, *A Humument*, unpag.

27 Phillips, *A Humument*, 246.

28 Pierre Alechinsky, *Alechinsky from A to Y* (Tielt: Lannoo, 2007), 242.

29 Alechinsky, *Alechinsky from A to Y*, 115.

30 Alechinsky, *Alechinsky from A to Y*, 268.

31 Phillips, *A Humument*, unpag.

32 James L. Maynard, "'I Find / I Found Myself / and / Nothing / More than That': Textuality, Visuality, and the Production of Subjectivity in Tom Phillips' 'A Humument,'" *The Journal of the Midwest Modern Language Association* 36, no. 1, 2003), 86.

33 For more information on the different versions of Phillips's book, see the book's official website at: www.humument.com/.

34 The author himself calls them "rivers." Phillips, *A Humument*, unpag.

35 Phillips, *A Humument*, unpag.

36 Marcel Proust, *The Captive & The Fugitive: In Search of Lost Time*, vol. 5, trans. t C. K. Scott-Moncrieff, Terence Kilmartin, and D. J. Enright (New York: The Modern Library, 2003), 244.

37 Given the one-directional nature of the textual "rivers" or "clusters" (a feature further enhanced by the recent recorded version of Phillips' text) it is difficult to agree with Katherine Hayles that Phillips's book operates as a hypertext and allows readers to enjoy a "readerly" form of freedom in their apprehension of the text (Maynard, "'I Find / I Found Myself / and / Nothing / More than That,'" 95).

38 Didi-Huberman, *Devant l'Image*, 280.

39 Didi-Huberman, *Devant l'Image*, 23. According to Steve McCaffery it is possible to read the writing throughs of Pound's *Cantos* performed by Jewish writer Jackson Mac Low as an act of symbolic revolt against his anti-Semitic master (Steve McCaffery, *The Darkness of the Present: Poetics, Anachronism, and the Anomaly* (Tuscaloosa: University of Alabama Press), 2012, 45).

40 Schor, "Details and Realism," 109.

41 On the usefulness of an understanding of the *effet de pan* as a phenomenological and semiological symptom, see Didi-Huberman, *Devant l'Image*, 308–310. On the Freudian notion of the detail, see also Schor, "Details and Realism," 101–120.
42 Phillips, *A Humument*, unpag.
43 Phillips, *A Humument*, 39.
44 W. H. Mallock, *A Human Document: A Novel* (London: Chapman and Hall, 1892), 182. Phillips's *A Humument* and Mallock's original text can be viewed here, accessed October 15, 2025: www.tomphillips.co.uk/humument.
45 Didi-Huberman, *Devant l'Image*, 41.
46 Didi-Huberman, *Devant l'Image*, 39.
47 Didi-Huberman, *Devant l'Image*, 41.
48 Phillips, *A Humument*, 26.
49 Phillips, *A Humument*, 100.
50 Arasse, *Histoires de peintures*, 11.
51 Arasse, *Histoires de peintures*,, 11.
52 This would seem to be a feature shared by both the detail and the fragment, pace Didi-Huberman's claim that "contrary to the fragment which only refers to the whole to deny its presence, or declares it absent or enigmatic or forever lost in memory, the detail *imposes the whole*, legitimizes its presence, its response and reference value, which is liable to become hegemonic" (Didi-Huberman, *Devant l'Image*, 274).
53 William Hurrell Mallock, *A Human Document*, London: Adamant Media Corporation, 2001, iii.
54 Mallock, *A Human Document*, vii.
55 Mallock, *A Human Document*, xiii.
56 Mallock, *A Human Document*, xiii.
57 Mallock, *A Human Document*, xiii.
58 Mallock, *A Human Document*, x.

Chapter 5

1 Mark Fisher, "The Metaphysics of Crackle," *Dancecult: Journal of Electronic Dance Music Culture*, vol. 5, no. 2, 2013, 52.
2 Mark Fisher, *Ghosts of My Life: Writings on Depression, Hauntology and Lost Futures* (London: Zero Books, 2014), 8.
3 Fisher, *Ghosts of My Life*, 6.

4 Fisher, "The Metaphysics of Crackle," 47. Fisher attributes the term to Reynolds, who doesn't recall coining it ("Not sure if it's Mark's dreaming or an actual philosophical term. Sounds plausible." [X, June 1, 2021, x.com/SimonRetromania/status/1399821023055290370?mx=2].)

5 Fisher, "The Metaphysics of Crackle," 131.

6 Fisher, "The Metaphysics of Crackle," 44.

7 Dyschronia, while being at the center of many recent artists' hauntological plunderphonic efforts, is of course not irrelevant to music produced in the predigital age. One thinks, for instance, of Charles Ives's simultaneous musics or similar experiments led by John Cage (*Radio Music*, 1956) and others in the course of the second half of the twentieth century. Frank Zappa's 1960s degenerate doo-wops created a similar sense of uncanny disorientation thriving on the breakdown of unmediated, immanent temporality. As for his detuned ballroom music in "Overture to a Holiday in Berlin" from the 1970 album *Burnt Weeny Sandwich*, it cannot but resonate with the music played in the haunted Gold Room of Kubrick's *The Shining*. Zappa's use of harmonic dissonance, mechanical detunings, and speed changes—in anticipation of later technologies of digital warping and hyper-reverbing—stirs the spooky undertones of a melodic line under the threat of collapse and dissolution, vacillating between melodrama and terror. That the song's title was inspired by the riot caused by student rebels disrupting one of the Mothers of Invention's 1968 West Berlin shows to advocate the liberation of Maoist activist Fritz Teufel returns us to the geopolitical origins of Derridean hauntology, a model which was in part intended as a critique of Francis Fukuyama's then recent predictions of the coming triumph of global liberal democracies known as the end of history.

8 Jacques Derrida, *Of Grammatology*, trans. Gayatri Spivak (Baltimore: Johns Hopkins University Press, 2016), 11.

9 Derrida, *Of Grammatology*, 13.

10 Fisher, "The Metaphysics of Crackle," 44.

11 Fisher, "The Metaphysics of Crackle," 53.

12 See his discussion of Kanye West's album *808s & Heartbreak* in *Ghosts of My Life*, 174–176.

13 Fisher, *Ghosts of My Life*, 11–12.

14 Fisher, "The Metaphysics of Crackle," 48.

15 Fisher, *Ghosts of My Life*, 21.

16 Emilie Friedlander, "Interview: William Basinski," *Fader*, September 11, 2012, unpag.

17 Sianne Ngai, *Ugly Feelings*, Cambridge, MA, Harvard University Press, 2007, 255.

18 Cited in Fisher, "The Metaphysics of Crackle," 49.

19 William Gaddis's *The Recognitions* features a singular example of counter-ruinic erasurism and cracklology. Its protagonist, the forger-restorer of Renaissance paintings Wyatt Gwyon, becomes so obsessed with "the crackle on the surface…from the wood panel expanding and contracting" that he eventually decides to remove all traces of pigment from the canvases in order to restore the original works to their primal nudity. William Gaddis, *The Recognitions* (New York: Harcourt, Brace & Company, 1955), 874.

20 W. H. Mallock, *A Human Document: A Novel* (London: Chapman and Hall, 1892), 7. Tom Phillips's *A Humument* and Mallock's original text can be accessed here: www.tomphillips.co.uk/humument.

21 "Doctoring Victorian Literature—A Humument: An Interview with Tom Phillips," in *Book Destruction from the Medieval to the Contemporary: New Directions in Book History*, ed. G. Partington and A. Smyth (London: Palgrave Macmillan, 2014), 114.

22 Cited in N. Katherine Hayles, *Writing Machines* (Cambridge, MA: MIT Press), 88.

23 Cited in Sheila Paine, *Artists Emerging: Sustaining Expression through Drawing* (New York, Routledge, 2019), xi.

24 Georges Bataille, Œuvres complètes, Vol. 6 (Paris: Gallimard, 1973), 295.

25 Stan Brakhage, Interview with Bruce Kawin, in *By Brakhage: An Anthology*, The Criterion Collection, 2003 (DVD).

26 Eric Rondepierre, Artist's statement, accessed October 19, 2025, www.ericrondepierre.com/en/dsl.html.

27 Rondepierre, Artist's statement.

28 And not necessarily in the aesthetic sphere: one thinks of Victorian "hidden mothers" keeping their children still during long exposure times. See also Claire Raymond's reconsideration of Woodman as responding to a lineage of nineteenth-century women artists including Julia Margaret Cameron and Clementina, Viscountess Hawarden in *Francesca Woodman and the Kantian Sublime* (London: Routledge, 2010).

29 See our discussion of Didi-Huberman in chapter four.

30 Gilles Deleuze and Félix Guattari, *A Thousand Plateaus: Capitalism and Schizophrenia*, English edition (Minneapolis: University of Minnesota Press, 1987), 115.

31 Craig Dworkin, *No Medium* (Chicago, IL: MIT Press, 2013), 107.

32 Grafton Tanner, *Babbling Corpse: Vaporwave and the Commodification of Ghosts*, (London, Zero Books, 2016), 25.

33 Kenneth Goldsmith, *Uncreative Writing: Managing Language in the Digital Age* (New York: Columbia University Press, 2011), 218.

34 Fisher, *Ghosts*, 16.

35 Hal Foster, *The Return of the Real: The Avant-Garde at The End of the Century* (Cambridge: MIT Press, 1996), xii.

36 Jameson cited in Fisher, *Ghosts*, 9.

Chapter 6

1 Charles Olson, "Projective Verse," *Poetics of the New American Poetry*, eds. Donald Allen and Warren Tallman, New York: Grove, 1973, 152.

2 Olson, "Projective Verse," 154.

3 Walter J. Ong, *Orality and Literacy: The Technologizing of the Word* (London: Routledge, 1982); Ernest Fenollosa, *The Chinese Written Character as a Medium for Poetry*, ed. Ezra Pound (San Francisco: City Lights, 1986 [1919]); Marshall McLuhan, *The Gutenberg Galaxy: The Making of Typographic Man* (Toronto: University of Toronto Press, 1962).

4 ῥυθμός, cadence or written character.

5 Ludwig Wittgenstein, *The Blue and Brown Books: Preliminary Studies for the Philosophical Investigations* (New York: Harper, 1958), 6–7.

6 Wittgenstein, *The Blue and Brown Books*, 7.

7 What "happens in the brain" is rather an index of these contingencies, constellated as a set of neural events.

8 Michel Foucault, *The Archaeology of Knowledge and the Discourse on Language*, trans. A. M. Sheridan Smith (New York: Pantheon, 1972 [1969]), 85.

9 Foucault, *The Archaeology of Knowledge* , 86.

10 Foucault, *The Archaeology of Knowledge*, 85.

11 Jonathan Swift, *Gulliver's Travels* (London: Wordsworth Edition, 1992 [1726]), III. iv, 195f.

12 *Rules of Hypergraphy*, ed. Paul Gangloff (Nijmegen: Extrapool, 2014), 11.

13 Raluca Lupu-Onet, "Christian Dotremont's logograms: an intermedial work avant la lettre," in *Disrupting, Remembering and Transforming Media*, ed. Leena Eilittä and Liliane Louvel (Newcastle: Cambridge Scholars Publishing, 2012), 34.

14 Raluca Lupu-Onet, 34.

15 Dotremont was regarded as CoBrA's "poet and philosopher." He formulated CoBrA's manifesto "The Case Was Heard" during the inaugural meeting at the Hotel Notre Dame café in Paris in 1948 and he was the group's primary spokesperson and secretary until 1951.

16 Roland Barthes, *The Rustle of Language*, trans. Richard Howard (Berkeley: University of California Press, 1986), 323.

17 Roland Barthes, *The Responsibility of Forms*, trans. Richard Howard (Berkeley: University of California Press), 1985, 220.

18 Peter Schwenger, *Asemic: The Art of Writing* (University of Minnesota Press, 2019), 1.

19 Francesco Aprile and Cristiano Caggiula, "About Asemic Writing," trans. Valentina Rettaroli, accessed September 21, 2025, www.utsanga.it/about-asemic-writing/.

20 The mathematical means by which Turing conceived of what was ultimately the foundational logic of modern computing derives from the proofs of the Czech mathematician Kurt Gödel, in response to Hilbert's positivistic claims (coded as four questions) regarding, in the first two instances, the completeness and consistency of mathematics (*Uber formal unentscheidbare Sätze der Principia Mathematica und verwandter Systeme* [1931]). Gödel's method was to treat mathematic statements as integers—in other words, to take advantage of the fact that mathematical propositions assume no external meaning beyond abstract symbolization—thereby treating "theorems in the same manner as '"numbers."' It was in a similar spirit that Turing's Computable Numbers responded to Hilbert's third question regarding determinability (the Entscheidungsproblem), and that Turing chose to treat computing "instructions" as though they were "numbers." This mode of transversality (disposing of Russell's insistence upon a rigid hypotaxis of classes and types) was not a mere theoretical posture but a practical demonstration of the fact that arithmetic processes in computing are merely an imitation—there are no numbers in the machine, only electrical impulses: an input representing a numerical value and an output representing a function of that value. This point is something

which Wittgenstein (and Sondheim) failed to grasp—Wittgenstein insisting in his discussions with Turing that mathematical propositions must have a meaning (just as Sondheim insists that "codework is not an instance... of mathematical Platonism or Gödelian-Platonism; if anything it relies on the breakdown of the ideal, pointing out the meaning-component of computation, programme, protocol, even the strictest formalisms"—which appears to belie a serious confusion between the materialism of both Gödel's and Turing's approaches to number and the Platonistic insistence upon symbolic meaning in the relation of form to idea).

21 Metzger later chaired the Honorary Committee of the London "Destruction in Art Symposium" (DIAS), September 9–12, 1966, which also included Bob Cobbing, Roy Ascott, and Wolf Vostell.

22 Mez, "The Datableeding Texts" (2001), accessed October 15, 2025, netwurkerz.de/mez/datableed/complete/index.htm.

23 Alan Sondheim, "Introduction," *American Book Review* 22, no. 6: "Codework" (October 2001), 6.

24 Marshall, Richard. "The Nude Brain: An Interview with Kenji Siratori," *3:AM* magazine (June 2002): www.3ammagazine.com/litarchives/2002_jun/interview_kenji_siratori.html.

25 See Rita Raley, "Interferences: [Net.Writing] and the Practice of Codework" www.electronicbookreview.com/thread/electropoetics/net.writing

26 Alan Sondheim, "Codeworld," *Rhizomes* 6: Codework and Surveillance, ed. Louis Armand (Spring 2003): www.rhizomes.net/issue6/sondheim.htm.

Chapter 7

1 Neo-avant-gardism distinguishes itself from "philosophy" by virtue of the latter's general indifference to the question of medium. That is, of the philosophical medium, which is of course in no way unique to philosophy, since the medium of philosophy is itself language, or more broadly the semiosphere, though it may claim special privileges over particular segments of it, logic for instance. As Wittgenstein unhappily pointed out, there really are no linguistic exceptions—"poetic language," for example, or "philosophical language"—there is only language in general. (See Wittgenstein, 1922: §5.6ff).

2 Michael Blankfort, cited in Sidra Stich, *Yves Klein* (London: Hayward Gallery/Cantz Editions, 1995), 156.

3 Douglas Khan and Gregory Whitehead, "Preface," *Wireless Imagination: Sound, Radio and the Avant-Garde* (Boston: Massachusetts Institute of Technology, 1992), ix–x.

4 As with Lyotard's displacement of the binaries of "post-" discourse, vis-à-vis *postmodernism*, as neither a historically discontinuous, nor incomplete project, but rather a modernism in a constant nascent state (Jean-François Lyotard, *The Postmodern Condition: A Report on Knowledge*, trans. Geoff Bennington and Brian Massumi, Manchester: Manchester University Press, 1979, 79), so here the question of the "post- " obtains vis-à-vis *medium*, as neither Platonic vehicle of *eidos*, nor the mute *stuff* of "base materiality." Krauss's terminology needs to be viewed within this particular constellation, against the naïve temporality of, for example, Bürger's historical/neo dualism. Krauss's frequent collaborator Hal Foster makes this something of an article of faith for those critics/theorists associated with *October* magazine, when he states that "the project of the avant-garde is no more concluded in its neo moment than it is enacted in its historical moment. In art, too, creative analysis is *interminable*" (Hal Foster, "What's Neo about the Neo-Avant-Garde?" *October* 70 (1994), 16). See also Derrida's "Videor," in which, discussing the video art of Gary Hill, the question of post-mediumism is shown to reinscribe a certain mimetic fallacy: "perhaps the video event, among others, reveals precisely the problematic fragility of this distinction between internal determination and an external determination..." (Jacques Derrida, *Thinking Out of Sight: Writings on the Arts of the Visible*, eds. Ginette Michaud, Joana Masó, and Javier Bassas, trans. Laurent Milesi, Chicago: University of Chicago Press, 2020, 202).

5 Richard Whitelaw, "Cut and Splice: *Transmission*," introduction to *Cut and Splice: Transmission* (London: Sound Threshold, 2010), 2.

6 Radio, for example, though invented in the late nineteenth century, aired its first regular programmed content only in the 1920s (prior to this, from the 1890s, live music hall performances were domestically available via telephone line—a kind of proto-internet connection which would then evolve through the development of broadcast infrastructure and the availability of mass-produced radio sets, TVs, and personal computers into what has since been termed "new media"). (For more on experimental TV, hypermedia, and the avant-garde see, e.g., Louis Armand, *Helixtrolysis:*

James Joyce & Cyberology, Prague, Litteraria Pragensia Books, 2014.) The term "new media" has always been fraught in its temporality, as well as its attempted media-specificity: the public consciousness of "computer art" begins in 1968, although limited experimentation in the multidisciplinary field of cybernetics stems from the 1940s and, while the internet originated in the 1970s, the term "digital art" wasn't used until it was coined by Aaron Cohen in the early 1980s. The affiliation of the term "new" with electronic computers is somewhat arbitrary, considering the entangled prehistory of electronic computation and digital media in general, from telegraphy to the automated telephone exchange and onward (a movement anticipated by the programmable machines of the industrial revolution, from the Bouchon loom—controlled by punched holes in paper tape [1725]—to Babbage's hypothetical "analytic engine" [1833]). Within the historical framework of print media, radio and television are hardly "old,' either, rendering the term "old media" bemusingly anachronistic, while Gutenberg technology itself is utterly intertwined with the conception of a programmability itself (the Universal Turing Machine) and the abstract functionality of digitization (see Jonathan Swift's prototype of a random text generator in *Gulliver's Travels*). In this respect it is necessary—as in Mallarmé's *Un coup de dés* (1897)—to recognize that "new media" must above all relate to the *longue durée* of the Gutenberg event: that it marks not a "conceptual" discontinuity in the actuation of technical artifacts across an arbitrary timeframe, but rather a general technicity constellated within the same evolutionary moment. It is no less trivial to suggest that Mallarmé's poem is already prefigured in the "technology" of the Gutenberg press than to point out that all digital media *and its associated cultures* are prefigured in the invention of alphanumeric writing (ancient Mesopotamia's "new media"). Just as ideology is indistinguishable from logistics, so too the "conceptual" and "technological" are bound together as expressions of *the possible*—a thesis elaborated in relation to *signifying materiality*, *constellation*, and *vortext* throughout two of Louis Armand's earlier books, *Technē* (1997) and *Literate Technologies* (2006). Failure to grasp this relation has inevitably led back to various species of technicist fallacy infused with metaphysics (Stiegler, Laruelle, Latour)—see his *Entropology* (Grand Rapids, MI: Anti-Oedipus Press, 2023).

7 Spike Milligan, *Adolf Hitler: My Part in His Downfall* (London: Penguin, 1972), 77.

8 Rick Cousins, *Spike Milligan's Accordion: The Distortions of Time and Space in 'The Goon Show'* (Amsterdam: Rodopi, 2016), 145.

9 Alex Seago, *Burning the Box of Beautiful Things: The Development of a Postmodern Sensibility* (Oxford: Oxford University Press, 1995), 7.

10 Jeff Nuttall, *Bomb Culture* (London: Paladin, 1970), 115–116.

11 Nuttall, *Bomb Culture*, 116.

12 Cousins, *Spike Milligan's Accordion*, 2–3.

13 James Joyce, *Finnegans Wake* (London: Faber, 1941), 482.31-483.01.

14 Jean-François Lyotard, *The Postmodern Condition: A Report on Knowledge*, trans. Geoff Bennington and Brian Massumi (Manchester: Manchester University Press, 1979), 81.

15 A mode echoed in Philip K. Dick's depiction of an abortive Martian radio broadcast of *Finnegans Wake*, in his novel *The Divine Invasion.* On the *tele*-effect, and the overarching *techno-poetics* of the avant-garde, see Donald F. Theall, *Beyond the Word: Reconstructing Sense in the Joyce Era of Technology, Culture, and Communication* (Toronto, Toronto University Press, 1995).

16 Joyce, *Finnegans Wake*, 341.18.

17 Gene Youngblood, *Expanded Cinema* (New York: Dutton), 1970, 78.

18 James Joyce, *Finnegans Wake* (New York: Viking, 1958), 41.28.

19 John Cage, *Roaratorio: An Irish Circus on Finnegans Wake*, ed. Klaus Schöning (Königstein: Athenäum, 1985), 89.

20 Gregory Bateson, "Cybernetic Explanation," in *Steps to an Ecology of Mind* (St. Albins: Paladin, 1973), 379.

21 Marjorie Perloff, "John Cage's Dublin, Lyn Hejinian's Leningrad: Poetic Cities as Cyberspaces," *in Classical, Renaissance, and Postmodern Acts of the Imagination: Essays Commemorating O.B. Hardison*, ed. Arthur F. Kinney, Newark, University of Delaware Press, 1996, 61-62.

22 John Cage, *Writing for the Second Time through Finnegans Wake* (New York: Printed Editions, 1978), 1ff.

23 Cage, *Roaratorio*, 29.

24 Ulrich Schönherr, "Intermediale Grenzgäge: Technologie, Sprache und Musik in Georges Perecs Hörspiel *Die Maschine*," *Monatshefte* 106, no. 3 (Fall 2014): 426–451.

25 Schönherr, "Intermediale Grenzgäge.

26 The game ended within half an hour with Cage (black) conceding despite Duchamp's one-knight handicap. This result was rather predictable for an otherwise chance-procedural set-up. The remaining three and a half

hours of the performance were then taken up by Cage and Duchamp's wife, Teeny, playing a second match in front of an increasingly diminishing audience (according to Cross, fewer than ten remained by 1:00 a.m.).

27 Lowell Cross, "*Reunion*: John Cage, Marcel Duchamp, Electronic Music and Chess," *Leonardo Music Journal* 9 (December 1999): 35–42.

28 Jacques Derrida, *Writing and Difference*, trans. Alan Bass, London, Routledge, 1982, 292.

29 Derrida, *Writing and Difference*, 289.

30 See Daniela Cascella and Lucia Farinati, *Cut and Splice: Transmission*, London, Sound Threshold, 2010, 6.

31 From the soundtrack of Guy Debord's 1959 film, *Sur le passage de quelques personnes à travers une assez courte unité de temps*, Debord, 1981, 33. [AW: What are the year and page number referring to in this Debord 1981 cite? Include full cite.]

32 Jacques Lacan, *The Seminar of Jacques Lacan. Book III: The Psychoses 1955–1956*, trans. S. Tomaselli (London: Cambridge University Press, 1988), 318.

33 Yves Klein, "Overcoming the Problematics of Art" [1959], *Overcoming the Problematics of Art: The Writings of Yves Klein*, trans. Klaus Ottmann (Putnam, CT: Spring Publications, 2007), 45.

34 Klein, "Overcoming the Problematics of Art," 45–46.

35 Klein's signature ultramarine whose intensity derived from the use of a polyvinyl acetate binder.

36 Cited in Peake, 2011: 196. [AW: Give full cite for this Peake source.]

37 Ibid., 2011: p.515—emphasis added.

38 Ibid., 511.

39 Jarman, *Smiling in Slow Motion*, unpublished diary (cited in Peake, 2011, 506).

40 Jacques Derrida, *Memoirs of the Blind: The Self-Portrait and Other Ruins*, trans. Pascale-Anne Brault and Michael Naas, Chicago: Chicago University Press, 1993, 45.

41 Jonathan Dawson, "British Sounds," *Sense of Cinema* (October 2005): sensesofcinema.com/2005/cteq/british_sounds/

42 Derek Jarman, *Blue: Text of a Film by Derek Jarman*, London: Channel 4 Television and BBC Radio 3, 1993.

43 Derek Jarman, "Into the Blue," *Chroma* (Woodstock: Overlook Press, 1995), 103.

44 Peake, 398. [AW: provide title in this short cite]

45 Jarman, "Into the Blue," 111.

46 Roland Wymer, *Derek Jarman* (Manchester: Manchester University Press, 2005), 173.

47 Jacques Derrida, *Of Grammatology*, trans. Gayatri Spivak (Baltimore: Johns Hopkins University Press, 2016), 3–5.

48 Spike Milligan, "The Dreaded Piano Clubber," *The Goon Show*, vintage series, episode 12 (recorded 1958), *Goon Show Compendium* 9 (London: BBC Physical Audio, 2014).

49 *A Void*: the English title of the translation of Georges Perec's *La Disparition* (1963).

Chapter 8

1 Philip K. Dick, *The Divine Invasion* (New York: Simon and Schuster, 1981), 15. "You think James Joyce was crazy, is that what you think? Okay; then explain to me how come he mentions 'talktapes' which means audio tapes in a book he wrote starting in 1922 and which he completed in 1939, before there were tape recorders! You call that crazy? He also has them sitting around a TV set—in a book started four years after World War 1…"

2 Jacques Derrida "Two Words for Joyce," in *Post-structuralist Joyce: Essays from the French*, ed. Derek Attridge and Daniel Ferrer (Cambridge: Cambridge University Press, 1984), 147–148.

3 Claude Shannon, "A Mathematical Theory of Communication," *Bell System Technical Journal* 27 (July, October, 1948): 394.

4 Derrida "Two Words for Joyce," 148.

5 As marking a convergence upon a proto-artificial intelligence, this generative interdependence may also be thought of as what Julia Kristeva calls "intrapsychic identifications"—see "Joyce 'the Gracehoper' or the Return of Orpheus," in *James Joyce: The Augmented Ninth*, ed. Bernard Benstock (Syracuse: Syracuse University Press, 1988), 169.

6 James Joyce, *Finnegans Wake* (London: Faber, 1939), 83.12.

7 "The proteiform graph itself is a polyhedron of scripture. There was a time when naif alphabetters would have written it down the tracing of a purely deliquescent recidivist, possibly ambidextorous, snubnosed probably

and presenting a strangely profound rainbow in his (or her) occiput." Joyce, *Finnegans Wake*, 107.08-12.

8 Michel Foucault, "What is an Author?" *Essential Works of Michel Foucault: Aesthetics, Method and Epistemology*, ed. James D. Faubion (New York: New Press, 1998), 206.

9 Samuel Beckett, "Texts for Nothing" [Text 3], *The Complete Short Prose 1929–1989*, ed. Stan Gontarski, (New York: Grove, 1995), 109.

10 An engendered-engendering "difference minimum" whose theoretical genealogy has been mapped from Hélène Cixous's *écriture féminine* to the "Cyberfeminist Manifesto" of VNS Matrix and Laboria Cubonik's *xenofeminism.*

11 See John von Neumann and Oskar Morgenstern, *Theory of Games and Economic Behavior*, (Princeton: Princeton University Press, 1944).

12 Karl Marx, *Grundrisse der Kritik der Politischen Ökonomie* (posthumous 1939–41), published in English as *Outlines of the Critique of Political Economy*, trans. Martin Nicolaus (London: Penguin, 1973).

13 "His [Joyce's] writing is not *about* something; *it is that something itself* [...] when the sense is sleep, the words go to sleep [...] when the sense is dancing, the words dance." Samuel Beckett, "Dante... Bruno, Vico.. Joyce," *Our Exagmination Round His Factification for Incamination of Work in Progress* (New York: New Directions Press, 1962), 14.

14 Gilles Deleuze and Félix Guattari, *Anti-Oedipus: Capitalism and Schizophrenia*, trans. R. Hurley, M. Seem, and H. R. Lane (New York: Viking, 1977).

15 Alec Williams and Nick Srnicek, "#Accelerate: Manifesto for an Accelerationist Politics" (2013): §3. [AW: add journal name?]

16 Samuel Beckett, "The Calmative" [1946], *Nouvelles et Textes pour rien* (Paris: Éditions de Minuit, 1958), 69.

17 Slavoj Žižek, *Absolute Recoil: Towards a New Foundation of Dialectical Materialism* (London: Verso, 2014), 393–394.

18 Žižek, *Absolute Recoil*, 386—emphasis added.

19 Gilles Deleuze, *L'epuisé* (Paris: Minuit, 1992), 57–78.

20 Félix Guattari, "Planes of Consistency' [1971], in *The Anti-Oedipus Papers*, ed. Stéphane Nadaud, trans. Kélina Gotman (Los Angeles: Semiotext(e), 2006), 283.

21 François Dosse, *Gilles Deleuze and Félix Guattari: Intersecting Lives*, trans. Deborah Glassman (New York: Columbia University Press, 2007), 448.

22 Cited in Dosse, *Gilles Deleuze and Félix Guattari*, 448.

23 Sigmund Freud, *Beyond the Pleasure Principle*, trans. C. J. M. Hubback [1919] (London: Hogarth Press, 1922).

24 Samuel Beckett, *The Complete Dramatical Works* (London: Faber, 1986, 213).

25 Gilles Deleuze, "Schizophrenia and Society," *Two Regimes of Madness,: Texts and Interviews 1975–1995*, ed. D. Lapoujade, trans. A. Hodge and M. Taormina (Los Angeles: Semiotext(e), 2006), 24—emphasis added.

26 A parody of Sartre's pebble-on-the-beach materialist ontology in *La Nausée* (1938).

27 Of this schizophrenic character of semio-capitalist desire, Deleuze notes, "Beckett and Artaud have said all there is to say about it." Gilles Deleuze, "Schizophrenia and Society," 25. See also e.g., Hito Steyerl, "Politics of Art: Contemporary Art and the Transition to Post-Democracy," *The Wretched of the Screen* (2012). [AW: provide publisher information]

28 In effect, allegory is here an engine of *ideological regulation* (meaning-production), endlessly repeatable.

29 This self-perpetuating compulsion assumes, in Beckett, the form of a "plus one": n+1 (n=0, 1, 2, …, ∞); i.e., this day and/or all preceding days, *plus* tomorrow; this word and/or all proceeding words, *plus* the next word—any word whatsoever, etc.

30 Beckett, *The Complete Dramatical Works*, 453.

31 Beckett, *The Complete Dramatical Works*, 445–446.

32 Foucault, "What is an Author?" 221.

33 See Murray Gell-Mann, *The Quark and the Jaguar* (New York: W. H. Freeman, 1994), 180.

34 Donald F. Theall, *Beyond the Word: Reconstructing Sense in the Joyce Era of Technology, Culture and Communication* (Toronto, Toronto University Press, 1995).

35 Joyce, *Finnegans Wake*, 271.21-24.

36 Jacques Derrida, *Of Grammatology*, trans. Gayatri Spivak (Baltimore: Johns Hopkins University Press), 1976, 6ff.

37 Joyce, *Finnegans Wake*, 185.29, 186.02.

38 Derrida, *Of Grammatology*, 8.

39 Derrida, *Of Grammatology*, 6–7.

40 Georg Lukács, *History and Class Consciousness*, trans. Rodney Livingstone (Cambridge, MA: MIT Press, 1971), 86.

41 Lukács, *History and Class Consciousness*, 87—emphasis added.

42 Joyce, *Finnegans Wake*, 482.31-483.01.

43 Cf. Jacques Lacan, "A Materialist Definition of the Phenomenon of Consciousness," *The Seminar of Jacques Lacan. Book II: The Ego in Freud's Theory and in the Technique of Psychoanalysis 1954–1955*, trans. S. Tomaselli (London: Cambridge University Press, 1988), 51.

44 Jacques Lacan, "Homeostasis and Insistence," *The Seminar of Jacques Lacan. Book II: The Ego in Freud's Theory and in the Technique of Psychoanalysis 1954–1955*, trans. S. Tomaselli (London: Cambridge University Press, 1988), 54.

45 Jacques Lacan, "Of the Subject of Certainty," *The Seminar of Jacques Lacan. Book XI: The Four Fundamental Concepts of Psychoanalysis*, trans. Alan Sheridan (London, Hogarth Press, 1977), 54.

46 Derrida, "Two Words for Joyce," 147–148.

47 John Cage, *Year from Monday: Lectures and Writings* (London: Calder, 1968), 50.

48 Invisible Committee, *The Coming Insurrections* (Los Angeles: Semiotext(e), 2009), 10.

49 Derrida, "Two Words for Joyce," 147–148.

50 Invisible Committee, *The Coming Insurrections*, 9.

51 Aldous Huxley, *Brave New World* (London: Chatto and Windus, 1932).

52 Samuel Beckett, "Dante… Bruno. Vico.. Joyce," *Our Exagmination Round His Factification for Incamination of Work in Progress* (New York: New Directions Press, 1962), 14.

53 Joyce, *Finnegans Wake*, 118.11-30.

54 See Stephen Heath, "Ambiviolences: Notes for Reading Joyce," trans. Isabelle Mahieu, in *Post-structuralist Joyce: Essays from the French*, ed. Derek Attridge and Daniel Ferrer (Cambridge: Cambridge University Press, 1984), 46.

55 Joyce, *Finnegans Wake*, 185.29; 186.02.

56 Lyotard, *The Postmodern Condition*, 80–81.

57 Slavoj Žižek, "Ecology against Mother Nature," *Verso* (May 26, 2015): www.
versobooks.com/
blogs/2007-ecology-against-mother-nature-slavoj-zizek-on-molecular-red/

Chapter 9

1 Rosalind Krauss, *The Originality of the Avant-Garde and Other Modernist Myths* (Cambridge, MA: MIT Press, 1985), 247.

2 Krauss, *The Originality of the Avant-Garde*, 248.

3 Krauss, *The Originality of the Avant-Garde*, 247.

4 Krauss, *The Originality of the Avant-Garde*, 249.

5 Krauss, *The Originality of the Avant-Garde*, 247.

6 Ann Quin, *Berg* (London: Calder, 1964), unpag.

7 Quin, *Berg*, 1;168.

8 Ann Quin, *Passages* (Chicago: Dalkey Archive, 2003), 110.

9 Quin, *Passages*, 111.

10 Dan Smith, "Iain Sinclair's Lights Out for the Territory," *Richmond Review* (1996): www.richmondreview.co.uk/lightsou/.

11 Cited in Iain Sinclair, *Lights Out for the Territory* (London: Granta, 1997), 7.

12 Sinclair, *Lights Out for the Territory*, 15.

13 Richard Makin, *Dwelling* (Hastings: Reality Street, 2011): www.realitystreet.co.uk/richard-makin.php.

14 Richard Makin, *Mourning* (London: Equus, 2018), 14; 262; 279; 89.

15 Richard Makin, *Concussion Protocols* (Prague: Alienist, 2015), 55.

16 Makin, *Concussion Protocols*, 40.

17 Adam R. Brown and Leonard Susskind, "The Second Law of Quantum Complexity," *High Energy Physics – Theory* (January 4, 2017): arxiv.org/abs/1701.01107.

18 Or as the number of Planck areas in the black hole's horizon area.

19 George Musser, "In New Paradox, Black Holes Appear to Evade Heat Death," *Quanta* (June 6, 2023): www.quantamagazine.org/in-new-paradox-black-holes-appear-to-evade-heat-death-20230606/—bold and italics added for emphasis.

20 James Joyce, *Finnegans Wake* (London: Faber, 1941), 185.35.

21 Georges *Bataille*, "Informe," *Documents* 7 (December 1929): 382.

22 Quoted by Yve-Alain Bois, "The Use Value of 'Formless,'" in *Formless: A User's Guide*, Rosalind Krauss and Yve-Alain Bois (New York, Zone Books, 1997), 18.

23 Richard Makin, *Work* (London: Equus, 2022), 334.

24 Makin, *Work*, 380.

25 Makin, *Work*, 226.

26 Makin, *Work*, 385.

27 Makin, *Work*, 232.

28 Makin, *Work*, 235.

29 Amy Catanzano, "Poetry in Superposition: An Essay-Poem in Quantum Poetics," *Crisis and Critique* 9, no. 1 (August 31, 2022): www.crisiscritique.org/storage/app/media/2022-08-31/amy-catanzano.pdf.

30 Makin, *Work*, 140.

31 Makin, *Work*, 167.

32 Makin, *Work*, 230.

33 Makin, *Work*, 228.

34 Robert Smithson, "Entropy and the New Monuments" (1966), accessed October 14, 2025, holtsmithsonfoundation.org/entropy-and-new-monuments.

35 Makin, *Work*, 199.

36 Samuel R. Delany, *Dhalgren* (London: Gollancz, 2010), 329.

37 Postselection is an operation that allows an experimenter to rig a random process in order to obtain a desired outcome. "Say you want to flip a coin and get 10 heads in a row. You can do it, provided you have the patience to start over every time it comes up tails. Similarly, the encoding program begins measuring the semiclassical qubits but reboots every time it gets a 1. Eventually, when it has measured most of the scrambled qubits and successfully gotten a string of zeros, it throws those qubits away. The few remaining, unmeasured qubits represent the pixels of the quantum image of the black hole as viewed from the exterior. Thus, the code squeezes a large semiclassical RAW file into a compact quantum JPEG." Charlie Wood, "Quantum Complexity Shows How to Escape Hawking's Black Hole Paradox," *Quanta* (August 2, 2023): www.quantamagazine.org/new-calculations-show-how-to-escape-hawkings-black-hole-paradox-20230802.

38 Cited in Philip Ball, "A New Idea for How to Assemble Life," *Quanta* (May 4, 2023): www.quantamagazine.org/a-new-theory-for-the-assembly-of-life-in-the-universe-20230504.

39 Makin, *Work*, 199.

40 Cited in Ball, "A New Idea for How to Assemble Life."

Chapter 10

1 Japanese Aerospace Exploration Agency (Tokyo).

2 Barbara Auclino & Dianne Timblin, "The Making of a Xenotext," *American Scientist* (June 22, 2016): www.americanscientist.org/blog/science-culture/the-making-of-a-xenotext/

3 Darren Wershler, "The Xenotext Experiment, So Far," *Canadian Journal of Communication* 37, no. 1 (2012): 50—emphasis added.

4 Christian Bök, "The Xenotext Works," *Poetry* (April 2011). [AW: add page number?]

5 Tony Godfrey, *Conceptual Art* (London: Phaidon, 1998), 4.

6 See Primož Krašovec, "Alien Capital," trans. Miha Šuštar (*Vast Abrupt*), accessed October 14, 2025, vastabrupt.com/2018/07/11/alien-capital/.

7 Sol LeWitt, "Paragraphs on Conceptual Art," *Artforum* (1967).. [AW: I can't find that on the Artforum site using this link or a search]

8 Christian Bök, *The Xenotext Experiment* (New York: /ubu Editions, 2007), 4.

9 Christian Bök in Kenneth Goldsmith, "The Xenotext Experiment: An Interview with Christian Bök," *Postmodern Culture* (July 28, 2007).

10 "The Cybernetic Hypothesis," *Tiqqun* (2001): theanarchistlibrary.org/library/tiqqun-the-cybernetic-hypothesis.pdf.

11 Harvey Wheeler, *Democracy in a Revolutionary Era,* (Santa Barbara, CA: Center for the Study of Democratic Institutions, 1968), 14.

12 Christian Bök, "Aleatory Writing: Notes Towards a Poetics of Chance," *Public 33 Errata* (2006): 26–emphasis added.

13 Bök, *The Xenotext Experiment*, 7.

14 I.e., as the defining contour of "language"—see Claude Shannon and Warren Weaver, *The Mathematical Theory of Communication* (Champaign: University of Illinois Press, 1963), 43.

15 Bök, *The Xenotext Experiment*, 4.

16 Katherine Hayles, "Literary Texts as Cognitive Assemblages: The Case of Electronic Literature,"
Electronic Book Review (2018): electronicbookreview.com/essay/literary-texts-as-cognitive-assemblages-the-case-of-electronic-literature/

17 Maurice Merleau-Ponty, "Indirect Language & the Voices of Silence," *Signs*, trans. Richard C. McCleary (Evanston, IL: Northwestern University Press, 1964), 39.

18 Jacques Derrida, "Différance," *Margins of Philosophy*, trans. Alan Bass (Chicago: Chicago University Press, 1982).

19 Bök, *The Xenotext Experiment*, 4—emphasis added.

20 See Paul Davies, "Do We Have to Spell It Out," *New Scientist* 2459 (August 7, 2004): 30–31.

21 Bök, "Aleatory Writings," 26—emphasis added.

22 Bök, "Aleatory Writings," 25.

23 Jacques Derrida, "Two Words for Joyce," *Post-structuralist Joyce: Essays from the French*, ed. Derek Attridge and Daniel Ferrer (Cambridge: Cambridge University Press, 1984), 148.

24 Jacques Derrida, *Of Grammatology*, trans. Gayatri Spivak (Baltimore: Johns Hopkins University Press, 2016), 6.

25 Derrida, *Of Grammatology*, 24.

26 Derrida, *Of Grammatology*, 68.

27 Bök, "Aleatory Writings," 3.

28 Bök, "Aleatory Writings," 3. See Pak Chung Wong, et al., "Organic Data Memory Using the DNA Approach," *Communications of the ACM* 46, no. 1 (January 2003): 95–98.

29 André Leroi-Gourhan, *Le geste et la parole* (1965), cited in Derrida, *Of Grammatology*, 85.

30 Derrida, *Of Grammatology*, 65.

31 Derrida, *Of Grammatology*, 23.

32 Jacques Lacan, "A Materialist Definition of the Phenomenon of Consciousness," *The Seminar of Jacques Lacan. Book II: The Ego in Freud's Theory and in the Technique of Psychoanalysis 1954–1955*, trans. S. Tomaselli (London: Cambridge University Press, 1988), 46. Lacan's engagement with cybernetics, and his treatment of the status of the thing in Freud ("A Materialist Definition of the Phenomenon of Consciousness," "Homeostasis and Insistence," "Freud, Hegel and the Machine," "The Circuit"), is conspicuous for the way it eschews any easy gesture of transcendence of the category of the human or of Humanism in approaching a definition of consciousness not seated in the I of Cartesian subjectivity, but instead positing an antecedent subjective condition of an apparently paradoxical post human/ism. That is to say, the positing of a post Human/ism as the condition for any Human/ism, by which subjectivity is grasped as an operation, or set of operations; in short, we might say, a poiēsis. Not simply an inversion of the classical dichotomy of technē and poiēses, but a thinking

anew of a techno-poetic foundation of subjectivity: techno to the extent that subjectivity always involves a logic of prosthesis and is aim-orientated, poetic in the sense that subjectivity is tropic.

33 Derrida, *Of Grammatology*, 6.

34 Derrida, *Of Grammatology*, 68.

35 See Joshua Schuster, "On Reading Christian Bök's 'The Xenotext Book 1' Ten Thousand Years Later," *Jacket 2* (February 2016): jacket2.org/reviews/reading-christian-boks-xenotext-book-1-ten-thousand-years-later.

36 Jacques Rancière, "Documentary Fiction: Chris Marker and the Fiction of Memory," *Blackout ((poetry & politics))* (2018): my-black-out-com/2018/10/10/jacques-ranciere-documentary-fiction-chris-marker-&-the-fiction-of-memory/.

INDEX

ABOUT THE AUTHORS

LOUIS ARMAND directs the Centre for Critical & Cultural Theory in the Philosophy Faculty of Charles University, Prague. His theoretical works include *Homo Catastrophicus* (2024), *Feasts of Unrule* (2024), *Entropology* (2023), *Videology* (2015), *Solicitations* (2013), *Event States* (2007), *Literate Technologies* (2006), *The Organ-Grinder's Monkey: Culture after the Avantgarde* (2013), *Helixtrolysis* (2014), *Incendiary Devices: Discourses of the Other* (2001), & *Techne* (1997).

www.louis-armand.com

•

MICHEL DELVILLE teaches literature and comparative literature at the University of Liège, Belgium. He is the author or editor of some thirty books pertaining to contemporary poetics and intermedial studies, including *The American Prose Poem, Food, Poetry*, and the *Aesthetics of Consumption: Eating the Avant-Garde, Crossroads Poetics, The Politics and Aesthetics of Hunger and Disgust* (with Andrew Norris), *Le roman de la faim : du Hungerkünstler au schizoflâneur,* and *The Edinburgh Companion to the Prose Poem* (w. Mary Ann Caws).

www.micheldelville.com